THE NATURAL HISTORY OF BRITAIN
AND NORTHERN EUROPE

COASTS AND ESTUARIES
RICHARD BARNES

Editors JAMES FERGUSON-LEES & BRUCE CAMPBELL

Contributors Franklyn and Margaret Perring (Plants);
Tegwyn Harris (Marine Invertebrates); Paul Whalley (Insects);
Frederick Wanless (Arachnids); Alwyne Wheeler (Fish);
James Ferguson-Lees (Birds); Tim Halliday (Amphibians and Reptiles);
Gordon Corbet (Mammals)

Illustrators Deborah King (Plants); Joyce Tuhill (Invertebrates);
Annabel Milne and Peter Stebbing (Fish);
Hilary Burn (Amphibians, Reptiles, Birds and Mammals)

D0276907

Hodder & Stoughton
LONDON·SYDNEY·AUCKLAND·TORONTO

This book was designed and produced by
George Rainbird Limited,
36 Park Street, London W1Y 4DE
for Hodder & Stoughton Limited,
Mill Road, Dunton Green,
Sevenoaks, Kent

House Editors: Karen Goldie-Morrison,
                Linda Gamlin
Designer: Patrick Yapp
Indexer: Annie Bednarska
Picture Researcher: Karen Gunnell
Cartographer: Tom Stalker Miller
Cover Illustrator: Hilary Burn
Endpapers Illustrator: Joyce Tuhill
Diagrams: David Watson
                The Garden Studio
Production: Jane Collins

Printed and bound by
W. S. Cowell Limited
28 Percy Street, London W1P 9FF

ISBN 0 340 23154 8

CONTENTS

FOREWORD

With increased travel and an expanding interest in Europe as a whole, many books and field guides on its natural history have been published in the last two decades, but most either treat a wide field in general terms or cover a single class or group of animals or plants. At the same time, inspired by the need for conservation, the pendulum is swinging back from the specialization of the post-war years to a wish for a fuller appreciation of all aspects of natural history. As yet, the traveller-naturalist has to be armed with a variety of volumes and, even then, has no means of understanding the interrelations of plants and animals. We believe that this new series will help to fill that gap.

The five books cover the whole of the northern half of Europe west of Russia and the Baltic States, and include Iceland: the limits are shown by the map on pages 66–67, which marks the individual countries, and the various subregions with the abbreviations used for them. Four of the volumes deal with (a) towns and gardens; (b) coniferous forests, heaths, moors, mountains and tundra; (c) broadleaved woods, hedgerows, farmland, lowland grassland and downs; and (d) lakes, rivers and freshwater marshes. This book is about coasts, dunes, sea-cliffs, salt-marshes, estuaries and the sea itself. Thus, in broad groupings, the series covers the whole rural and urban scene.

Each book is divided into two. The first half is an ecological essay about the habitats, with examples of plant and animal communities as illustrations of interrelationships. The second is a field guide of selected species, each illustrated and described, with its habitat, the part it plays in food webs, and its distribution. Obviously there are limitations: about 600 species are illustrated in each book, or around 3000 in the series, but the north European total is probably at least 50,000. Whereas good proportions of the characteristic vertebrates (148 mammals, 364 birds, 18 reptiles, 22 amphibians and more than 300 fish) are included, some single *families* of insects have more species than the total of these; there are over 4000 different beetles in Britain alone, and probably 8–9000 in the whole of our area, while some 3500 plants are also native or naturalized in north Europe. On the other hand, the identification of many insects and some groups of plants is a matter for the specialist and we believe that many readers will be satisfied if they can identify these at the family level. So our list of invertebrates and plants is selective, but we hope that it will form a useful groundwork from which interest in particular groups can be developed.

All plants and animals are grouped into classes (*eg* Angiospermae, Insecta, Aves), orders (*eg* Campanulatae, Lepidoptera, Passeriformes), families (*eg* Compositae, Nymphalidae, Turdidae) and genera (*eg Aster, Inachis, Turdus*), groups of increasingly close affinity. Each plant or animal has two scientific names, the first of which is the genus and the second the species. These are often considered to be outside the scope of a work of this kind, but many invertebrates and some plants have no vernaculars and, at the same time, such names are invaluable in showing relationships. Consequently, each species is given its scientific name at the first mention in each essay chapter and again in the field guide, where the family name is also inserted in capitals.

The specially commissioned colour paintings which illustrate the field guide are a delight in themselves. It has become customary to illustrate plants and animals in field guides as individual specimens, but here they are arranged in attractive compositions. Scale has had to suffer, but the sizes are always given in the facing descriptions, as are the correct food plants of the invertebrates.

All the other books in the series deal with land habitats or fresh water; this is the only marine book, but it ranges from the splash zone on cliffs and rocky shores, and from river estuaries, down to the flat continental shelf which is found some 200 metres below the present sea-level. It is perhaps fair to claim that in this meeting place of land and sea the concept of zonation is most clearly seen and can be realized in a way not always possible in terrestrial habitats much modified by man. Not that man is without his influence at sea; indeed, the threat of various forms of marine pollution, from oil spills to the subtler infiltration of industrial chemicals into the oceans, is one of the great problems of conservation today.

But this book is not primarily about conservation problems: it is about the living creatures of the transitional zones between land and sea and we have been fortunate to secure as author of the essay Dr Richard Barnes, lecturer in aquatic ecology at the University of Cambridge and a Fellow of St Catharine's College. He is also a consultant to the Open University. He has written a book on *Estuarine Biology* and edited a most impressive volume on *The Coastline* (1977); he is secretary of the Estuarine and Brackish-water Sciences Association. In spite of all these commitments he finds time to carry out research on coastal lagoons in Cornwall and on intertidal invertebrates. He has also conducted research in other continents and so brings to this book no parochial outlook. The sea shore was the happy hunting-ground of the Victorian naturalists and collectors. Richard Barnes, assisted by the field guide section of representative plants and animals, shows how their descendants can enjoy and understand the complex relationships of coastal ecology, either as holiday visitors or as students.

JAMES FERGUSON–LEES
BRUCE CAMPBELL

INTRODUCTION

Northern Europe has a long, varied and often spectacular coastline along which, with the exception of mangrove-swamps and coral-reefs, all the world's major types of coastal habitat may be found. In several areas, towering cliffs, sandy beaches, shingle spits, lagoons, sand-dunes and salt-marshes may all be seen within a 100-kilometre journey. But because this region is characteristically windy, and because the seas around our shores are often very shallow, it is a little difficult to decide which coastal habitats should be included in such a book as this, and which should be omitted. The coast is after all a transitional zone between land and sea, and not a clearly delineated region. Salt-spray, for example, can travel many kilometres inland and can impart a subtle and indefinable coastal appearance to inland areas. These zones are often termed submaritime, and can be characterized by the presence of such plants as alexanders *Smyrnium olusatrum* in the south, and sea plantain *Plantago maritima* in the north. Similarly, out at sea, it is usually possible to tell when one is near a coastline by the murkiness or colour of the water, or by characteristic current patterns.

Rather than try to force arbitrary limits, it is better to let nature set her own by including certain characteristic habitat types within the definition 'coastal', regardless of how far from the shoreline they may extend. Intertidal zones, such as rocky shores, sand or shingle beaches and mud-flats, must obviously be included, and so must salt-marshes which are covered by some though not all tides. The very names of other habitats betray their coastal nature: sea-cliffs, coastal dunes and coastal lagoons, for example. Then we have the continental shelf, that gently sloping plain stretching out up to 1200 kilometres (although generally much less) from the nearest coastline until depths of some 200 metres are reached. Continental land masses rise from the ocean floor as large blocks with steeply sloping sides, but at 200 to 250 metres below the present sea-level they flatten out to form shelves which are in part cut into the land by the action of water and in part areas drowned beneath a rising sea-level. These areas, with their shallow coastal seas, must also be included.

We shall, however, omit areas of reclaimed land and the submaritime fringe referred to above. Land reclaimed from the sea is all too quickly used for building purposes or agriculture and it soon loses its (specifically coastal)

Coastal scene with salt-tolerant vegetation including lichens on the rocky cliff, and wracks on the rocks below; Orkney.

natural history interest; but because of the widespread occurrence of land reclamation we must look at its extent and significance later in this section. The submaritime fringe is in most respects a normal terrestrial habitat – in the form of woods, heaths and fields – and the comparatively subtle effects of the nearby sea are not sufficient to warrant its detailed treatment here.

Coastal regions are thus highly diverse, but they do share one very important feature which affects the lives of all their inhabitants: they are subject to rapid change, both in the climate to which they are exposed and in their very nature and structure. It is the background of continual change which we must consider in this introductory section. Changes take place at a variety of different time scales, but it is useful to distinguish two main categories which we shall call 'major' and 'minor', although paradoxically, it is the minor changes that have the greatest effects on the daily lives of coastal organisms. Major changes are comparatively long-term fluctuations brought about by variation in the height of the sea relative to the land. These will affect the general position of the coastline as, say, marked on a large scale map. For the last million years, northern Europe has experienced a series of ice advances interspersed with warmer 'interglacial' periods, in one of which we are now living. The water locked up in ice during the glacial phases is that which would otherwise have been in the sea and hence, at times of maximum ice cover, sea-level was much lower than it is now – at least some 150 metres lower probably. Conversely, at times of minimum ice cover, sea-level was possibly some 150 metres higher. A difference of 300 metres can cause very marked changes in the position of the European coastline.

Although sea-level has probably been fairly stable for the last 5000 years, the effects of the glaciations are still with us. This is because the height of the land is still moving relative to that of the sea: the weight of ice depressed the land in various areas and, now that much of this ice has melted, the land is bobbing back up again like a cork. Thus northwestern Scotland is rising at the moment, whilst, moving about an axis after the manner of a see-saw, southeastern England is slowly sinking (at a rate of two millimetres per year). Of course, we tend to assume that the height of the land is constant and so we notice or interpret these changes as further rises or falls in sea-level. In geographical terms, these changes in relative land- or sea-level are clearly 'major' but in terms of the life spans of coastal organisms such changes are of comparatively small importance. They have been important, however, in creating favourable habitats for marine organisms, notably the many large, sheltered inlets or natural harbours formed by the drowning of river valleys, and other coastal features, some 12,000 to 15,000 years ago.

The coastal changes to which animals and plants must be adapted, and which in some cases they can positively exploit, are more local, short time-scale phenomena caused by the powers of wind, wave, current and, for example, frost. These are the processes of erosion and accretion, which may combine to produce 'long-shore drift'. The nature and speed of action of these processes vary greatly around the world, depending on the prevailing climate (using that word in a very broad sense), and so we must first look briefly at the marine climate of the northern Atlantic.

The world's coastal regions can be divided into a number of geographical areas on the basis of such features as windiness, tidal range (vertical distance between high- and low-tide levels), wave heights, and so on. The whole area covered by this book (with the exception of the brackish and land-locked Baltic Sea which is a case unto itself) falls into a single one of these regions. It can be characterized by high winds, large waves, large to very large tidal ranges, two periods each of high and low tide each day (semi-diurnal tides), freedom from extensive development of coastal ice (except in Iceland) although coastal frosts occur throughout the region, and by the relative importance of pebbles as beach or sea-bed material. We shall return to many of these features later as they have a profound effect on the nature and natural history of our coastlines, but it is sufficient at the moment to point out that these characteristics will result in considerable erosion of unprotected coastlines: 'wave energy' is high, storm waves will be frequent, and the water may be armed with small pebbles which greatly increase its battering power.

Erosion is the removal from a given area of the material of which it is built. Rocks, for example, are broken down by repeated wetting and drying, or heating and cooling, by the expansion on freezing of water in crevices, by being dissolved, or by the force of waves breaking against them (this force may exceed 26,000 kg per sq m, or 2 tons per sq ft). Once particles are loosened they may drop to the foot of the cliff, be carried by ground-water flow, be washed off by rainwater, or be directly carried away by the sea. Thus cliffs may be undermined by the waves and the overlying material collapse on to the beach, or the cliffs may be eroding anyway as a result of the aerial climate to which they are exposed and the sea then merely removes the debris accumulated at the cliff base. Of course the animals and plants living on the rock surface suffer the same forces as the rock and so they must possess powerful means of attachment to prevent their being dislodged and swept away.

Such forces are acting all the time, although soft rocks will clearly be more easily eroded than hard ones. Whilst hard igneous rocks may show little change over the passage of centuries, there are many examples of rapid loss of soft sandy cliffs. The comparatively soft cliffs of the Holderness region of Humberside have been retreating at a rate of one to six metres every year for over 1000 years, involving losses of the order of one million cubic metres of cliff each year. Rather more spectacular and disastrous for the communities inhabiting coastal regions are the erosive powers of storm surges, onshore-wind-driven banks of water which can breach coastlines and flood adjacent low-lying areas. That of the 31st January/1st February 1953 caused severe flooding, damage and loss of life around the southern shores of the North Sea. During this surge, the cliffs at Covehithe on the East Anglian coast were cut back 10·7 metres in two hours.

Margate jetty crashes into the sea during the storm surge of 1953.

These few examples should suffice to show the extent to which the sea itself can alter the position of a coastline by removing material from cliffs and low-lying ground. The material removed in this manner is deposited on the intertidal zone or forms part of the sea-bed, where it is joined by material brought down by rivers. The sea-bed also forms a reservoir of pebbles, many of them eroded from chalk cliffs or derived from material scraped from the land by glaciers. Some of this sediment may find its way back to the immediate coastline by the process of accretion.

There are basically two ways in which this is possible. Either, in comparatively exposed areas, waves may move sand or shingle from below low-tide level on to the shore or, in sheltered areas, mud can settle out of suspension in water at times of high-water slack tide. It may seem surprising, having previously considered waves as agents of destruction, to be suggesting now that they also have constructive powers. The answer, of course, is that there are different kinds of waves and different situations in which they can act. Cliff erosion is a result of violent waves striking a vertical or near-vertical solid surface; here the impact of the waves has much more force than it would have on a more nearly horizontal surface composed of many small particles, a surface, furthermore, through which some of the water can drain. Waves which plunge vertically downwards and have little swash are destructive, and

This shingle spit, which is growing at a rate of 12 metres a year, continues to deflect the mouth of the River Alde southwards. Lagoons have been created (left); Orfordness, Suffolk.

tend to move material seawards from the shore; waves with a powerful and extensive swash, much of which percolates down into the shore (thereby minimizing the backwash), can build up a beach by the addition of material temporarily carried in suspension or moved along the bottom. In a similar manner, offshore ridges or barriers of sand or shingle may be constructed and, perhaps, moved on to the shore during storms. Cycles often occur in which beaches are built up in summer and the increments are removed again in winter.

The second means by which beaches can be built occurs only in the sheltered waters of harbours, estuaries and the like. When water movement is negligible, small particles of silt and clay can settle out of the water on to the bottom. If this happens at high tide, much of the 'bottom' will be the intertidal zone in these shallow areas, and, if more mud settles out than is removed again on the ebb tide, the level of the mud-flat will slowly rise. It is here that the presence of plants in the intertidal zone is of particular importance in these otherwise physical processes. Sinking mud particles stick to the mucus produced by minute algae living on or near the mud surface and they are therefore less easily washed away, and large plants, such as those characterizing salt-marshes and some mud-flats, markedly reduce water movements in their immediate vicinity, allowing more fine material to settle. Without the aid of these plants, to which we shall return in a later section, upward growth rates of a mud-flat surface of less than two millimetres a year would be possible; when they are present, the accretion rate may rise to 20 centimetres a year.

Much of this discussion will also apply to sand-dunes if we substitute wind for water. Dunes are built of grains of sand blown from sandy beaches at low tide, the sand being trapped by sand-dune plants. Phases of accretion and erosion occur, in this case in different areas of the same dune system at any one time, and they often give rise to the movement of whole dunes. This subject will also be discussed in more detail later, but it does serve here to introduce the importance of wind as a feature of coastal climates. Wind speeds are, amongst other things, a function of the openness of the regions across which they blow and most coastal areas will therefore be windy. Besides this general exposure to wind, coastal regions may also generate their own winds as a result of the different capacities of land and water to retain heat. The land heats more quickly than the sea, but it also loses heat more rapidly. During the day, therefore, the land becomes hotter than the sea and the air over it rises, to be replaced by air moving in from the sea. The result is an onshore breeze. At night, the reverse situation applies. The sea is now the hotter of the two and an offshore breeze is generated. Such breezes are particularly marked in summer and, of course, when no strong winds are masking or obliterating the effect.

The final natural process moulding the shoreline which we must consider is long-shore drift. Waves do not always approach parallel to a beach; they often come in at an angle. Their swash will then carry pebbles obliquely up the shore. The backwash will, however, travel straight down the beach slope perpendicularly to the water line, and hence material will be transported along the beach. This simple effect can result in the mass movement of whole structures along the coast, and it causes the growth of such complex forms as shingle spits at places where the coastline makes a sharp change in orientation. Shingle migrating along a stretch of beach will tend to continue along the line set by that beach even though the coast no longer follows the same line. Offshore islands aligned with a beach may be connected to the mainland by causeways of shingle formed in this manner. Shingle spits have other effects on local geography. They may deflect the entrances to harbours (a number of small, but formerly important, ports can no longer operate because spits have all but sealed them off from the sea); like offshore barrier islands, they provide conditions of shelter in their lee so that mud deposition or salt-marsh formation can occur; and they may dam the mouths of small rivers or estuaries, thereby creating coastal lagoons. Their advance may be rapid: Orfordness in Suffolk has lengthened at an average rate of about 12 metres per year during the last eight centuries.

One intriguing feature of spits is that their ends are often recurved. How this comes about is somewhat controversial, but one possible explanation relies on the observation that the direction from which winds and waves usually approach a shore is not necessarily the same as that from which storm waves approach. If we imagine that pebbles are normally rolled southeastwards along a beach by waves approaching from the west, then if storms tend to produce waves approaching from the southeast, they will batter the end of the spit round into a recurved position. After the storm, shingle may continue to move southeastwards and, if a long interval occurs before the next severe storm, further growth will take place, until once again the growing tip may be bent round. In this manner, multiple recurved ends may form.

By considering erosion, accretion and long-shore drift in some detail, I have tried to convey an impression of the short-term mobility of coastal features and of the catastrophic effects of sporadic storms. Thus are habitats created, destroyed and created anew. Before proceeding to look at the coastal organisms which must be able to adjust to and tolerate these changes, it is necessary to look at man's reaction to these phenomena because he is not so tolerant of their effects and not so adaptable, and by seeking to control or modify them he alters the nature of many coastal habitats.

Much of the land around the southern shores of the North Sea (southeastern England, the Low Countries, Germany and Denmark) is low-lying and some of it, as in the fens of East Anglia and, especially, in the Netherlands, is below sea-level. Hence if coastal barriers are breached, extensive flooding will result. The storm surge of 1953 inundated some 250,000 hectares. For this reason, man has endeavoured to protect low-lying regions with a series of sea-walls, and much of the coastline of such areas is now partly artificial. Most frequently the sea-wall is an earth or clay bank raised to a level above that of the highest expected tide, with to landwards a parallel ditch or 'borrow drain' from which the earth was dug. In exposed areas, the bank is constructed at an angle of about 20° to the horizontal and is faced with rectangular or polygonal, interlocking, concrete slabs (or sometimes stone or sandbags). A parapet designed to keep out the surge from breaking waves may also be added. This form of wall is specifically constructed to dissipate wave energy and prevent direct erosion, whilst the earth banks are more usually mere protection from flood-waters and the erosion due to material carried away in suspension.

Plant species may be planted as an aid to the stabilization of natural coastal defences. Marram *Ammophila arenaria* can be planted to encourage the natural growth and repair of dune systems and older dunes can be stabilized by afforestation. Two conifers, Corsican pine *Pinus nigra* ssp *laricio* and Scots pine *P. sylvestris*, have been widely used for this purpose. The value of these natural defences was made clear after the storm surge of 1953: sand-dunes withstood the onslaught much better on the whole than did man-made structures; they are also much cheaper. Mobile sand-dunes may also cover public roads and houses which provides an additional incentive for stabilization.

A second, and in many ways the best, natural barrier against erosion is a well-developed sloping beach topped by shingle; such a beach can very effectively dissipate wave energy. Before the value of shingle for coastal defence was realized, shingle was mined from the shore at Hallsands in Devon for the construction of dockyards at Plymouth. Erosion of the cliffs behind the beach started almost immediately thereafter: between 1907 and 1957 they retreated six metres, and the village of Hallsands was attacked by wave action and reduced to ruins. Beach development in front of soft cliffs or in resort areas can be maintained by the building of groynes, low wooden fences extending down the shore from the high-water mark. These are designed to intercept long-shore drift and keep a beach 'where it is wanted'. The construction of groynes (or piers or breakwaters) may, however, lead to increased erosion further along the coast since sand or shingle eroded from the far side of the groyne can no longer be replaced.

The problem of coastal defence is particularly acute in the Netherlands, first because much of that country is liable to flooding and secondly because of the great length of its coastline in relation to its land area. It is also a small country with a high population density (3·75 people per hectare) and therefore land is in short supply. Land reclamation from the sea solves both problems, since by reclaiming estuarine and coastal bay areas the length of coastline can be greatly reduced. Since 1930 many of these areas have been enclosed: the former Zuider Zee was enclosed by a 32-kilometre barrage in 1932, the former Lauwers Zee was enclosed in 1969, and the enclosure of the Rhine–Meuse Estuary (the embayments of Haringvliet, Grevelingen and Oosterschelde) is well under way. Enclosure of part of the Waddenzee is also now being discussed.

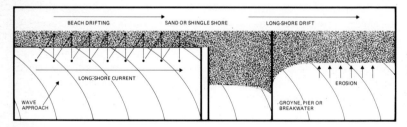

LEFT *The action of long-shore drift and* RIGHT *its interception by groynes.*

OPPOSITE *Land reclaimed for agriculture. The layout is well ordered since the constraints of history and separate ownership have been avoided; Noord Oost polder, the Netherlands.*

From these enclosures, a total of over 300,000 hectares has or will be re-claimed for agriculture, and many smaller reclamations for agriculture have been made both in the Netherlands and in the other countries bordering the North Sea – 30,000 hectares of the Wash in England, for example. But coastal defence and agriculture are not the only reasons for enclosing arms of the sea. La Rance Estuary in France has been dammed for the tidal genera-tion of electrical power, and proposals have been put forward for a similar tidal barrage across the Severn Estuary in England. Many intertidal flat and salt-marsh areas have been reclaimed for port installations (Europort and Southampton Docks), for industry (parts of the Tees Estuary and the south-western shores of Southampton Water in England), and for freshwater reser-voirs (the Delta region of the Netherlands); numerous other schemes have been mooted. These reclamations have all been entirely 'artificial' processes in which a barrage, of similar structure to a sea-wall, is built across the bay or estuary, and the region behind the barrage is then pumped dry and infilled with pumped slurry from the adjacent sea-bed, with domestic and industrial refuse, or whatever else is required to achieve the desired end.

Not all reclamation is so artificial, however. Man has also taken advantage of the ability of salt-marsh plants to increase accretion rates by deliberately planting Townsend's cord-grass *Spartina anglica* on various mud-flats to promote sedimentation. It has even been exported to Australia and New Zealand for this purpose. But *Spartina anglica* behaves as an invasive weed, and is giving rise to considerable alarm because of its ability to invade native European salt-marsh communities. *Spartina anglica* is a vigorous fertile hybrid derived from the original sterile hybrid *S.* × *townsendii* which first appeared in Southampton Water in 1870 as a cross between the native Euro-pean *S. maritima* and the immigrant American *S. alterniflora*. Salt-marsh growth is also encouraged by embanking and draining.

Man's influence on the nature of the coastline is increasingly being felt, and several types of habitat are under severe pressure: mud-flats, salt-marshes and whole estuaries and lagoons are being reclaimed; the natural coastline is being replaced in low-lying areas by sea-walls, and near harbours and docks by sheet piling; whilst in addition sand-dunes are being converted into golf courses, and the submaritime fringe is in some areas becoming over-burdened with caravan parks and other 'amenities'. Large areas, however, of unspoilt coastline do still exist, several of them protected in nature reserves and national parks, and examples of the various types of coastal habitat can still be found in most areas. To these we shall now turn, although it is pos-sible only to sketch briefly the nature of each habitat and mention the more characteristic or important of its organisms.

SANDY BEACHES

Sandy shores range in size from only a few square metres tucked away in a rocky headland to vast stretches of sand, tens or even hundreds of kilometres long and hundreds of metres wide. These beaches, which must surely be the most heavily visited parts of the coast, may appear barren and lifeless to the visitor at low tide. If the shore is exposed to heavy wave action, such a view would be substantially correct, but in more sheltered regions it would certainly be an illusion, which would be dispelled if the visitor could examine the sand surface at high tide. At low tide, the inhabitants of sandy shores burrow or bury themselves deep in the sediment to gain protection from desiccation and to avoid attracting the attention of predatory birds.

Except along the strand-line, higher plants are noticeably absent from clean sandy beaches, although small algae, particularly diatoms, live there, attached to the sand grains. These require light and so can only photosynthesize in the top few millimetres of the sand; but because of the mobility of beach sand they may be buried as deep as 20 centimetres, where they may lie dormant for several months, coming to life again when wave action brings them to the surface. Only along the strand-line do flowering plants encroach on to the beach. There, in the sands enriched with nutrients from the decay of flotsam, may be found prickly saltwort *Salsola kali*, sea rocket *Cakile maritima*, sea sandwort *Honkenya peploides*, oraches *Atriplex*, and sand couch *Agropyron junceiforme*. These mostly annual species are important in initiating sand-dune development.

Also near the strand-line may be seen small pin-prick holes in the dry sand. These are the burrows of sand-hoppers *Talitrus saltator*, large scavenging amphipods which emerge at night to consume anything edible that the tide has brought in. New burrows are created every morning in which to spend the day, and although they may roam well down the beach at night, the animals are able to return to the same level of the beach the next morning using complex station-fixing behaviour patterns.

Exposure to wave action is the single most important factor determining the variety and abundance of life on the sand-beach proper. When waves pound an exposed stretch of sand, the surface particles (down to a depth of several centimetres) are whirled into suspension as in a submarine sandstorm, and few organisms could manage to prevent themselves being swept away in the water or being sand-blasted by the dancing grains. A few species which include the small crustaceans *Eurydice pulchra*, *Haustorius arenarius*, and *Bathyporeia*, the spionid worm *Nerine cirratulus* and the banded wedge

Strand-line on a sandy beach. The sand-dunes have been heavily eroded by January storms; North Norfolk.

shell *Donax vittatus* do survive in such habitats however, albeit in small numbers. The cat-worm *Nephtys* may sometimes accompany them. The various crustaceans mentioned are good swimmers and/or burrowers. (*Haustorius*, in particular, is well-adapted for digging rapidly through sand with its broad, flattened legs; when swimming its body is held upside-down.) They are probably carrion-feeders and scavengers seizing any small particles, living or dead, brought in on the tide, although *Haustorius* can filter-feed. *Donax*, in contrast, is a suspension-feeder and lives with its beautiful, highly-polished shell buried just below the sand surface whilst it draws a current of water into its shell, passes it through its gills so that planktonic algae and other suspended matter may be filtered out, and then expels the filtered stream of water. In common with most other suspension-feeding bivalves, *Donax* possesses short siphons.

As the exposure to wave action lessens, so more and more species enter the fauna and that of sheltered, though still clean, sands can be rich. Here more diatoms and other algae can colonize the sand grains, and more edible debris can settle out of the water and become incorporated into the beach. This debris or detritus is broken down by bacteria, protozoa and fungi, and the whole complex of detritus and its decomposers, besides being consumed by sediment-eating animals, forms the basis for a food-web of minute organisms (0·05 to 3 mm long) some too small to be seen without a microscope, but of great importance in the ecology of sandy shores. These interstitial or meiofaunal animals inhabit the spaces between the sand grains (which may comprise 40 per cent of the volume of the beach) in numbers to be counted in millions per square metre of shore surface. Although many groups of animals have representatives in the meiofauna, such interstitial animals have evolved a very similar general body shape in response to the need to move through the sand without displacing the grains and to be protected against sand mobility. They are all small, elongated animals, often with strong or armoured body-walls, with the ability to contract into small blobs and to attach themselves to individual sand grains by hooks or suckers.

The larger resident animals of sheltered sandy shores fall into three categories: suspension-feeders, deposit- or sediment-feeders, and carnivores and scavengers. Most species live only near low-water level, but some – like the lug-worm *Arenicola marina* – extend over much of the exposed sand, and others, such as the various species of *Bathyporeia*, divide the beach between them so that a distinct zonation can be found.

Suspension-feeders use the beach as a support and a safe retreat whilst, like *Donax*, filtering suspended material from the overlying water at high tide. The majority of suspension-feeders are, like *Donax*, bivalve molluscs, for example *Venus, Pharus*, the trough-shells *Spisula* and *Mactra*, the sunsetshells *Gari*, and, most importantly, the razor-shells *Ensis* and *Solen* and cockles *Cerastoderma* (*Cardium*) and *Acanthocardia*. Razor-shells – so called because of their resemblance to a closed cut-throat razor – are large, long bivalves (up to 20 cm) living at or near low water, whose whole structure appears geared to rapid burrowing. They are greatly elongated along the axis of entry into the sand, and the whole of the posterior half of the shell is occupied by a muscular foot capable of exerting a pull approaching one kilogram. When the foot is pushed into the sand its tip is pointed, but when some progress has been made, this pointed shape is converted into a large, swollen anchor holding the tip of the foot firmly in place. Muscular contraction then draws the rest of the animal down too. The valves of the shell now open slightly, wedging the razor-shell's body against the sand, whilst the foot is again pointed and pushed farther down into the burrow-to-be; and so the process is repeated. The animal can burrow upwards with equal facility by pushing with its foot instead of pulling. When quietly feeding, the anterior end of the shell is near the sand surface and the short siphons draw in and expel a current of water. A slight vibration in the sand or a shadow passing overhead, however, causes the razor to descend rapidly, faster than it is possible to dig with a spade. The most frequent clue to this animal's presence is the spouting of small jets of water as it retreats at the approach of one's footsteps. If the descent is slightly too late and a bird has grasped the fleshy siphons, these can be cast off along special fracture planes, and the razor can regenerate a new set. *Pharus legumen* is a bivalve which has independently evolved the razor-shell way of life and has convergently attained a similar body shape.

Cockles, such as *Cerastoderma edule*, have much stouter, almost spherical shells and hence they cannot burrow nearly as quickly or nearly as deeply as the razors. They often lie only just below the surface and rely on the strength of their shells to protect them from waves and predators. They are quite mobile, however, and can leap over a beach by using the foot as a spring. Cockles occur over the greater part of many sandy beaches and can attain densities of 3·6 million per hectare. Not surprisingly, man harvests these abundant molluscs for food, but many other animals have had the same idea: the small pea crab *Pinnotheres pisum*, for example, often lives inside the cockle shell and helps itself to the food collected by its host's gills, and the gill tissue itself. Cockles living relatively high up a beach will be covered by the tide for a smaller proportion of the day than those living lower down, and hence they can spend less time feeding. They are therefore often smaller than their more fortunate peers.

The deposit-feeding category includes all those animals which, so to speak, wait for material to settle out of the water before they consume it. They may either collect their food specifically from the sand surface or else consume the sediment itself; in either case they also consume many bacteria, interstitial algae, protozoa and meiofauna. Thus many different potential food items undoubtedly pass into their mouths and it is a matter of great scientific debate which ones they actually digest and on which they are most dependent. In any event, since edible materials comprise a minute fraction (some 0·05 per cent by weight) of the ingested sediment, they must consume large quantities of sandy material (*eg* 5–10 grams) each day in order to obtain sufficient food. The lug-worms, for example, may pass all the sand in their immediate habitat down to a depth of 10 centimetres through their guts once every two years. Deposit-feeders are a large category of animals and include the lug-worm *Arenicola*, sand mason *Lanice conchilega*, some cat-worms *Nephtys* and other polychaete worms *Nerine*, *Spio filicornis*, *Ophelia*, *Magelona papillicornis* and *Scoloplos armiger*; the amphipod crustacean *Corophium arenarium*; the thin tellin *Tellina tenuis*; the acornworm *Saccoglossus ruber*; and the seapotato *Echinocardium cordatum*.

The lug-worm *Arenicola marina* lives in a deep L-shaped burrow, comprising a tail shaft, a gallery and, from the closed end of the gallery to the surface, a sand-filled head shaft. The worm feeds by consuming the sand at the base of the head shaft and as it does so more sand collapses down the shaft to replace that eaten. A depression in the sand surface therefore marks the location of this head shaft. Every three-quarters of an hour or so, the worm backs up the tail shaft to defaecate on the surface, leaving the familiar coiled worm-cast. Lug-worms sometimes suffer the indignity of having their tails pecked by birds whilst so engaged, and hence individuals with short tails are not uncommon. Their whole life may be spent in the one burrow, although the worms can swim clumsily if forced to do so and can build new burrows. Water is drawn into the burrow by waves of muscular contraction passing along the body from tail to head. This provides oxygen for respiration, helps to keep the gallery aerobic, and possibly loosens the sand in the head shaft. It also encourages the growth in the head shaft of certain diatoms and meiofauna of particular food value, and certainly enriches the sand there with material filtered out of suspension. During low tide, feeding can still continue if the sand remains wet. The sand mason, in contrast, feeds upon surface deposits. This red and white worm constructs a very characteristic tube from sand grains, the top of which projects a few centimetres above the sand surface and ends in a series of tassels. These projecting tubes, with their coronets of branched filaments, form miniature forests over the lower half of some sand-flats. At high tide, the worm climbs up its tube with the aid of minute hooks set in rows down the anterior segments of its body and extends its 'head' of numerous fine tentacles to writhe over the sand surface. Food particles, and sand grains to extend or repair the tube, are conveyed back along these translucent tentacles. Food particles are carried to the mouth, whilst the sand particles are coated with mucus and become added to the tube where necessary.

Our final example of a deposit-feeder must be the sea-potato or heart-urchin, an inhabitant of low tidal levels. Unlike most other sea-urchins, the shell or test of this species is not hemispherical; instead it is flattened, possesses a distinct 'head' and 'tail' end, and is covered with golden, adpressed spines. The animal lives 15 to 20 centimetres down in sand in a mucus-lined cavity connected to the surface by a narrow respiratory tube, built and maintained in good repair by a series of very long tube-feet. The food of the sea-potato comprises organic matter on the surface of the sand grains lying immediately below its anteriorly-placed mouth. These are picked up by a second series of tube-feet and held against the mouth, where the organic coating is scraped off. The faeces pass into a specially constructed sanitary tube – a short, blind-ending cavity created by a special series of spines and tube-feet encircling the anus. Unlike *Arenicola*, the sea-potato cannot occupy the same burrow for very long. It moves slowly through the sand, eating as it goes and creating new respiratory and sanitary tubes.

Sandy shores also possess their resident carnivores and omnivorous scavengers. *Glycera gigantea*, a turgid worm pointed at each end, which coils into a spiral when disturbed and swims with its back end forwards, and other polychaetes with large eversible probosces, prey on still other polychaetes, as probably does the large muscular and pale yellow or fawn ribbonworm *Cerebratulus*. This beautiful and impressive creature unfortunately breaks into large fragments when handled. Bivalve molluscs are the prey of necklace shells *Natica* which are burrowing gastropods. In life, the smooth shell of

Lug-worm casts on a sandy beach; the Wash.

Natica is partly covered by fleshy extensions of its foot, which streamline it for passage through the sand. On finding a suitable bivalve, the snail grips it by the strong foot and bores a small hole through the shell until the flesh is reached. The sand-burrowing starfish *Astropecten irregularis* also consumes bivalves, but this voracious creature eats almost anything which it comes across, ingesting the organism whole. The burrowing anemone *Peachia hastata* is worthy of special mention because unlike most other anemones it does not attach itself to rocks or stones. Instead, it has a free-living existence, burrowing in sand and using the bulbous base of its body in a similar manner to the foot of a razor-shell. At high tide, it climbs towards the surface and projects its 12 long tentacles out into the water; at low tide it retreats down into its burrow which may descend 25 centimetres or more.

Omnivores or scavengers include the large burrowing brittle-star *Acrocnida brachiata*, and a number of decapod crustaceans of which the shrimps *Crangon* and the burrowing masked crab *Corystes cassivelaunus* may be mentioned. Next to the common cockle, the common shrimp *Crangon crangon* is the most important sandy-shore organism from the point of view of man's stomach. This flattened and sand-coloured animal is largely nocturnal and hides during the day just below the surface of the sand, often beneath shallow pools of water. During the night-time high tides it ventures out, crawling across the surface or more rarely swimming, and seizes any small animals which it can find, including worms larger than itself. On the approach of day-light, it buries itself by a peculiar shuffling motion of its legs and sides, so that it seems to sink, vibrating, down into the sand.

An equally peculiar method of burrowing is adopted by the masked crab. In contrast to other crabs, this species burrows backwards into the sand whilst sitting bolt upright. The posterior pairs of legs dig away at the sand and the animal slowly sinks in; in association with this mode of entry, its shell or carapace is much longer than broad. Another difference is its extremely long pair of hair-fringed antennae, as long as the rest of the body (most crabs have inconspicuous antennae): these are also associated with its burrowing habit. Although the masked crab is mainly sublittoral, it can occasionally be found near the low-tide mark, buried in the sand with only the tips of its antennae visible above the surface. The hairs on these appendages are in two rows, both directed inwards and towards those of the other antenna, such that the hairs of the two antennae interlock to form a tube. It is down this tube that the respiratory water current passes to the crab's gills.

Numerous other predators enter the sand-beach habitat only at certain states of the tide. Wading birds are typical low-tide additions to the fauna, and several species may be seen following the tidal water down and up the beach, probing the surface with their bills. Few species are restricted to sandy shores and the role of this important group of coastal birds will mainly be defined in the section on mud-flats. Oystercatchers *Haematopus ostralegus*, however, may be mentioned as important consumers of lug-worms, cat-worms, cockles and other bivalves. Smaller waders, such as sanderlings *Calidris alba* and ringed plovers *Charadrius hiaticula*, also take amphipods and other small organisms found near to the surface of sandy beaches or disturbed by the rising tide.

Several fish, of which the sand goby *Pomatoschistus minutus*, sand-eels *Ammodytes*, the lesser weever *Echiichthys vipera* and young flatfish (especially plaice *Pleuronectes platessa*, dab *Limanda limanda*, sole *Solea solea* and turbot *Scophthalmus maximus*) are most characteristic, invade sandy beaches at high tide and consume most small crustaceans, molluscs and polychaetes that they can find. Sand-eels, largely feeders on other fish, may often be found buried just below the sand surface near low tide, as may the lesser weever with only its eyes and dorsal spines exposed. The weevers should on no account be touched: their dorsal and opercular spines can deliver a poison with a more virulent effect than that of a wasp sting.

Other temporary immigrants from the sublittoral zone which may be found stranded near low water are the whelk *Buccinum undatum*, the spider-crab *Macropodia longirostris* and the common hermit-crab *Pagurus bernhardus*. Hidden below the surface of the sand, but otherwise coming into the same category, may be found the small swimming-crab *Portumnus latipes* and the most massive of our northern European polychaetes, the sea-mouse *Aphrodita aculeata*. Also temporarily stranded, although this time voluntarily, may occasionally be seen those most spectacular of sandy-shore visitors, the grey seals *Halichoerus grypus* and common seals *Phoca vitulina*, which often haul out on quiet sandy beaches whilst fishing. Young calves may also haul out when separated from their parents by storms at sea.

MUD-FLATS

As shelter from wave action increases still further, silts can settle out of suspension as described earlier and become important constituents of beach
sediments. In fact we have a continuum from clean sandy beaches, through
muddy sands and sandy muds, to soft mud-flats. Because the input of organic
detritus to a beach also increases with increasing shelter, we find too that the
food available to deposit- or sediment-feeders is largest when the shore is
muddiest, and hence this category of the fauna becomes progressively more
numerous. In the extreme case of soft muds, the quantity of silt present in
the water at high tide may clog the delicate feeding-structures of suspension-
feeders and so these species may decrease in actual as well as relative importance. The addition of this detrital food has one further consequence.
Bacterial decomposition of organic matter uses oxygen and this is removed
from the interstitial water. But the muddier the sediment, the less permeable
to water and dissolved gases it is, and so, if the bacteria remove oxygen faster
than it can be replaced, the sediment will become anoxic except at or very
near the surface. The bacteria can still obtain their required oxygen from
dissolved sulphates, but in the process they liberate sulphides and hence
anoxic muds are black and sulphurous. At depth, clean sands are also anoxic,
but the muddier the sediment, the nearer to the surface will anaerobic conditions extend and therefore the more crucial will be the abilities of animals to
draw a respiratory current down from the overlying water. Several of the
meiofaunal organisms living under these conditions can respire anaerobically.

In this section, we shall consider two further points along the sand-mud
continuum: the firm muddy sand-flats characteristic of fully marine though
highly sheltered situations; and the soft mud-flats typical of estuaries and
other areas of maximum shelter. Many of the animals which we mentioned
in the last section have ranges which also encompass muddy sand, although
in a few cases the species in the two habitats may be different; polychaete
worms such as *Nerine*, *Nephtys*, *Glycera*, *Scoloplos*, the lug-worm *Arenicola
marina* and sand mason *Lanice conchilega*, bivalve molluscs such as venuses
Venus, razor-shells *Ensis/Solen* and cockles *Cerastoderma*, and shrimps *Crangon*, for example, may all be common in muddy sand. But if sufficient shelter
occurs to add appreciable quantities of mud without altering the basically
firm and sandy nature of the beach, these species may be joined by a host of
others, making such shores one of the most biologically rich and diverse of
all northern European intertidal areas.

The suspension-feeding bivalve molluscs, for example, are joined by others of the same basic type as the cockles, such as the rayed artemis *Dosinia exoleta*, carpet shell *Venerupis decussata* and common otter shell *Lutraria lutraria*. Although the otter shell is a suspension-feeder it possesses siphons more than twice as long as the rest of its body; these cannot be completely withdrawn into the shell and are covered by a thick, protective, horny layer. The otter shell lives deeply buried in the sand and relies on these siphons to maintain its connection with the water at high tide. It cannot burrow rapidly like razor-shells; indeed, apart from slowly burrowing deeper as it grows, it does not burrow at all and its sole means of protection from potential predators is the 40 centimetres of sand between it and the surface.

Some fan-worms, such as the peacock *Sabella penicillus* and *Megalomma vesiculosum*, construct tubes near low water variously of mud set in a mucous matrix, of sand grains, and even of jelly, dependent on species. These tubes descend vertically into the sediment and often project a little beyond the surface. At high tide, the worms inhabiting them extend into the water a feathery and often beautifully coloured crown of tentacles which collect and transport food particles to the mouth. The crown may bear small simple eyes, and the worms may retreat rapidly into their burrows should a shadow pass over them. The peculiar, fragile and phosphorescent chaetopterid worm *Chaetopterus variopedatus*, now sadly rare between the tide marks, is also a suspension-feeder. This it carries out by drawing a water current through its large, U-shaped, parchment-like tube by the beating of three large fans. The current is then filtered through a mucous bag which the worm secretes and consumes.

Amongst the suspension-feeding crustaceans of muddy sand are the large, pale burrowing-shrimps *Upogebia* and *Callianassa*. These excavate extensive burrow systems near low tide and sublittorally, and draw a water current through by beating their abdominal swimmerets. The first two pairs of legs are fringed with long hairs, forming a basket which retains any small particles in the water. These are wiped off by the mouthparts, sorted and swallowed.

Similarly, the surface-deposit feeding *Lanice* is joined by a host of other polychaete worms feeding in essentially the same manner: for example, *Amphitrite*, *Nicolea venustula*, *Eupolymnia*, *Owenia fusiformis* (which can also suspension-feed) and *Cirriformia tentaculata*. And the numbers of sediment-feeders are increased by the capitellid worm *Notomastus latericeus* and many small bamboo-worms *Clymenura*, the peanutworms *Golfingia* and the burrowing sea-cucumbers *Leptosynapta inhaerens* and *Labidoplax digitata*. *Golfingia* was so called because the first specimens to be found were discovered by a scientist whilst playing golf on a coastal sand-dune.

With the increase in the number of potential food items, it is not surprising to find that the number of predators and scavengers is also larger. Several omnivorous worms probably include animal prey in their diet, whilst

A creek running through an estuarine mud-flat bordered on the right by salt-marsh.

also consuming debris and even the sediment. Polychaete species such as the rag-worms *Perinereis cultrifera* and *Platynereis dumerilii*, the eunicid *Marphysa sanguinea*, all with strong, chitinous jaws, and the elongate *Phyllodoce* and *Sthenelais boa* with soft probosces, are common in muddy sand, as are the ribbonworms *Lineus* and *Tubulanus annulatus*. The unique, worm-like *Priapulus caudatus*, with its annulated body, its large, barrel-shaped, spine-bearing proboscis and its cluster of terminal egg-like structures, is a voracious carnivore. Lastly, the types of burrowing anemones also increase, with species of *Halcampa* and *Cereus* (in the south and west) entering the fauna. The daisy anemone *C. pedunculatus* is not a true burrowing anemone since its base is attached to a stone or shell beneath the surface.

Higher plants make their first appearance on the shore in muddy-sand habitats, in the form of eelgrasses *Zostera*, relatives of the freshwater pond-weeds. The largest of these grass-like perennials, *Z. marina*, with leaves of up to one metre in length, can be found near low water and sublittorally, whilst the two smaller species, *Z. noltii* and *Z. angustifolia*, extend further up the shore; all three have creeping underground stems and inconspicuous petal-less flowers in the bases of some of the leaves. *Z. marina* suffered a wasting disease in the 1930s and some eelgrass meadows have still not recovered their former glory. A well-developed fauna is, or was, associated with this plant, including several small gastropod molluscs, the chameleon prawn *Hippolyte varians*, several opossum-shrimps (*eg* the chameleon

Eelgrass growing on muddy sand. The cockle has also been uncovered by the ebbing tide.

shrimp *Praunus flexuosus*) and the small stalked jellyfish *Haliclystus auricula*, which we shall meet again on the rocky shore.

In contrast to this species richness, the fauna of mud-flats with an insignificant sand component is very poor in terms of numbers of species probably resulting from the uniformity, liquidity and anoxic state of most of them, together with the low and fluctuating salinities often prevailing. Those few species which can survive these conditions, however, can achieve huge densities because of the abundance of food. These soft mud-flats may be found in estuaries, lagoons, harbours and land-locked bays, and in the lee of offshore barrier islands such as those fringing the southern North Sea coasts. The small eelgrasses may still occur in these habitats, but more important are the seaweeds which can grow attached to small stones or even on the mud-flat surface under these highly sheltered conditions. The green seaweeds – sea-lettuce *Ulva lactuca*, *Enteromorpha* and *Ulothrix* – and various mat-forming blue-green algae are characteristic, and several dwarf and often bladderless forms of some of the rocky-shore wracks *Fucus* may also be found.

Apart from a few very small sea-slugs (*Limapontia* and *Alderia*) which graze the algal mats, the fauna is almost entirely mud-eating. Of course, it is the high detritus content of the sediment, together with the bacteria, meiofauna and microscopic diatoms which provides the real food source. The laver spire shell *Hydrobia ulvae* crawls over the mud and seaweed (in densities of over 300,000 per sq m on *Enteromorpha*), eating as it goes, whilst the other common species live in the mud itself. The amphipod *Corophium volutator*, for example, constructs a U-shaped burrow, out of which it partially emerges to pull in surface sediment with its very large antennae. The mud is sorted by the mouthparts before swallowing. Like the burrowing-shrimps, it can also filter food from its respiratory water current using setae on its anterior limbs.

Two thin-shelled bivalves, the Baltic tellin *Macoma balthica* and the peppery furrow shell *Scrobicularia plana*, burrow well down below the sediment surface – *S. plana* as much as 25 centimetres below – and extend a long, mobile, inhalent siphon up to vacuum-clean the surface, often leaving characteristic star-shaped suction marks. As with other bivalves, material is filtered by the gills, and the filtered current passes out through the somewhat shorter exhalent siphon. Long, independently mobile siphons are typical deposit-feeding adaptations in bivalves. The common rag-worm *Neanthes* (*Nereis*) *diversicolor* also inhabits a vertical burrow, but each burrow has several oblique shafts running to the surface, creating multiple entrances and exits, and a series of mucous tunnels may lie on the mud surface as an extension of the burrow system. This rag-worm is one of the mud-flat opportunists and will poke its anterior end out of its burrow to seize and consume small living animals such as amphipods, dead or moribund fish and other carrion, or pieces of green algae. It will also rasp away at the sediment surface to consume the micro-algae and meiofauna, and can suspension-feed in a manner reminiscent of the chaetopterid worm *Chaetopterus*. A cottonwool-like plug of mucus is secreted in one of the entrances to its burrow system, and the worm positions itself so as to draw a current of water through the plug by undulatory movements of its body. When the plug has collected particles from the water current, it is seized and eaten.

Other deposit-feeding organisms live in the mud, including the cat-worm *Nephtys hombergi*, and various other polychaetes (spionids and *Ampharete*), tubificid worms such as *Peloscolex benedeni*, and even insect larvae such as those of crane-flies (Tipulidae); but the mud-flat also has a few specialist suspension-feeders. The sand gaper *Mya arenaria* and blunt gaper *M. truncata*, for example, are large bivalves very similar in general shape to the otter shell *Lutraria* mentioned earlier: both have permanently extended siphons encased in a tough skin, and live deep (some 60 centimetres) in the sediments near low-water level.

Eelgrasses, the green algae and the large numbers of invertebrates attract many wading birds and wildfowl at low tide, especially from the late autumn to early spring. Amongst the wildfowl, brent geese *Branta bernicla* and shelducks *Tadorna tadorna* are particularly characteristic, brent geese consuming eelgrass and *Enteromorpha*, and shelducks taking *Hydrobia* and, less frequently, amphipods and small polychaetes. Shelducks feed by slowly waddling along the shore, swinging their bills to and fro in the surface layers and sifting out any small organisms. One shelduck from Kent contained 3000 individual *Hydrobia ulvae*. This small gastropod is also taken in large quantity by other ducks, for example by shovelers *Anas clypeata*, pintails, *A. acuta* and teal *A. crecca*; whilst wigeon *A. penelope* also eat eelgrass and *Enteromorpha*. Although predominantly herbivorous in winter, mallards *A. platyrhynchos* may feed on mud-flats where they consume a wide range of small polychaetes, molluscs and crustaceans.

It is, however, for the waders that these beaches are best known; indeed, large percentages of the world populations of several species are dependent on these areas of northern Europe in winter. Curlews *Numenius arquata* and black- and bar-tailed godwits *Limosa limosa* and *L. lapponica*, with long, downcurved or straight bills, take the deeper-burrowing polychaetes and the softer-shelled molluscs. The stout bill of the oystercatcher can equally be used to catch rag-worms and similar-sized polychaetes as to hammer open cockle shells. Waders with medium-sized bills, such as many species of *Tringa* and *Calidris* (the redshanks, greenshank, sandpipers, knot and dunlin), consume more shallowly-burrowing polychaetes, molluscs and crustaceans, for example the various spionids, tellins and amphipods. Redshanks *T. totanus* can eat 40,000 *Corophium*, and knot *C. canutus* over 700 *Macoma* per bird per day. The small-billed waders and particularly the plovers (*Pluvialis*, *Vanellus*, *Charadrius*) then take the surface fauna of *Hydrobia* and such amphipods and other small crustaceans as they can find. Some waders rely not so much on probing the beach as on stirring the surface sediment and catching the uncovered animals as they endeavour to make for safety: avocets *Recurvirostra avosetta* and phalaropes *Phalaropus* are examples. Gulls *Larus*, crows *Corvus* and several other birds also make use of the opportunity to feed on exposed, muddy beaches. Gulls and crows will pick up hardshelled bivalves and drop them until they strike a hard surface which breaks the shells and enables the birds to reach the flesh.

At high tide, the flocks of birds leave the beach and roost on adjacent high ground, and it is then the turn of fish to invade the rich feeding area, together with shore crabs *Carcinus maenas* and other scavenging crustaceans. A few fish, the grey mullets *Chelon labrosus* and *Liza ramuda* for example, swim in to browse on the films of blue-green algae, leaving marks for all the world like those made by the front teeth of some gigantic rabbit; but the majority of the fish seek the invertebrates which will be resuming their normal activity on being covered by the tide. As on sandy shores, it is the flatfish and the gobies (Gobiidae) which are particularly abundant. Dabs *Limanda limanda* specialize in biting off the tentacular crowns of the fan-worms whilst also taking some crustaceans; brill *Scophthalmus rhombus* take gobies and shrimps *Crangon*; plaice *Pleuronectes platessa* consume mainly polychaetes; and flounders *Platichthys flesus* concentrate on swimming crustaceans. The characteristic goby of these shores, *Pomatoschistus microps*, eats almost anything – meiofauna, small shrimps, amphipods, small polychaetes and young *Hydrobia*.

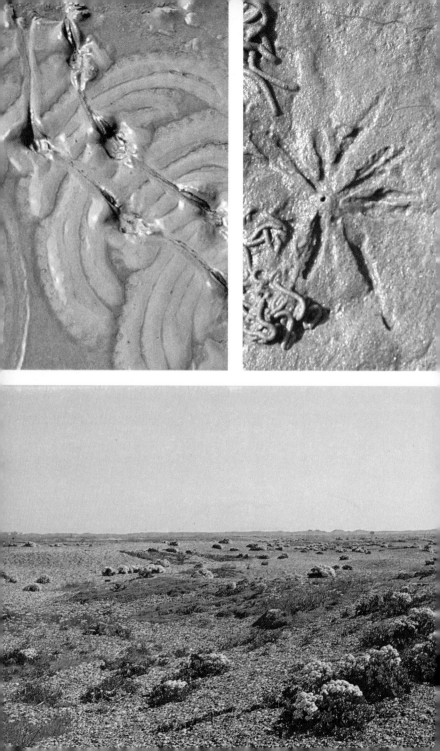

SHINGLE BEACHES

Wide expanses of intertidal shingle, such as occur along parts of the Atlantic coast of France, the southern shores of the Baltic, and along several stretches of the British coastline, appear desolate in the extreme. Because individual pebbles are rotated one against another by wave action, the intertidal zones are lifeless. Only when the pebbles are set into a sandy or muddy beach can they be colonized by animals and plants, and then the shores largely conform to the descriptions given earlier. But a few species are characteristic of such situations: for example, the lug-worm *Arenicolides ecaudata* and the cirratulid worm *Cirriformia tentaculata* live under the pebbles.

Above the high-tide line on shingle beaches, organisms may be scarce but they are present. Some accumulation of humus or fine particulate matter between the pebbles is required before higher plants can establish themselves, and hence they are often associated with the strand-line and with areas which mosses and, more importantly, lichens have already colonized. Continuous swards are hardly ever formed; instead, individual plants occur as isolated mats or clumps, a total of six different species along any one stretch of beach being a good score. Characteristic shingle species are sea campion *Silene maritima*, the maritime variety of curled dock *Rumex crispus* var *trigranulatus*, yellow horned-poppy *Glaucium flavum*, sea pea *Lathyrus japonicus*, sea beet *Beta vulgaris*, sea-kale *Crambe maritima*, yellow stonecrop *Sedum anglicum*, herb-robert *Geranium robertianum* and, in the north, the rare oysterplant *Mertensia maritima*. Several of these are typical strand-line species and also occur on other beach types. Other members of the strand-line flora can colonize shingle if its interstices contain appreciable quantities of their preferred sediment: thus sea sandwort *Honkenya peploides*, sea couch *Agropyron pungens* and red fescue *Festuca rubra* are present where wind-blown sand has accumulated between the pebbles, and Babington's orache *Atriplex glabriuscula* occurs when the strand-line is muddy.

In sheltered regions, for example along the lee side of shingle spits, the drift-line may be colonized locally in south Britain and France by shrubby

TOP LEFT *The feeding arcs created by the bill of a shelduck as it waddled along the shore in search of small gastropods.* TOP RIGHT *The suction channels of a peppery furrow shell where its siphon has surfaced to vacuum-clean the surface for food particles.*

BELOW *Shingle beach with the characteristic patchy vegetation which here includes sea-kale (white), hawk's-beard (yellow) and ivy-leaved toadflax (purple).*

sea-blite *Suaeda fruticosa*, a large heather-like species requiring well drained and well aerated soils, requirements admirably met by shingle. It can also be found in the small, flat pockets of stable shingle associated with dune systems on a shingle base (as in areas from which the sand has been eroded), where it occurs in company with rock sea-lavender *Limonium binervosum*, sea heath *Frankenia laevis* and the prostrate variety of a typically salt-marsh species, sea-purslane *Halimione portulacoides*.

Little is known of the animals of these habitats, although from the scanty information available it would appear that they are all visitors from adjacent terrestrial areas and that truly coastal species are lacking. Stable shingle, however, is used as a breeding site by ringed plovers *Charadrius hiaticula*, oystercatchers *Haematopus ostralegus*, and Sandwich *Sterna sandvicensis*, common *S. hirundo*, arctic *S. paradisaea* and little terns *S. albifrons*.

Shingle masses often contain small ponds or lagoons between their component ridges, and shingle bars or spits may enclose lagoons in their lee. These natural aquaria, as they have been called, bear a fauna and flora closely related to that described in the section on mud-flats but in which several mud-flat species are replaced by typical lagoon forms. For example, other species of *Hydrobia* replace *H. ulvae*; the thinner-shelled *Cerastoderma* (*Cardium*) *glaucum* replaces the common cockle *C. edule*; and the prawn *Palaemonetes varians* replaces the common shrimp *Crangon crangon*. Isopods and amphipods elsewhere living under stones or in seaweed are represented by *Sphaeroma* and *Gammarus zaddachi*.

The lack of wave action and the fact that these lagoons do not experience low tide has enabled a number of basically terrestrial or freshwater organisms to be represented there by specialist maritime species. Pulmonate snails (the characteristic group of land snails) occur, for example, as do numerous insects; the damselfly *Ischnura elegans*, various water-boatmen *Sigara stagnalis*, *S. selecta*, *S. concinna*, *Corixa panzeri* and *Notonecta viridis*, several beetles and the pondweeds *Ruppia*, *Zannichellia* and *Potamogeton pectinatus* are but a few of these species. Such lagoons may also be fringed by reeds *Phragmites australis* and sea club-rush *Scirpus maritimus*. As on mud-flats, detritus is central to the ecology of lagoons and, as we shall see later, these areas show many similarities to the small pools found on salt-marsh surfaces, salt-pans. In passing, we can also note the resemblance to the northern limb of the Baltic, the Gulf of Bothnia, where various freshwater animals, such as pond snails and the isopod *Asellus*, live in what geographically is the sea.

ROCKY SHORES

Rocky shores are the most diverse of all coastal habitats, ranging from exposed boulder beaches, the feet of vertical cliffs and horizontal rock platforms to quiet, seaweed-strewn areas and closely vegetated estuarine headlands. They are also the commonest coastal habitat-type, especially in the west and north (only along the southern shores of the North Sea are they rare or absent), and the richest biologically, with species lists of seaweeds and animals running into the thousands.

Before we proceed too far it is necessary to define some abbreviations and terms for use in this section. Many more rocky-shore species may be found in the south and west of northern Europe than in the north and east. This is because, while sand- and mud-dwellers can burrow down into the sediment to gain protection from, for example, cold spells, animals of rocky shores are more exposed to the vagaries of the weather, and warmth-loving species can therefore inhabit only the western and southwestern shores of Ireland and Britain and the northwestern shores of France (*ie* the southern part of our region and those areas bathed by the Gulf Stream). Species thus restricted in their distribution will be indicated by the appropriate compass points after their names – the rock-urchin *Paracentrotus lividus* (W), for example. The extreme southwestern regions are sufficiently warm to form a transitional zone between northern Europe on the one hand and the richer, warm temperate coasts to the south on the other, and a number of 'Lusitanian species' from the Mediterranean and adjacent areas also manage to extend into Brittany, Cornwall, Dyfed and Munster, making these regions especially rich. In contrast, there is an impoverishment of the fauna and flora as one proceeds northwards into progressively colder climates. In north and east Iceland, however, and in Norway north of the Lofotens, arctic species, there at their southernmost limit, enter the fauna, thus creating the northern natural boundary zone of our region.

We shall also see that the organisms of rocky shores often show a well-marked vertical zonation which can be related to certain tidal heights or to the height to which spray is cast. We shall describe the fauna and flora against a background of five zones. The supralittoral fringe extends from the highest point covered or wetted by spring tides (EHWS) to the average high-water level of spring tides (MHWS); the upper eulittoral zone from MHWS to the lowest point on the shore left uncovered by high water of neap tides (E(L)HWN); the mid-eulittoral zone from E(L)HWN to the highest point on the shore left uncovered by low water of neap tides (E(H)LWN); the

ABOVE *Barnacle line on West Dale beach, Pembrokeshire. Sand-blasting keeps the base of the rock clear of vegetation and animals.* BELOW *Variation in predicted high and low tide levels (measured in metres above datum) at St Helier, Channel Islands, January–June 1978, showing the different tidal zones and their broad classification into upper, middle and lower shore. (– – – high-water mark, · · · low-water mark.)*

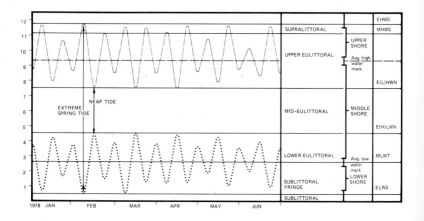

lower eulittoral zone from E(H)LWN to the average low-water level of all tides (MLWT); and the sublittoral fringe from MLWT down to and below the lowest point on the shore ever exposed at low tide (ELWS). This zonation scheme sounds complex, but is really very simple. The supralittoral fringe is covered by only a few high tides; the upper eulittoral is left exposed by some high tides; the mid-eulittoral is covered by all high tides and exposed by all low tides; the lower eulittoral is exposed by most low tides; and the sublittoral fringe is exposed by only a few low tides. At any one place, the tidal range varies during the month, depending on the relative positions of the sun and moon; periods when the tidal range is large are called springs and when it is small are called neaps. There are two sets of springs and two neaps in each lunar month.

As on the sandy beaches, we shall begin our look at rocky shores with the simplest type – those exposed to severe wave action. Two features of exposed rocky shores immediately strike one: the eulittoral zone is animal-dominated, and, owing to the surge, splash and spray of breaking waves, all the tidal zones and particularly the supralittoral fringe extend farther up the shore than would be predicted entirely on the basis of tidal range. The zones on these beaches are therefore determined not in relation to tidal height but to the heights to which wave spray is normally hurled.

In the supralittoral fringe, a black belt of 'oil' or 'paint' with patches of 'soot' at comparatively high levels is characteristic. Both phenomena are lichens: the thin black film is *Verrucaria maura*, while the sooty patches are *Lichina confinis*. In crevices or holes in the rock at this level will be found the small periwinkle *Littorina neritoides* and its larger relative, the rough periwinkle *L. saxatilis*, and a maritime woodlouse, the sea-slater *Ligia oceanica*; near the base of the film of *Verrucaria*, a dark band of slippery blue-green algae is not uncommon. Both periwinkles graze the lichens and algae and show a number of adaptations for semi-terrestrial life, the small periwinkle by being resistant to the water-loss resulting from the long bouts of exposure to the air (although it still has planktonic larvae and can spawn only at the times of high spring tides), and the rough periwinkle by having suppressed its planktonic larval phase.

Both periwinkles also occur in the upper eulittoral zone, in which the two lichens mentioned above are replaced by the spiky tufts of *Lichina pygmaea*, although the dominant organism here is the star barnacle *Chthamalus stellatus* (W). On shores where the similar species *Balanus balanoides* is also present, these two acorn-barnacles have been shown to compete for the available space on the rocks. In such circumstances the faster-growing *Balanus* is the victor. *Chthamalus*, however, is more tolerant of desiccation and so can survive in a zone above that to which *Balanus* is restricted, free of any competition. On some shores, stunted seaweeds can colonize this zone in the form of sprigs of *Fucus distichus* (N and NW) and small tufts of the dwarf variety of spiral wrack *Fucus spiralis* var *nanus*. Rarely, however, do these algae cover much of the available space.

The mid-eulittoral zone remains a barnacle domain, with *Balanus balanoides* usually dominant and covering much of the rock surfaces, although in some areas dense populations of small common mussels *Mytilus edulis* carpet the rocks either almost to the exclusion of barnacles or else as a number of discrete patches interspersed with similar patches of *Balanus*. The mussels may be draped by purple laver *Porphyra umbilicalis* (which looks like a red version of the sea-lettuce *Ulva*) and they may occur in company with a stunted, bladderless form of bladder wrack *Fucus vesiculosus*. The young stages of these algae are consumed by the common limpet *Patella vulgata*, which enters the fauna near the top of this zone and increases in importance through it; whilst a predator of both mussels and barnacles, the dog-whelk *Nucella lapillus*, may be found aggregated in comparatively sheltered hollows and pockets. Limpets, including *P. intermedia* (SW), may be particularly abundant in any rock pools present at this height on the shore, and in these pools or in crevices the beautiful anemones *Sagartia elegans* (perhaps commonest in the SW) and *Metridium senile* (the plumose anemone), together with the beadlet anemone *Actinia equina*, seek relative shelter.

This fauna and flora may continue through the lower eulittoral, with perhaps the replacement of the common limpet by *P. aspera* (SW), but not infrequently a number of red seaweeds, *eg* common coralweed *Corallina officinalis* and *Gigartina stellata*, form a short turf through which the long straps of the brown thong-weed *Himanthalia elongata* issue from their basal 'buttons'. In pools, often lined by encrusting coralline algae, or in crevices at this height may dwell the rock-urchin *Paracentrotus lividus* (W) or green sea-urchin *Psammechinus miliaris* whilst they await the return of the tide to venture up the shore in search of food.

Finally, the sublittoral fringe is dominated by the large, strap-like murlins *Alaria esculenta* and in less exposed areas, the tangle *Laminaria digitata*. The surge of waves tends to make examination of this zone hazardous.

The fauna of exposed, rocky shores is largely a sessile, suspension-feeding one; mussels and barnacles are both suspension-feeders. Barnacles, in contrast to their appearance, are crustaceans and not molluscs. They begin life as small planktonic larvae, typically crustacean, but when they reach a later stage of development they descend from the plankton and prospect suitable places on rocks or stones to which they can cement themselves, head first. After attachment, the hard plates of the 'shell' are secreted rapidly to protect the young barnacle from wave action and predators, and from then on these small crustaceans are permanently affixed to the rock and spend their lives 'kicking' food into their mouths when covered by water. If one watches a group of barnacles in a rock pool, one will see a feathery net issue from the mouth of the shell, sweep through the water and retract into the shell again, only to emerge once more and repeat the performance. This feathery structure is the barnacle's legs or cirri, and in sweeping through the water the cirri can filter from it particles down to 0·03 millimetres in size. The catch is then cleaned from the cirri by other appendages and passed to the mouth.

The other important component of the rocky-shore fauna, the grazers of living plants, are represented on exposed shores by the periwinkles, limpets and some sea-urchins (for example *Paracentrotus*). These graze the young sporeling stages of the larger algae and in so doing rasp away the rock surface as well, by as much as 1·5 millimetres per year. The larger wracks and kelps are too tough, rubbery and indigestible to be eaten by the majority of grazers, and so it is only by consuming the very young stages of these seaweeds that the grazers can live, and it is only through their activities that the larger algae are prevented from carpetting all but the most exposed of rocky shores. The smaller, softer algae growing on the broader blades of the larger wracks and kelps can, however, also be eaten.

The resident carnivore population of rocky shores is usually more numerous than on sandy or muddy beaches. On exposed rocks, dog-whelks bore through the shells of barnacles and mussels in a similar fashion to the necklace shell *Natica* mentioned earlier. Barnacles are also eaten by the green sea-urchin and, it is said, by the long, green paddle-worm *Eulalia viridis*, to be seen crawling across the wet surface of barnacle-covered rocks.

Much of this pattern persists on more sheltered shores, but in general, dominance by seaweeds increases with increasing shelter, whilst animal diversity is greatest on the intermediate, semi-exposed to moderately sheltered shores which we shall consider now. On shores about half way along the exposure–shelter gradient, the supralittoral fringe differs little in essence from that described earlier. The zone is, however, greatly reduced in height (as wave splash and spray are less here) and the small periwinkle becomes progressively more scarce, especially in the north, whilst the rough periwinkle is more abundant. In the upper eulittoral, the sparse cover of *Lichina pygmaea* and the two dwarf wracks is replaced by an upper band of channelled wrack *Pelvetia canaliculata*, and sometimes by a lower belt of full-sized spiral wrack. Star barnacles may still be present in considerable numbers, but barnacles generally decline from their position of dominance as the seaweed cover becomes greater.

It is at low tidal levels, however, that the effects of the greater shelter are most marked. The mid-eulittoral is characteristically clothed in the normal form of bladder wrack (except where streams run down the shore and at the head of estuaries, where it is replaced by the related horned wrack *Fucus ceranoides*). On bladder wrack lives the flat periwinkle *Littorina littoralis*, and under seaweed, in rock pools and on the bare rock may be found the fourth northern European periwinkle, the edible winkle *L. littorea*, in company with the thick top-shell *Monodonta lineata* (SW), the purple top-shell *Gibbula umbilicalis* and the ubiquitous common limpet. All these gastropods browse and graze algal sporelings and epiphytes. The carnivorous dog-whelks and beadlet anemones also occur in this and in lower zones.

A sheltered rocky shore with an upper band of channelled wrack, and spiral wrack bordering the rock pool.

A final type of *Fucus*, the saw wrack *F. serratus*, occurs in the lower eulittoral together with *Gigartina*, *Corallina* and many other red seaweeds such as pepper dulse *Laurencia pinnatifida*, dulse *Palmaria palmata*, carragheen *Chondrus crispus* and *Lomentaria articulata* – which continue the development of the red algal turf found on exposed shores. These small red algae, especially when present in rock pools, provide a home for a multitude of minute invertebrates too small to be seen without the aid of a microscope. Where rocks jut into sandy bays, all these algae may be replaced by reefs of the honeycomb worm *Sabellaria alveolata* (SW), which may completely dominate large areas of the lower eulittoral zone. The reef consists of the massed tubes, built of sand grains, of these small worms; the mouth of each tube is partially closed by a shelf with a central round hole through which the worm pokes its head, when covered by the tide, to collect suspended food materials and sand grains. Exceptionally, the large acorn-barnacle *Balanus perforatus* (SW) may also dominate this zone, although more usually it occurs together with the red algae or with the honeycomb worm. This zone, and the kelp-dominated sublittoral fringe with its forests of *Laminaria digitata* and cuvie *L. hyperborea*, support a wealth of animal species – amongst the seaweeds, on rocky overhangs, under boulders, and in rock pools – in increasing diversity the nearer one gets to the regions permanently covered by the sea.

These numerous species – too numerous to mention even all the common ones – can be broadly divided into three categories: grazers, suspension-feeders (including some carnivores which catch minute animals suspended in

The underside of a boulder carpeted by sponges (blue and red), a sea-squirt Ciona intestinalis, *and tube-worms.*

the water), and predators and scavengers. As on exposed rocky shores, the grazers are mainly gastropod molluscs which are represented near low water by the top-shells *Gibbula cineraria, G. magus* (S and W), *Tricolia pullus* (SW) and the handsome painted top-shell *Calliostoma zizyphinum,* and by the limpets, *eg Acmaea* and the blue-rayed limpet *Patina pellucida* which may be found on the stipe and frond of *Laminaria* when juvenile and in the holdfast when adult. Chitons, *eg Lepidochitona cinereus,* are also grazers, as are the sea-urchins *Echinus esculentus* and *Strongylocentrotus droebachiensis* (E) which may be found at extreme low-water levels.

Many of the suspension-feeders are sessile and colonial: they characteristically carpet the underside of boulders, giving rise to a multicoloured patchwork of different encrusting species, hang from shady rocky overhangs and encrust or attach to seaweeds. Three common encrusting types are the sponges, sea-squirts and bryozoans or sea-mats. Perhaps the most abundant sponge is the green, yellow and brown breadcrumb sponge *Halichondria panicea.* Water is drawn into this almost inanimate animal over much of its surface, suspended particles are captured by special cells which line its internal cavity, and the water is then ejected through the visible, small volcanoes or oscula over its surface. Other sponges encrusting rock and boulders, such as *Hymeniacidon perlevis* and *Ophlitaspongia seriata* (S), may be bright red. Yet further sponges do not encrust but have characteristic vase-like shapes attached at their bases to seaweeds or rocks. The purse-sponge *Grantia compressa* and *Sycon coronatum* are examples.

Also divisible into encrusting forms (although 'enjellying' might be more apt) and hanging or upright types are the often brightly-coloured colonial sea-squirts, although a single species may occur in both growth forms. The common star ascidian *Botryllus schlosseri*, for example, encrusts the under-side of boulders but hangs pendant from overhangs or the roofs of caves. The background colour of this species may be yellow, green, blue or violet. The individual animals, set in the communal jelly and arranged in the form of a star, are bright yellow or red. *Botrylloides leachi* and *Morchellium argus* (SW) are common, as indeed are a host of others, including the solitary *Dendrodoa grossularia*, which resembles nothing so much as a small reddish blob of stiff jelly, and the much larger translucent *Ciona intestinalis*, so common on piers and jetties.

A comparable division of growth types is also found amongst the bryo-zoans. Some like the sea-mat *Membranipora membranacea* encrusts seaweeds whilst the hard sea-mat *Umbonula littoralis* covers rocks. *Bugula*, however, hang as miniature trees from any suitable support. These tufted bryozoans are very similar in appearance to several of the colonial hydroids, which hang or arise feather-like from seaweeds or rocks. Hydroids are not strictly suspension-feeders: the microscopic, anemone-like polyps, which are the food-catching elements of the colony, extend tiny tentacles into the water and individually catch small planktonic animals which bump against them. In species such as *Dynamena pumila* and *Obelia geniculata*, one only sees the external skeleton of the colony, the individual polyps being too small; but some, like *Tubularia*, have large brightly-coloured polyps and have been called sea-flowers.

Their larger, solitary relatives, the sea-anemones, are also frequent at low tidal levels: species such as the snakelocks anemone *Anemonia sulcata* (W) with its violet-tipped tentacles which cannot be retracted into the body, the larger dahlia anemone *Tealia felina*, which frequently has small stones and pieces of shell adhering to its sides, and the small wartlet or gem anemone *Bunodactis verrucosa* (SW), with its six rows of warts, join *Sagartia*, *Metridium* and *Actinia*.

In the southwest may also be found this region's only intertidal corals, the Devonshire cup coral *Caryophyllia smithi* and the scarlet-and-gold star coral *Balanophyllia regia*, small solitary species secreting one-centimetre-high skeletal cups attached firmly to the rock. The southwest also boasts northern Europe's only stalked jellyfishes – including *Lucernariopsis* and *Haliclystus auricula* – tiny, trumpet-shaped animals attached by a sucker, arising from the upper side of the bell, to *Laminaria* and other seaweeds, and sometimes to rocks. Unlike other jellyfish, they never swim free in the water.

Not all true suspension-feeders are colonial, neither are they necessarily sessile. On the underside of boulders, two small species of porcelain-crabs are common, *Porcellana platycheles* and *P. longicornis*; these flattened relatives of hermit-crabs feed, like the burrowing-prawns of muddy sand, by filtering particles from water currents with hairs on their mouthparts. The related squat-lobsters *Galathea* also feed in this manner, but like the hermit-crabs *Pagurus*, which abound in low-level rock pools, they scrape material off the rocks into suspension and then retain it in their filtration apparatus. Most other suspension-feeders are sessile. Seaweeds and rocks may be covered by the small, frequently tightly coiled tubes of the tube-worms *Spirorbis* and *Pomatoceros triqueter*, which can close the mouths of their calcareous tubes with a special 'lid' borne on one of their head appendages. Like their relatives, the fan-worms, some of which live under stones or in crevices on rocky shores (for example *Branchiomma bombyx*, *Bispira volutacornis* (SW) and *Amphiglena mediterranea*), spirorbid tube-worms feed using a crown of feathered tentacles. Attached to the rock one may find saddle oysters *Anomia* and the variegated scallop *Chlamys varia*, whilst other suspension-feeding bivalves like *Hiatella* bore into the rock. Large acorn-barnacles, such as *Balanus crenatus*, extend up from the sublittoral zone into the sublittoral fringe.

The sessile suspension-feeders are preyed on by a host of carnivores, which dwell with them on the underside of boulders. Important predators of the sponges, bryozoans, sea-squirts, hydroids and sea-anemones are the nudibranch molluscs or sea-slugs. The common grey sea-slug *Aeolidia papillosa* feeds on sea-anemones. The sea-slug is not affected by the stinging threads of its sea-anemone prey, indeed it puts them to good use: they become lodged in the papillae covering its upper surface, so that potential predators of this sea-slug may find themselves on the receiving end of the offensive armoury of an anemone. The cowries *Trivia arctica* and *T. monacha* also feed on sea-squirts, whilst the small sea-spiders, *eg Nymphon* and *Pycnogonum littorale*, consume hydroids and sea-anemones. Barnacles and mussels are the prey of other molluscs besides *Nucella*; the sting winkles *Ocenebra erinacea* (S) and *O. corallina* (S), and the small sea-slug *Onchidoris bilamellata*, for example.

Many of the remaining carnivores are rather general predators and scavengers, and, again, most can be found under boulders awaiting the return of the tide. Into this category can be placed the many scale- and paddle-worms; the shore crab *Carcinus maenas* and its larger, more handsome relative the velvet swimming-crab *Macropipus puber* (SW); various brittle-stars like *Ophiothrix fragilis* and *Amphipholis squamata*; the cushion star *Asterina gibbosa* (SW) and common starfish *Asterias rubens*; the netted dog-whelks *Nassarius*; and a multitude of amphipods, such as *Gammarus locusta*. Other species are more typical of rock pools, the prawn *Palaemon elegans* for example, while the rocky-shore fish may occur in either habitat. These include the rock goby *Gobius paganellus* (S), the clingfish *Lepadogaster* (mainly SW), the sea scorpions *Taurulus*, the five-bearded and the shore rocklings *Ciliata mustela* and *Gaidropsarus mediterraneus*, the shanny *Lipophrys pholis*, the butterfish *Pholis gunnellus* and the viviparous blenny *Zoarces viviparus* (NE). The shore fish take a wide range of crustaceans, polychaetes, molluscs and other fish; blennies can even bite barnacles from the rocks.

A few deposit-feeders are also present: relatives of several of the muddy-shore polychaetes may be found under stones and, if one is very lucky, the small sea-cucumbers (*Pawsonia*, *Aslia* and *Ocnus*) may be seen on the underside of boulders uncovered by low spring tides.

Two other small microhabitats deserve a special mention. The holdfasts of *Laminaria* support a microcosm of rocky-shore life. Small polychaetes (scale-worms, syllids and *Nereis pelagica*), ribbonworms and brittle-stars, generally of a predatory or scavenging nature, hide and shelter in these structures at low tide. There they join a sedentary or sessile fauna of even smaller gastropod and bivalve molluscs, and serpulid polychaetes, which live permanently within the safety of the holdfast. Unfortunately, in common with the inhabitants of the other micro-habitat, rock crevices, these animals are all too small to be seen properly without the aid of a microscope. Deep cracks or crevices in the rock support a comparable microcosm, but here a number of different terrestrial animals manage to find a home on the otherwise inhospitable shore. Small pulmonate snails, with lung chambers instead of gills, pseudoscorpions *Neobisium maritimum*, centipedes *Strigamia maritima*, beetles *Aepus robini*, the springtails *Anurida maritima* and the bristletail *Petrobius maritimus*, which can also be found on the rock surface at high tidal levels, live here in company with small marine molluscs *Cingula cingillus* and *Lasaea rubra*, isopod and amphipod crustaceans, and polychaetes like *Amphitritides gracilis* (SW).

The final type of rocky shore to be considered is that occurring in highly-sheltered situations, as, for example, at the heads of sea-lochs and fjords. The most noticeable features of these shores are the much reduced supralittoral fringe, which may even be partially replaced by terrestrial vegetation, the dense carpet of seaweeds across the eulittoral zone, and the frequently muddy sublittoral fringe occurring as a result of silts settling out of the quiet, sheltered water.

The upper eulittoral is occupied by a higher-level blanket of channelled wrack which merges into a lower zone of spiral wrack. Almost the only animal to be seen is the rough periwinkle although it may be abundant. Drifts of rotting seaweed may, however, shelter the sand-hopper *Orchestia gammarella* – the rocky-shore equivalent of *Talitrus*. The fronds or ropes of the knotted wrack *Ascophyllum nodosum* – which may be up to four metres long – replace bladder wrack in the mid-eulittoral and lie as tangled masses all over the zone. On the fronds the flat periwinkle is abundant, and beneath them the widespread common limpet, edible periwinkle and acorn-barnacle *Balanus balanoides* still persist. Knotted wrack itself supports an abundant fauna of attached hydroids like *Clava squamata* (mainly SW), bryozoans like *Bowerbankia imbricata*, and the coiled tubes of serpulid worms; whilst the red epiphyte *Polysiphonia lanosa* may occur as dense tufts. The green *Enteromorpha* will usually be found on temporarily bare areas of rock.

The lower eulittoral is usually totally dominated by saw wrack although some red algae may still be found in the position of their characteristic turf on more exposed shores: pepper dulse *Laurencia pinnatifida* and carragheen are two persistent species. The sublittoral fringe is the most variable of the zones on these shores. Tangle may still be present, but the dominant species is normally sea belt *Laminaria saccharina*, together with the sea oak *Halidrys siliquosa* and, more locally, the green *Codium*. Occasionally, the laminarians are replaced by a low-level red algal turf of *Furcellaria fastigiata* and carragheen, or, rarely, by the massed tubes of the serpulid worms *Pomatoceros triqueter*. Where the shores are not too silty these seaweeds bear a rich covering of epiphytic red algae, hydroids, bryozoans and sea-squirts; the grey top-shells *Gibbula cineraria* and snakelocks anemones are common on the rock. Where it is muddy, however, few of the suspension-feeders can colonize, leaving only the more tolerant mussels and their predator the shore crab to represent the already impoverished fauna.

Shore birds are less common on rock than they are on mud and muddy sand, but there are a few characteristic species. Turnstones *Arenaria interpres*, purple sandpipers *Calidris maritima*, and the larger oystercatchers *Haematopus ostralegus* commonly pick over rocky shores; the two smaller birds taking small crustaceans and molluscs, and the oystercatchers concentrating on mussels. Purple sandpipers will consume shore crabs, periwinkles, dog-whelks and mussels. Mussels are also taken by sea-ducks such as eiders *Somateria mollissima*, and the ubiquitous gulls *Larus*. Most other birds use rocky shores only as a convenient resting place: prime examples are cormorants *Phalacrocorax carbo* and shags *P. aristotelis* which fish offshore and often rest on rocks to preen and digest their meals.

A mammal which may be seen on sheltered, rocky coasts, such as there are on the west coast of Norway and the northern isles of Britain, is the otter *Lutra lutra*. Although primarily inhabitants of freshwater, some otters live permanently on coasts, where they feed on fish and crabs.

An otter with a conger eel amongst knotted wrack on a sheltered rocky coast ; Shetland Isles.

SALT-MARSHES

The final intertidal habitat to be considered is the salt-marsh – the most peculiar of all intertidal zones with the exception of its tropical counterpart, the mangrove-swamp. For a start, salt-marshes are dominated by salt-tolerant representatives of otherwise terrestrial plant and animal groups, and, secondly, they can only occur above the average level of high neap-tides; the remainder of the shore being occupied by sand or mud-flat. Yet at the same time, salt-marshes epitomize the coast as a transitional zone between land and sea; in marsh creeks and salt-pans, the fauna and flora are essentially marine; those above the level of the sediment surface are almost entirely terrestrial; only the marsh surface itself supports organisms of both ancestries, and here spiders and beetles meet and mingle with seaweeds and winkles.

The ability to withstand both inundation by sea water and the high salinity of marine sediments is rarely found in higher plants: there are few salt-tolerant species and even fewer species requiring abundant salts. Most species which colonize the fringe of the sea do so in spite of the salt not because of it, except insofar as it keeps other (competing) species away. Plants must therefore possess mechanisms for dealing with the unwanted salts taken up by their roots. Some, such as the sea-lavenders *Limonium*, excrete salts through special glands in their leaves (the undersides of sea-lavender leaves may sparkle with excreted salt), others – the fleshy or succulent species – tolerate high internal levels of salt by virtue of their succulence. This is a complex and controversial phenomenon. Succulence was once thought to be a means whereby water could be stored, analogous to the situation in desert cacti, but it is now considered to be a way of minimizing and localizing potential damage to the tissues as a result of high internal salt concentrations. Yet further species, including several rushes, appear to accumulate salt internally without any ill effects. Not surprisingly, different species are differentially susceptible to tidal immersion, to the amount of salt in the soil, to wave action, and to other intertidal variables.

Although the species may change somewhat from area to area, basically salt-marshes form in sheltered regions (bays, estuaries, areas in the lee of shingle spits or offshore barrier islands) by the following sequence of events. A number of salt and submersion tolerant plants are distributed by seeds (or vegetative fragments) released into and carried by coastal seawater. These will settle out with the silts in sheltered regions and, if conditions are favourable, they will germinate. One of the necessary conditions is a minimum period of at least 50 hours of continual exposure to the air, and hence germination can only occur at high tidal levels. One of the most characteristic pioneer colonists is the annual glasswort *Salicornia*.

Small fleshy spikes of glasswort thus spring up over high level mud-flats or beds of eelgrass *Zostera*, and they have two important effects. They act as a comb or screen preventing the removal of some of the deposited sediment by the ebbing tide, and they reduce water movement in their immediate vicinity, thereby encouraging the deposition of silt and causing the level of the surrounding beach to become raised. This, of course, will have the effect of exposing that area to the air for longer and longer periods, until eventually plants less tolerant of submersion can germinate. This they do, and outcompete glasswort in the originally colonized area. Many of these later arrivals are large, perennial and sometimes bushy species and they are even more effective at trapping sediment, and so rendering the habitat suitable for invasion by yet more species. Meanwhile, the pioneers will have spread out laterally and initiated salt-marsh formation slightly to seaward of the original site. Eventually, the level of the marsh surface will be raised to such a height that the tide now rarely covers it; its upward growth will then slow down as the tidal supply of sediment is reduced. But it will slowly continue to increase in height until its level is above that of all but the highest of spring tides, by which time the salt-marsh may have effectively changed into a terrestrial habitat.

How long this whole process takes will depend upon the tidal range, the supply of sediment, and a number of other factors – and man often steps in to encourage this 'reclamation' – but upward growth rates of a half to two centimetres per year are usual (up to a maximum of 20 centimetres per year) and 150 to 350 years might be a reasonable estimate. Complete natural reclamation is, however, probably a very rare phenomenon: such is the rapidity of coastal change that, without man's intervention, salt-marshes would suffer phases of erosion leading perhaps to the loss of all the land gained.

Two important points for us to notice in this process are the phenomena of succession, in which one community of plants replaces another at any one point as the marsh height increases, and zonation whereby different plant species are characteristic of different tidal levels or heights above the original mud-flat, so that a series of zones of different species may be present. To some extent, the zonation in space is a reflection of the succession in time, such that the plants nearest the sea are the pioneer colonists, those immediately landward of the pioneers are those which will displace them in time, and so on.

The salt-marshes of northern Europe form a single fairly uniform group, although there are some regional differences. Those of eastern Ireland, western and northeastern Britain, Scandinavia and Schleswig-Holstein are pre-

Salt-pans (foreground) surrounded by glasswort and saltmarsh-grass have here been succeeded, at a later stage in salt-marsh formation, by sea-purslane (the paler vegetation) which characteristically forms a margin to creeks. The whole area is flooded by high spring tides.

dominantly sandy and grassy (with abundant common saltmarsh-grass *Puccinellia maritima* and red fescue *Festuca rubra*). These grasses are less important – though still present – on the siltier marshes of southeast Scotland, eastern England, the Low Countries and northern Germany. The marshes along the English Channel are, or were, similar to the North Sea ones, but are now all too frequently dominated by the hybrid cord-grasses *Spartina anglica* and *S. × townsendii*. Finally, the marshes of southwestern Ireland are somewhat atypical in that they are growing on peat, and algae are particularly numerous; some of those in the Baltic also form a rather special subgroup, to which certain sedges, the club-rush *Desmoschoenus bottnica* and the rush *Juncus bufonius* are restricted, and in which the club-rush *Scirpus maritimus* and spike rush *Eleocharis parvula* act as pioneer colonists. These Baltic saltings are in many respects intermediate between marine and freshwater marshes. These differences are, however, comparatively minor variations on a theme and it is possible to give a unified description of that theme. Salt-marshes are not found north of about Trondheim in Norway, nor on the northwest or southern shores of the Baltic.

Three broad zones or successional stages can be distinguished: low marsh, high marsh, and a region near and above mean high-water spring which we can call the supralittoral fringe. Low marsh is created by the pioneer colonists: glasswort where the shore is silty, the tufted and perennial common saltmarsh-grass in sandy areas (sometimes together with glasswort and, along Channel coasts, the tall and coarse cord-grass). Having established themselves, these species can spread vegetatively; cord-grass in particular covering the erstwhile mud-flat very rapidly. Very few other species can invade pioneer cord-grass stands. They encourage very rapid sedimentation and produce a soft, wet, muddy habitat inimical to other species. Hence, as the available space is covered and a dense meadow is formed, a high marsh is created without the addition of further immigrants. Hectare after monotonous hectare of up to one-metre-high erect stems, with 3–6 flowering yellowish spikes per plant, are formed.

In contrast, once glasswort and saltmarsh-grass have initiated a low marsh, species such as annual sea-blite *Suaeda maritima* and sea aster *Aster tripolium* soon invade. Sea-blite is a small fleshy annual, with inconspicuous flowers although, like some *Salicornia* species, the whole plant turns an attractive red in autumn. Sea aster is a relative of the garden Michaelmas daisy and, like it, is a largish perennial. Its fleshy oblong and somewhat bluish leaves and, in August and September, its yellow disc and blue-purple ray-florets are a conspicuous feature of low marshes. Along the southwest shores of the North Sea the var *discoideus* without ray-florets forms a high percentage of its populations. Several seaweeds also occur in low marshes: the unattached form of channelled wrack *Pelvetia canaliculata* var *libera* is perhaps the most common and, together with the red *Bostrychia scorpioides*, it forms a dense ground cover at the bases of glasswort and sea aster, and in salt-pans; whilst stunted varieties of bladder wrack *Fucus vesiculosus* are also common.

These pioneer communities are invaded by high-marsh species, although many of the pioneers can maintain their populations, albeit in reduced numbers, through into this phase. Saltmarsh-grass in particular, remains the – or one of the – dominant species in sandy high marshes. The following later arrivals may each separately dominate high-marsh stages, may share dominance with saltmarsh-grass or may together form a group of co-dominants, as in many muddy marshes: the perennial sea-lavenders *Limonium vulgare* (S and E) and *L. humile* (W), with their July and August display of lavender spikes; thrift *Armeria maritima*, the longest flowering of salt-marsh plants, from April to October; sea-purslane *Halimione portulacoides*, a large, bushy perennial commonest in the south, which characteristically forms a margin to creeks although it can also extend as a monoculture over whole marshes; and sea plantain *Plantago maritima*, like thrift a perennial with a woody root. Equally characteristic of high marshes, though never dominant, are the scurvy-grasses *Cochlearia*, the first salt-marsh plants to flower (early April); the trailing sea-spurreys *Spergularia*, whose pink flowers are much more obvious than their straggly stems; and sea arrowgrass *Triglochin maritima* which resembles the sea plantain in form and habit but which can be distinguished by the old face-flannel smell of its crushed leaves. Red fescue also invades comparatively mature saltmarsh-grass marshes and may even dominate the grassy sward. Several of the seaweeds of the low marshes persist into the high-marsh stage, where they may be joined by another variety of bladder wrack, var *muscoides*.

The highest levels of all salt-marshes are usually dominated by the rushes *Juncus gerardii* and *J. maritimus*, with their typical spiky leaves and stems, and dingy flowers. Associates of these rushes are many, most notably sharp sea couch *Agropyron pungens*, creeping bent *Agrostis stolonifera*, the highly aromatic sea wormwood *Artemisia maritima* and sea-milkwort *Glaux maritima*. Where freshwater emerges on to the supralittoral fringe, the salt-marsh may grade into (and, perhaps, ultimately be replaced by) reedswamp. Reedswamp is largely outside the scope of this volume, but we can note the presence in these coastal freshwater marshes of maritime plants such as sea club-rush *Scirpus maritimus*, parsley water-dropwort *Oenanthe lachenalii*, celery-leaved buttercup *Ranunculus sceleratus*, and the handsome marsh-mallow *Althaea officinalis*. In the Baltic marshes tall fescue *Festuca arundinacea* characteristically occupies this zone.

A number of salt-marsh flowers are visited, even at high tide, by bees, hover-flies and butterflies from the adjacent land, but few, if any, of these are part of the salt-marsh, or even coastal, fauna. Several salt-marsh plants, however, do have specific maritime insects associated with them which spend all or most of their lives on the marsh. The sap of scurvy-grasses is sucked by the aphid *Lipaphis cochleariae* and both larvae and adults of the beetle *Phaedon cochleariae* consume its tissues. The shoots and roots of sea asters are also tapped by aphids, and the roots parasitized by *Pemphigus trehernei*. The flowering stalks of sea plantain are sometimes deformed by the larvae of the beetle *Mecinus collaris*. Even the recently evolved cord-grass is consumed by a grasshopper, the short-winged cone-head *Conocephalus dorsalis*. Many other species of terrestrial ancestry frequent the marsh surface, sometimes with characteristic species in the various marsh zones. The predatory money-spider *Erigone arctica*, wolf-spider *Pardosa purbeckensis* and marine bugs (Saldidae) roam more widely in search of food.

On low marshes, the root-feeding aphid *Pemphigus trehernei* is found only on sea asters in well-drained areas, like the margins of creeks, although on high marshes, with their better-developed soil structure and more plant root-cavities, it can colonize such asters as have persisted into this later successional stage. Water-logged soil and the consequent poor aeration are conditions which most of the burrowing insects avoid. Such a distribution is shown by most of the salt-marsh beetles. Rove-beetles *Bledius* feed on algae and detritus, and excavate tunnels just below the level of the vegetation at the tops of the banks of creeks. Small piles of sediment around a central hole often betray the presence of a burrow. In turn, they are consumed by predatory ground-beetles (Carabidae). The abundant ground-beetle *Bembidion* catches amphipods such as *Corophium*, mites (Acari), collembolans and fly larvae, including those of the flies (Dolichopodidae) which skate over the surface of creeks, banks and salt-pans. Many of these insects can survive periods of tidal cover by retreating into their burrows, which retain bubbles of air, and they are therefore active only at low tide. Other basically terrestrial elements in the fauna of the marsh surface are pulmonate snails, *eg* mouse-ear-shelled *Phytia myosotis* and *Assiminea grayana* which may be joined by such marine species as the sand-hopper *Orchestia gammarella*, the shore crab *Carcinus maenas* and the rough periwinkle *Littorina saxatilis*. But it is in the creeks and salt-pans that the marine element in the salt-marsh fauna is mainly to be found. There, many of the original marine inhabitants of the sand or mud will still occur, and there the various temporary members of the sand and mud fauna (especially redshanks *Tringa totanus*, dunlins *Calidris alpina* and such fish as gobies *Pomatoschistus*, eels *Anguilla anguilla* and flounder *Platichthys flesus*) will feed on them. A few marine or brackish species are particularly characteristic of the salt-pans, rather than the creeks (many of them being lagoonal species): for example, the prawn *Palaemonetes varians*, the isopod *Sphaeroma rugicauda* and the ribbonworm *Tetrastemma melano-cephala*. The similarity of these small pools to lagoons is further emphasized by a freshwater element in their fauna: water-boatmen (Corixidae), beetles and other insects can be found in salt-pans, together with the larvae of the caddisfly *Limnephilus affinis* and of several midges.

As usual in intertidal zones, a number of species enter salt-marshes at low tide to feed, largely on the salt-marsh plants and on their seeds. Prominent amongst these are the browsing and grazing rabbits *Oryctolagus cuniculus*, brown hares *Lepus capensis*, voles like the root vole *Microtus ratticeps*, geese *Anser* and brent geese *Branta bernicla*; and the seed-eating ducks, especially teals *Anas crecca*, mallards *A. platyrhynchos* and pintails *A. acuta*.

SAND-DUNES

Sand-dunes are by no means confined to the coast; they occur wherever large areas of sand are found, and are thus present in regions such as the Sahara Desert and, on a much lesser scale, the Breckland of East Anglia. But dunes are characteristic of the landwards margins of sandy beaches along many coastlines (although several of the smaller ones have now disappeared beneath the car parks and promenades of resort towns). Apart from a supply of dry sand, the prime requirement for dune formation is wind. A minimum wind speed of about 16 kilometres per hour is required to move sand grains, and thereafter the rate of sand movement is proportional to the cube of the wind speed: a force 10 gale will therefore transport over 200 times more sand than a force 3 gentle breeze. If, on hot days when the surface layer has dried, strong winds blow across a beach at low tide, sand grains may be moved across the shore. They will be deposited when the wind speed at ground level drops below the threshold 16 kilometres per hour. Exactly comparable to the situation in salt-marshes, strand-line plants and flotsam at the high-water mark reduce the wind speed near ground level, and hence if sand is being moved up the beach it will collect as small 'embryo dunes' on plants like the sea sandwort *Honkenya peploides* and sea rocket *Cakile maritima*. Two perennial grasses which can spread vegetatively, sand couch *Agropyron junceiforme* and lyme-grass *Elymus arenarius*, typically grow in such areas and can grow up through the accreting sand, provided that the rate of accretion does not exceed about 30 centimetres per year. These tall, coarse grasses are even more effective than the smaller strand-line plants at reducing wind speed, and they also decrease the ability of the wind to remove accreted material by stabilizing it with their extensive horizontal and vertical root-systems: growth of the embryo dunes is thereby encouraged.

In facilitating the accretion of sand, however, these plants cause their own downfall. Their powers of rapid upward growth are limited and, if sand continues to accrete on and around them, they are replaced by a third and most important dune-grass, marram *Ammophila arenaria*. This can keep pace with sand being deposited at rates of up to one metre per year and, like the two former species, it is a tall, coarse grass with horizontal and vertical roots, so that it can both encourage accretion and bind those grains captured.

What happens after this stage depends on the supply of sand and on the pattern of wind speed and direction in a rather complex manner. As the dune grows higher, so the wind speed affecting it is likely to increase (winds being more gentle at ground level because of friction with the sand surface), and

A dune ridge with isolated clumps of privet and bramble, North Norfolk.

therefore if winds are generally strong and if the supply of sand is limited, sand will be eroded from the windward face of the dune and deposited on the sheltered leeward face, causing the dune to move landwards, in whole or in part, at speeds of up to seven metres per year. The dune will also attain a maximum height, over which the wind speed will be such as to balance the rates of accretion and erosion from its marram-covered surface. Alternatively, if a large supply of dry sand is available and if the predominant wind speeds are not large, the dune may be further stabilized by vegetation where it was formed originally and a new embryo dune may grow to seawards, itself becoming stabilized and replaced as the growth point by yet another embryo dune in front of it. A series of parallel dunes will thereby be formed. The mobile dune of very windy areas may also be stabilized eventually by a plant cover when it has moved inland and out of the strongest wind zones.

In both mobile and static dune ridges, the essential biological story, after the initial accretion of a dune, is one of increasing stabilization by plants and increasing colonization by animals. Let us return to the embryo dune after its invasion by marram. Whilst the supply of sand lasts, marram will spread laterally and grow upwards, and the dune will increase in size: a height of some 10 to 35 metres could be considered normal, although the largest coastal dune (near Brisbane, Australia) tops 275 metres. Because of its vegetative spread, the hundreds of individual marram plants clothing a dune may really be one single plant, the various shoots being connected by underground stems. Other plant species increasingly colonize this yellow (or white) dune stage. Typical maritime species are sea-holly *Eryngium maritimum*, a perennial umbellifer with spiky glaucous leaves and blue flowers resembling those of teasels *Dipsacus*; sea bindweed *Calystegia soldanella*, a more handsome relation of the bindweed pests of hedge and garden, with glossy kidney-shaped leaves and very large pink or pale purple flowers, which does not climb on other species but trails over and in the sand surface; the sea spurges *Euphorbia paralis* (mainly S) and *E. portlandica* (W), many-stemmed bushy species with glaucous leaves; sand sedge *Carex arenaria*, a small sedge with long underground stems, often spreading in straight lines, from which arise bunches of leaves and flowering stems at intervals; and sand fescue, a variety of red fescue *Festuca rubra*, also with extensive below-ground portions. Whilst marram stabilizes the sand some distance below the surface, several of these later arrivals are more efficient at binding the surface sand, both by the additional cover which they afford and by their near-surface horizontal root network. The areas of bare sand between these maritime species also provide a suitable habitat for widely dispersed, waste-ground plants, largely of the family Compositae with their parachute-like seeds, which colonize any temporarily bare ground. Groundsels and ragworts *Senecio*, thistles *Cirsium/ Carduus*, and the confusing numbers of cat's-ears *Hypochaeris*, hawkbits *Leontodon*, hawkweeds *Hieracium*, hawk's-beards *Crepis* and dandelions *Taraxacum* flourish on dunes and protect the surface with their rosettes.

At this early stage in the development of a plant cover, animal species are not noticeably abundant. Butterflies, hover-flies and moths, however, are conspicuous as they feed on the nectar provided by the flowers; and the yellow- and black-banded caterpillars of the cinnabar moth *Callimorpha jacobaeae* may provide a splash of colour as they defoliate the ragworts. Spiders and insects are the dominant animals of dunes in general, and many are highly mobile and can roam over wide areas. Few, however, are in any sense coastal species, although several are characteristic. Sand-wasps *Ammophila* may often be seen hunting their arthropod prey over sandy dune areas. They begin by digging a hole in the sand, and then set off to hunt for prey, often caterpillars, with which to stock it. They therefore need to remember where the hole was dug: this they do by memorizing the local geography. Not infrequently, dunes are subject to plagues of insects which have often migrated or been blown over wide stretches of sea before, famished, they make landfall on the sand: then for a week or more, the dunes may be coloured red by ladybirds (Coccinellidae) or be gaudy with migrant painted lady butterflies *Cynthia cardui*. In contrast, female horse-flies (Tabanidae) can make life unpleasant for the visitor with slow reactions.

One of the main problems faced by sand-dune plants is the lack of water in the highly porous dunes. Many therefore have root-systems which include a vertical component penetrating deeply into the sand. But the pioneer colonists provide, on their death and decay, a quantity of humus which, besides holding a certain amount of water, also increases the nutrient status of the incipient soil. The additional moisture and nutrient content of well-established marram dunes are exploited by a group of winter annuals – plants whose seeds germinate in the autumn, the seedling surviving through the winter and then flowering and shedding seed very early the next year (around

March/April) before the heat of the summer evaporates the small store of moisture gained by the surface layers in the winter. Common whitlowgrass *Erophila verna*, early forget-me-not *Myosotis ramosissima* and common corn-salad *Valerianella locusta* are examples. Mosses (like *Bryum* and sand-dune screw-moss *Tortula ruraliformis*) and lichens *Peltigera* and *Cladonia* also start their colonization process at this stage in a dune's evolution, and by so doing provide a further, and particularly important, sand-stabilizing force.

One must not give the impression that dunes are uniform in their plant cover or flora. Two factors, at least, serve to disturb any tendency to uniformity: the development of blow-outs, and the aspect of a dune slope. If the sand supply is cut off from a developing dune or if for any reason the vegetation cover is broken, more sand may be removed from an area than is being deposited, and once a bare area has been created the wind can progressively erode more and more sand, and form a blow-out. The local erosion hot-spots may be quickly repaired by sand fescue or sand sedge, or they may increase in extent until a whole dune becomes affected and moves as a parabolic dune across the ground. The second cause of local variation, that of aspect, results from the high latitudes in which northern Europe lies. Because the sun passes across the southern part of the sky, south-facing slopes will be relatively hot and dry, whilst northern slopes will be cooler and more moist. Light- and heat-demanding species, such as the spurges, will, for example, be commonest on southerly slopes.

Mosses and lichens herald the grey dune stage, in which the plant cover becomes complete and maritime plants are largely replaced by inland species. Whereas yellow dunes are so called because of the obvious yellow (or white) sand between the plants, grey dunes derive their name in part from the cover of grey-green lichens and in part from the dirty colour of the sand resulting from the addition of humus and from chemical changes to the iron compounds coating the grains. Marram shows reduced vigour and eventually dies when sand no longer accretes around it; on grey dunes, sand fescue and sand sedge replace it and form a denser grassy sward. Many beach sands contain appreciable quantities of lime in the form of pulverized fragments of mollusc shells. Hence the soil of dunes may often be calcareous, and plants and animals of dry, lime-rich inland areas may be equally common on stabilized dunes. Yellow feather-moss *Camptothecium lutescens*, yellow-wort *Blackstonia perfoliata*, gentians *Gentianella*, various centauries *Centaurium*, lady's bedstraw *Galium verum*, carline thistle *Carlina vulgaris* and a number of orchids (autumn lady's-tresses *Spiranthes spiralis*, common twayblade *Listera ovata*, and the pyramidal *Anacamptis pyramidalis* and bee orchids *Ophrys apifera*, amongst others) occur, often in abundance, on grey dunes, as do the snails *Cepaea nemoralis*, *Theba cantiana* and *Vitrina pellucida*. Such calcareous dune-pasture in the western Highlands and islands of Scotland forms a coastal habitat known as 'machair': it is a tree-less plain largely covered by marram, sand fescue and other grasses and sedges, and because of the particularly high shell-content of the sand, it is floristically rich. Its relatively high fertility especially when fertilized by seaweed, in relation to the peaty moors and mountains inland, causes it to be widely used for agriculture by the resident crofting community. Dunes, like other porous soils, are subject to leaching, however, and the relatively small amounts of lime normally present in the early stages may be progressively leached out. Somewhat older dunes, therefore, are often colonized by such species as heath dog-violet *Viola canina*, tormentil *Potentilla erecta*, harebell *Campanula rotundifolia*, wood sage *Teucrium scorodonia* and sheep's sorrel *Rumex acetosella* – plants generally characteristic of more acid grassland or heaths. Most of the other typically grey-dune flowers are grass- or waste-land species with a distinct submaritime preference: for example, hound's-tongue *Cynoglossum officinale*, wild pansy *Viola tricolor* ssp *curtisii*, great lettuce *Lactuca virosa*, the evening-primroses *Oenothera* and henbane *Hyoscyamus niger*.

The summits and hollows of stabilized dunes bear a dense but low covering of bushes – privet *Ligustrum vulgare*, hawthorn *Crataegus monogyna*, elder *Sambucus*, brambles *Rubus*, roses *Rosa rugosa* and *R. pimpinellifolia*, and sea-buckthorn *Hippophae rhamnoides* – all, it may be noted, species with berries distributed by birds. Sea-buckthorn occurs naturally from Bodø in Norway, around the shores of the North and Baltic Seas, to Yorkshire and Sussex in England; but it has been introduced by man on to many other dunes to stabilize the sand. Sea-buckthorn can achieve this even on young dunes low in nutrients because of the nitrogen-fixing nodules on its roots. But, similarly to cord-grass *Spartina anglica* on salt-marshes, sea-buckthorn can behave as an invasive weed and convert species-rich dunes into an impenetrable spiny thicket lacking a ground flora. It spreads by both seeds and suckers, and cut stems freely regenerate. These shrubs may eventually dominate the dunes, forming dune-scrub which is in turn succeeded by woodland. Man has frequently hastened this process – often, again, with sand stabilization mainly in mind – by planting conifers, usually various pines *Pinus*. Many large dune systems are now backed by conifer plantations, in which occasionally occur the orchids, creeping lady's-tresses *Goodyera repens* and narrow-lipped helleborine *Epipactis leptochila*. Alternatively, the dune-scrub phase may be replaced by dune-heath which, as on heaths in general, is dominated by gorse *Ulex*, heather *Calluna vulgaris* and bracken *Pteridium aquilinum*, although this too develops ultimately into woodland. Dunes maintained as golf-courses are kept in the dune grassland stage by mowing.

Pre-eminent amongst the grey-dune animals is the rabbit *Oryctolagus cuniculus*, and its burrowing activities have honeycombed many a dune and been responsible for blow-outs and local erosion. In medieval times, rabbits were introduced on to dunes to provide a convenient source of food requiring no maintenance or attention. The species is now regarded more as a pest, especially by coastal-defence authorities. As in inland areas, its influence on the vegetation can be marked: heavy grazing pressure can reduce the grassy sward to a close turf only two centimetres high. Other dune animals are also equally characteristic of inland areas: grasshoppers (Acrididae), caterpillars and plant-bugs (Homoptera) consume the vegetation; bees collect pollen and nectar (one leafcutter bee, *Megachile maritima*, is, however, specifically coastal); spiders and damsel-bugs (Nabidae) hunt their prey; skylarks *Alauda arvensis*, meadow pipits *Anthus pratensis* and linnets *Carduelis cannabina* sing and call in the air and nest on the ground; kestrels *Falco tinnunculus* and short-eared owls *Asio flammeus* feed on the larger insects, wood mice *Apodemus sylvaticus* and voles (Cricetidae). A characteristic coastal sound is added to the scene, however, by many gulls (particularly the black-headed *Larus ridibundus*, herring *L. argentatus* and lesser black-backed *L. fuscus*) and terns (esperially the sandwich *Sterna sandvicensis* and common *S. hirundo*) which nest in dunes, although to the gulls dunes are one of many potential nesting sites.

The final dune habitats to be considered are the valleys or hollows between dune ridges, which are for much of the year moist and for part of the year may have sheets of standing water. Depending on the normal degree of wetness of the ground, dune-slacks, dune-marsh or dune-lakes may occur; and if seawater can gain entry to a hollow, variants of salt-marsh vegetation can develop, in essence similar to that already described for stable shingled areas within dunes. The vegetation of the wetter marshes and lakes is almost entirely a freshwater assemblage.

The flora of dune-slacks is, however, highly characteristic of dune systems and does contain some typically dune forms. The dominant plant is the creeping willow *Salix repens*, a prostrate or hummock-forming species which may carpet much of the ground, but arising through its mat of stems, in wet grassy areas, occur a number of orchids – marsh helleborine *Epipactis palustris*, the dune variety of fen orchid *Liparis loeselii* var *ovata* and several marsh-orchids *Dactylorhiza* – and the equally, or more, attractive grass-of-Parnassus *Parnassia palustris* var *condensata* and large wintergreen *Pyrola rotundifolia* var *maritima*. Few coastal sights can be more impressive than an expanse of marsh helleborine in flower, and few can be more beautiful than the waxy blooms and shining leaves of large wintergreen.

One of Europe's few coastal amphibians is an inhabitant of dune slacks, although it may be encountered along the crest of dune ridges, running in its characteristic fashion. The natterjack toad *Bufo calamita*, grey, brown or green with a yellow line down its back, burrows in the sand of slacks during the day (and during the October to February hibernation period) and emerges at night to feed on insects. It breeds from April to May, laying eggs in fresh and brackish waters which develop into the smallest of European tadpoles. Besides its running gait, it is unusual amongst amphibians in that it can withstand long periods of drought. This gregarious toad is consumed by a variety of birds and mammals, as a protection against which it secretes from its skin a whitish substance which has been described as smelling like burnt gunpowder, sulphur, and boiled indiarubber.

The often spectacular cliffs of northern Europe have mostly been formed by marine erosion and, unless they plummet straight down into deep water, have rocky shores at their feet. Such cliffs are usually vertical walls of rock. Some of the softer cliffs of the southern North Sea and parts of the English Channel, however, are mainly being eroded by frost, rain and other aerial influences, and the sea is merely removing the rubble which collects or slips on to their base. Various intermediates exist, of which one of the more interesting is the slope-over-wall type of the southwest. At times of low sea-level in the past, these cliffs were eroded into a comparatively gentle rubble slope by the aerial processes referred to above, but, since the rise in sea-level over the last 12,000 years, waves have again attacked them and have cut out the lower portions to form the steep-sided wall.

Understandably, it is difficult for organisms to survive on the sheer vertical face and hence they are dependent on the presence of the occasional flatter areas and of ledges, crevices and other breaks in the rock surface. In turn, these will depend on the type of stone and, if sedimentary rock, on its angle of dip. As on sand-dunes, there will be additional variation related to the aspect of the cliff-face, with usually a greater luxuriance on sunny, south-facing slopes; whilst hardness of the rock is another variable, in that very soft rocks may be eroded too quickly for plants to colonize successfully. Of course the precipitous nature of cliffs also makes their study a difficult matter, and so binoculars are an essential tool of the naturalist. This places a lower limit on the size of organism for which we have much information.

We noted earlier that the more exposed the rocky shore, the higher the supralittoral fringe, with its black lichens, extended to points well above the high-water mark as a result of spray and wave surge. Therefore, on exposed cliffs, the more terrestrial vegetation will start to appear at levels considerably above that of the beach. Eventually, however, *Verrucaria maura* will give way to other lichens, of which orange encrustations of *Xanthoria parietina* are most characteristic. Here and there amongst the bright orange sheet, patches of the white *Ochrolechia parella* and fluffy, glaucous-green tufts of sea ivory *Ramalina siliquosa* will also be found.

At yet higher levels, flowering plants can colonize such crevices, gullies, ledges and flat areas as have weathered out of the rock and have accumulated some soil, itself largely the product of weathering processes. The plant cover will be sparse, but many species may be represented, including several of the maritime plants which we have previously encountered on salt-marshes and shingle banks. These may be joined by up to a dozen, rather more specifically cliff-dwelling species, although even some of these may occasionally be found on shingle.

In the southern part of the region, the edible rock samphire *Crithmum maritimum* grows from crevices and ledges, often in the company of the rock sea-spurrey *Spergularia rupicola* and the handsome gold-and-orange flowered golden samphire *Inula crithmoides*, which is particularly abundant on warm, south-facing ledges. Also southern in their distribution are the sea radish *Raphanus maritimus* and wild cabbage *Brassica oleracea*, both large biennials or perennials with thick rootstocks and big yellow flowers. The wild cabbage is the ancestor of the garden vegetable and indeed greatly resembles one that has been allowed to go wild and run to seed. Predominantly western in their range are the region's only strictly maritime fern, sea spleenwort *Asplenium marinum*, which inhabits moist, shady crevices, and the large tree-mallow *Lavatera arborea*, which can grow to almost two metres in height; whilst scots lovage *Ligusticum scoticum* is confined to the north, where it replaces the other cliff-face umbellifer, rock samphire. In northern regions a group of plants, which in more southerly latitudes are restricted to high mountains, descend to sea-level where they may be found on coastal cliffs. These arctic-alpine species include roseroot *Rhodiola rosea*, moss campion *Silene acaulis*, mountain avens *Dryas octopetala*, and the saxifrages *Saxifraga oppositifolia* and *S. hypnoides*. Conversely, mountain-tops also provide a home for species otherwise found only in the coastal zone: thrift *Armeria maritima*, sea campion *Silene maritima* and sea plantain *Plantago maritima* are well-known examples.

Cliffs also possess their share of botanical rarities: in the southwest the sea-lavenders *Limonium paradoxum*, *L. recurvum*, *L. transwallianum* and *L. auriculae-ursifolium*, and the hoary stock *Matthiola incana* may be found in a few localities. The stock may not be native, and the mesembryanthemums which blanket some southwestern cliffs are certainly introductions (mainly from South Africa).

These plants of ledges and crevices extend up the cliff-face to the cliff-top or the slope of slope-over-wall cliffs. There many of them may still occur, although the vegetation of cliff-tops is far more terrestrial in character, often being dominated by heath or grassy swards of bents *Agrostis*, sheep's-fescue *Festuca ovina* and Yorkshire-fog *Holcus lanatus*. A number of the inhabitants of cliff-top swards are genuinely submaritime species, however, of which some of the more characteristic are buck's-horn plantain *Plantago coronopus*, sea pearlwort *Sagina maritima*, scentless mayweed *Matricaria maritima*, the stork's-bills *Erodium*, the wild carrot *Daucus carota* and the squills *Scilla*.

The one group of cliff-inhabiting animals for which we have much information is the cliff-nesting bird fauna, and many northern and western cliffs and stacks are famous for their colonies of sea-birds. Comparatively few species are restricted to cliff-faces: it is possible that many species now mainly nest there because of their inaccessibility to egg and chick predators such as man and his accompanying rats and feral cats. Indeed on small rocky islands and in the arctic many species nest on the ground. Although it is the sea-birds which spring to mind, several land-birds also nest on ledges or in holes and crevices in sea-cliffs. Perhaps the most inspiring of these are the white-tailed eagle *Haliaeetus albicilla* and gyr falcon *Falco rusticolus* of the north, and the formerly more widespread peregrine *F. peregrinus*, which has been the victim of pesticides. Other typically cliff-nesting birds are jackdaws *Corvus monedula*, ravens *C. corax*, choughs *Pyrrhocorax pyrrhocorax* and rock doves *Columba livia*, the ancestor of the feral pigeon, still found on coastal cliffs of Ireland and western Scotland. The only small passerine (or song bird) uniquely adapted to life on the shore at all seasons is the rock pipit *Anthus spinoletta*. It breeds on sheltered rocky headlands in sea lochs or on exposed cliffs, but tends to winter on beaches where there is a wrackline of rotting seaweed full of invertebrate life. In the Isles of Scilly and other islands where there are no meadow pipits *Anthus pratensis*, the rock pipit occupies their niche inland.

The main colonially-nesting sea-cliff birds (with individual colonies holding from 10 to 100,000 pairs) are fulmars *Fulmarus glacialis*, gannets *Sula bassana*, kittiwakes *Rissa tridactyla*, razorbills *Alca torda*, guillemots *Uria aalge* and *U. lomvia*, and puffins *Fratercula arctica*; although puffins, together with Manx shearwaters *Puffinus puffinus* and Leach's petrels *Oceanodroma leucorhoa*, nest in burrows on the cliff-top rather than on the exposed face. Guillemots, Brünnich's guillemots, fulmars and razorbills nest on the most exposed cliff ledges, although fulmars have other sites, and razorbills do prefer the somewhat more sheltered corners of ledges and also nest in crevices. Since the single egg is laid directly on to the ledge, many eggs roll off into the sea, and only the sticky coating of guano which eggs soon collect prevents a higher loss rate. Gannets and kittiwakes, however, make definite nests: that of the gannet being up to half-a-metre high and composed of seaweed, flotsam and grass, and that of the kittiwake being a firm structure of grass and mud cemented to the ledge by a mixture of green algae and guano.

Puffins seem to have declined markedly during this century. On St Kilda, for example, it was estimated that at the end of the last century there were between one and three million birds; in 1971 only about 165,000 burrows were occupied. Similarly, the colonies on the Shiant Islands which used to house hundreds of thousands of birds have now declined to some 62,000 pairs. The cause of the decline – if indeed it has a single cause – is not known, but erosion brought about by the burrowing activities of the puffins themselves, climatic change and pollution have all been suggested to have played a part. Early estimates probably erred on the generous side. The fulmar, on the other hand, has undergone a great population increase and extension of range in the last 100 years: in the British Isles, for example, from 100 occupied nest sites in Shetland and the Outer Hebrides in 1889, to 270,000 such

Guillemots on a sea-cliff.

sites (excluding St Kilda) in 1969–70, extending southwards to the English Channel. Once again, the cause is largely unknown, although a climatic change and the provision of an additional supply of food, particularly perhaps over the critical winter period, from whaling and trawling activities, have been advocated.

The other specialist cliff-nesting sea-bird is the black guillemot *Cepphus grylle*, which nests in caves and holes in cliff-faces and, unusually amongst northern European auks, lays two eggs. The preference for secluded places on which to lay its eggs means that the black guillemot is far less colonial than its relatives. A further three species – the cormorant *Phalacrocorax carbo*, shag *P. aristotelis* and herring gull *Larus argentatus* – will nest on broad cliff ledges, amongst other sites; the shag is the most typical cliff-bird of the three, and its larger nest of seaweed, sea beet *Beta vulgaris* and bracken may be seen amongst, for example, colonies of kittiwakes.

COASTAL SEAS

It would be surprising if the coastal sea did not bear many resemblances to the open ocean, but apart from being much shallower it does show a number of very distinctive features. It is much more productive than the ocean, for example, largely because of all the nutrients (phosphates, nitrates and complex organic substances leached out of soil) discharged into coastal waters by rivers. Its shallowness is also relevant here. Dissolved nutrients are taken up by the minute plant cells, the phytoplankton, suspended in the surface waters of the sea. These may be consumed by animals or, in particularly rich areas, may die uneaten. But in any event, the dead bodies of animals and plants, and animal faeces, sink toward the sea-bed taking their incorporated nutrients with them. Bacteria may decompose some of this rain of debris en route, releasing the nutrients back into the water, but if the water is deep this rain may denude the surface waters of nutrients, which then accumulate in the permanently dark zones of the deep sea and in the bodies of animals living on and in the ocean floor. In the shallow coastal sea, much of the descending nutrients can be brought back into the sun-lit layers by mixing processes in the water which extend down to the continental shelf. The continual depletion of these essential chemicals required for plant growth is thereby alleviated.

Rivers also transport detritus in the form of leaves and other debris from the land to the sea, and waves and tides may remove dead seaweeds and salt-marsh plants from the intertidal zone and carry them out to sea. Some of this rotting material may be cast on to the shore again by the flood tide to form a strand-line, which soon attracts the small kelp-flies (Coelopidae and Heleomyzidae) that so annoy holiday-makers; but much of it sinks to the sea-bed where it provides additional food for the sublittoral detritus-feeders. The sublittoral fringe of laminarians on rocky shores is only the tip of the iceberg, in that dense kelp-forests can extend down to depths of 30 metres or more. Such kelp-forests are one of the most productive stands of vegetation in the world, although once they have passed the sporeling stage they are consumed by very few animals. The predominantly sublittoral sea-urchins *Echinus*, *Paracentrotus* and *Strongylocentrotus* and the sea-hares *Aplysia* are kelp-eaters, but otherwise the laminarians join the pool of detritus in the coastal sea. In the open ocean, of course, attached seaweeds do not occur in the lightless depths.

Lastly, most bottom-living marine animals have planktonic larvae – small, often bizarre forms suspended in the surface water layers and bearing little resemblance to the adult animals into which they will eventually metamorphose. Coastal-water plankton includes the many larval stages of intertidal and subtidal animals. In contrast, the plankton of open waters contains few of these temporarily planktonic organisms since 82 per cent of the ocean floor lies between depths of 2000 and 8000 metres, and only a small number of deep-sea species journey all the way to the surface waters to undergo their larval life.

The food-web of coastal seas is therefore typically complex and different parts of it may be separated by large vertical distances. Except for the immediately sublittoral eelgrass *Zostera* meadows and kelp-forests, plants in the sea are restricted to the algal phytoplankton – diatoms, dinoflagellates and many micro-algae – largely confined to the surface layers. These are consumed by permanently planktonic animals, the zooplankton, and by the planktonic larvae of polychaetes, molluscs, crustaceans and echinoderms. Several zooplankton species probably also consume small particles of suspended detritus, as well as the algae. These herbivores and omnivores are then eaten by carnivorous members of the plankton, such as arrow-worms *Sagitta*, larval fish, and several jellyfish and siphonophores (smaller relatives of the virulent Portuguese man-o'-war *Physalia* occasionally stranded on beaches). Members of the plankton are sieved from the water by filter-feeding fishes and mammals, like the 11-metre-long basking shark *Cetorhinus maximus*, and the huge baleen whales (Mysticeti), or are captured individually by fish such as herrings *Clupea harengus* and mackerel *Scomber scombrus*. The food-chain is extended by big fish and cephalopod molluscs eating smaller fish, which are in turn eaten by still larger fish, seals and toothed whales (Odontoceti). Common porpoises *Phocoena phocoena* and common dolphins *Delphinus delphis* take herring, mackerel and whiting *Merlangius merlangus*. Other whales may be seen occasionally. Killer whales *Orcinus orca*, which can catch seals and dolphins, are regular inhabitants of the coasts of northern Scotland, Iceland and the Atlantic coast of Scandinavia although scarcer in the North and Baltic seas and the Channel. The pilot whale or blackfish *Globicephala melaena* is also fairly common in the north, where schools of over 100 whales have been driven ashore and stranded by lines of boats manned by the most predatory species of them all. Diving birds, such as gannets *Sula bassana*, terns *Sterna* and auks (Alcidae), also take their toll of fish.

In spite of all these mouths waiting to snap up food, much detrital and faecal material and the occasional corpse do reach the sea-bed whilst in relatively shallow areas the plankton extends down to within range of suspension-feeders, on and in the bottom. Perhaps largely through the activities of bacteria, a bottom, or benthic, fauna is thereby supported. Most of the continental shelf is covered by gravels, sands and muds eroded from the land by waves, rivers and glaciers, and so the communities of animals dominating the benthos are similar to those found on sandy beaches or mud-flats. Indeed, many of the species mentioned in earlier sections extend down to depths in the order of 100 metres.

Close to the shore in muddy situations for example, the characteristic organisms of soft muddy beaches are found below low-water level. The Baltic tellin *Macoma balthica* and the other animals associated with it also dominate most of the Baltic (both along the shoreline and offshore) except in the north of the Gulf of Bothnia, where, in waters containing only one tenth of the salts normally found in sea water, a peculiar group of relict animals, many of which are crustaceans, replace them. These relicts date from the time during the Ice Age when arctic species penetrated into fresh or brackish seas situated, some 10,000–13,000 years ago, in the region now forming the Baltic. Today they survive only in a few adjacent lakes (like Vättern) and in the almost fresh waters of the Gulf of Bothnia, tending to occur in offshore areas and being replaced in shallower zones by more recent invaders such as midge larvae and oligochaete worms.

The fauna associated intertidally with the common mussel *Mytilus edulis* is also found in the shallow waters of estuaries and sheltered bays, although the commonest and most widespread community found on the surface of offshore sediments is that associated with the horse mussel *Modiolus modiolus*. Many of its species are those occurring intertidally on rocky shores, whilst other rocky-shore forms are replaced by related species. It is from this community that many of the common objects on the strand-line of northern European beaches have originated. A walk along a strand-line will frequently yield the dried bodies of the common starfish *Asterias rubens* or common sunstar *Crossaster papposus* (the latter eats the former), the carapace or claws of the mollusc-eating edible crab *Cancer pagurus* and, very abundantly, the flat plates of the cabbage-like hornwrack *Flustra foliacea*, the large, fingered masses of the sponge *Haliclona oculata* with, if the specimen is fresh, rows of oscula, like eyes, running the length of the 'fingers', and the sponge-like egg

A school of bottle-nosed whales, predators on cuttlefish and herring, swimming close to the shore.

masses of the common whelk *Buccinum undatum*. The cuttlebones of the common cuttlefish *Sepia officinalis* are another common item of flotsam.

This community, like the horse mussel itself, is largely a suspension-feeding assemblage and it includes one of the most famous and valuable of all suspension-feeders, the European oyster *Ostrea edulis*. Several inshore regions dominated by the horse mussel community are now farmed commercially for oysters, which is to say that they are raked to remove starfish or even ploughed to bury predators or competitors deeply into the seabed, and the young spat – often imported from elsewhere – are laid on the bed so created. The faster-growing and silt-tolerant *Crassostrea* has also been imported to increase yield. Unfortunately, imported *C. virginica* from the USA also served to bring in several pest species, including the oyster drill *Urosalpinx cinerea* (S), which can consume 10 young oysters per week, and the competing slipper limpet *Crepidula fornicata* (S). The slipper limpet grows on oyster shells and not only smothers them but also, since it too is a suspension-feeder with a large gill functioning like those of bivalves, removes from the water food which could otherwise be consumed by the more valuable mollusc. Large slipper limpets are female, whilst the small specimens which may be found, in chains, on the large ones' shells are males; these will change their sex as they grow and turn female. The whole chain of individuals may move as a unit, with the basal female doing all the work.

Other members of this rich and diverse fauna are numerous scale-worms (Polynoidae), rag-worms (Nereidae) and amphipod crustaceans; these hide in crevices in the mollusc shells (often honeycombed by the boring sponge *Cliona celata*), which accumulate and provide a pseudo-rocky substratum, to which seaweeds and bushy bryozoans can attach. Crustaceans are frequent, including the hairy crab *Pilumnus hirtellus*, and several spider-crabs of the genera *Hyas*, *Inachus* and *Macropodia* which are camouflaged against the seaweed background; some spider-crabs perfect the camouflage by attaching small algae to their carapaces and legs. The smooth, compact and finely-textured sulphur sponge *Suberites domuncula* may grow as an oval or spherical object attached to a small stone, which it may eventually envelop, but it is also found attached to shells occupied by hermit-crabs and, for many years, it was in this form known under a different name, *Ficulina ficus*. Shells inhabited by hermit-crabs are also colonized by a variety of hydroids and anemones: for example, the hydroid *Hydractinia echinata* and the large anemone *Calliactis parasitica* are typical fellow-travellers of common hermit-crab *Pagurus bernhardus*, whilst the strawberry anemone *Adamsia palliata* is associated with *P. prideauxi*.

The last community which space permits us to consider is restricted to rocky bottoms in deep water, of from 100 to 200 metres, off the western Swedish, Norwegian and Scottish coasts. This is dominated by the branched colonies of the stony corals *Lophelia* and *Amphihelia* which may attain heights of one metre. Entwined around these corals are basket-stars, relatives of the brittle-stars (Ophiuroidea), whose arms repeatedly branch to form a circular mass of tendrils. The tropical appearance of this deep, cold-water community is heightened by the presence of the sea fan *Paragorgia arborea*.

These bottom-living animals are the prey of bottom-living or demersal fish, of which the cod *Gadus morhua* and its allies the gadoids (Gadidae), the flat-fish, and the skates and rays (Rajidae) are of particular interest to man. The quayside of a fishing port, whether based on whelks or on finfish, is, incidentally, one of the best places for catching a glimpse of many of the organisms mentioned in this section, either scattered around the quay or in the piles of 'trash' which assail the nose in many a shellfishing village. The number of bottom-feeding fish is vast and space must restrict us to a consideration of a few of the more important and characteristic types. Skates, rays and dogfish *Scyliorhinus canicula* are all predators which hunt by smell and by the use of the sixth sense found in fish, the pressure-sensitive lateral-line system. Crustaceans and other fish appear to be the main food items taken, although comparatively little is known of their diet. The egg cases of these species are the well-known mermaid's purses. Those of the skates and rays have stout, curved projections at each corner, while those of dogfish have more delicate coiled tendrils, resembling the tendrils of vetches and other climbing plants, which serve an anchoring function.

Of the 15 gadoid fish which occur with any degree of frequency in northern European waters, the cod and the haddock *Melanogrammus aeglefinus* are bottom-feeders. The haddock feeds almost entirely on benthic polychaetes, crustaceans, molluscs, and, especially, the sea-urchins and brittle-stars, for which it roots around in the bottom somewhat in the manner of a pig. The cod also takes polychaetes, crustaceans and molluscs, although its main food consists of other fish, particularly small haddock, sand-eels *Ammodytes* and herring. Most of the 18 species of north European flatfish are bottom-living. As juveniles some frequent shallow coastal areas; when adult they tend to occur in deeper water, but their diet of benthic invertebrates and fish is maintained. The largest flatfish, the halibut *Hippoglossus hippoglossus*, which can attain a length of two-and-a-half metres, is restricted to deep water, from 100 metres to the edge of the continental shelf, and is entirely a fish-eater; it can swallow a haddock whole.

In turn, fish are preyed on by a number of marine mammals, of which seals are the most coastal and most familiar. Northern Europe possesses three breeding species of seals (whilst a further three and the walrus *Odobenus rosmarus* are not infrequent visitors, especially in the north). The ringed seal *Phoca hispida*, the smallest of our species and also distinguishable by the light-coloured rings on its back and sides, is generally found associated with ice in the Arctic; but like the relict crustaceans mentioned earlier, this species was trapped within the northern Baltic (and in some adjacent lakes) several thousand years ago, where it now successfully breeds on the March/April ice. The related common or sand seal *Phoca vitulina* is found throughout the northern parts of the North Pacific and North Atlantic Oceans (including the southern Baltic) and, as its alternative name suggests, it is associated particularly with sand-banks and sheltered coastal waters in general. Fish are the main prey, especially gadoids, flatfish and herring, although salmon *Salmo salar* and sea trout *S. trutta* are also taken. These seals have therefore attracted the opprobrium of fishermen, particularly for the damage they do to nets (bounties are still paid for common seals by salmon-fishing companies); the main odium of fishermen, however, is reserved for the next species.

The grey or Atlantic seal *Halichoerus grypus* is the largest of our resident seals, being half as long again as the common seal, unlike which it is typically an inhabitant of exposed rocky coasts, where the cows haul out to breed in the autumn, either in caves or in the open. It occurs from the North Cape of Norway and around Iceland to Brittany in the south (including the Baltic where a small population lives atypically in the Gulf of Bothnia and Gulf of Finland), although the majority (some 75 per cent of the European population) occur around the coasts of Britain and Ireland. Also, unlike the common seal, individuals disperse quite widely: calves marked on the Farne Islands off the Northumberland coast have been recovered from the Faroes, Hebrides, Norway, Denmark and the Netherlands. Grey seals eat gadoid and salmonid fish and cephalopod molluscs. Their consumption of salmon is of economic importance; one seal has been reported as killing 13 salmon in a single hour, and up to 15 per cent of salmon caught in Scottish waters bear claw-marks attributable to this species. Not surprisingly, therefore, fishermen kill grey seals whenever a chance presents itself and legal organized culls of cows and calves on the breeding grounds have been instituted in an attempt to reduce their numbers. This notwithstanding, and regardless of having become extinct as a breeding species in Denmark, grey seal numbers have continued to increase quite dramatically since the late 1950s.

THE VISITOR AND THE COAST

Although wholesale land reclamation and pollution are major threats to many coastal habitats, the effects of trampling and over-collecting are no less destructive. The 175,000 visitors each year to Kynance Cove in Cornwall have removed 500 square metres of vegetation and 150,000 kilograms of soil just in walking from the car park to the beach; while the activities of the 'collector' whether for bait, food, souvenirs or educational study are even more marked. The naturalist is therefore asked to follow these guidelines: do not subject easily damaged habitats to unnecessary trampling; do not move rocks unnecessarily, and always return those moved to their original positions; spread the area from which you collect bait or other specimens and fill holes afterwards; do not collect live animals, dead shells can usually be found, and take notes and photographs, not specimens, wherever possible.

The Seas of Northern Europe

Arctic Ocean

Arctic circle

34

ICELAND

Norw
Se

35   34   3

35

Atlantic Ocean

Faeroes

Shetland Is

Orkney Is

Hebrides

35

SCOTLAND

35

North Sea

34   3

IRELAND

Irish Sea

BRITAIN

WALES   ENGLAND

NETHERLANDS

BELGIUM

LUXEMBOURG

English Channel

35

Channel Is

| 0 | 50 | 100 | 150 | 200 | 250 | 300 Miles |

| 0 | 100 | 200 | 300 | 400 Kilometres |

Bay of Biscay

FRANCE

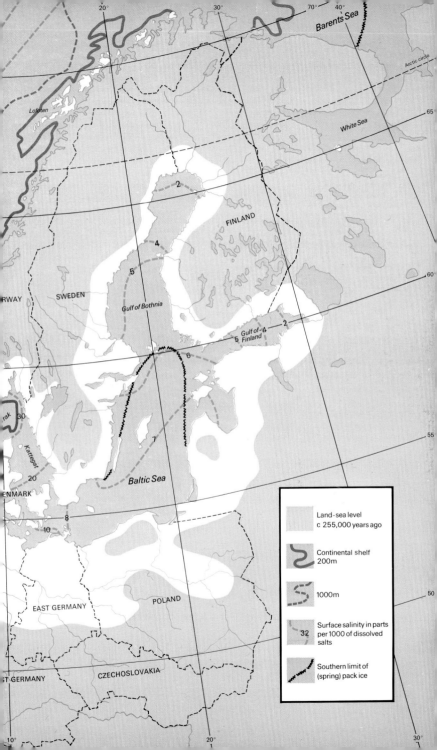

Barents Sea

Arctic circle

Lofoten

White Sea

65°

FINLAND

2

SWEDEN

4

5

60°

Gulf of Bothnia

NORWAY

Gulf of 4
Finland   2

5

6

55°

7

rak   30

Kattegat

20

Baltic Sea

DENMARK

8

10

EAST GERMANY

POLAND

50°

ST GERMANY   CZECHOSLOVAKIA

10°   20°   30°

	Land-sea level c 255,000 years ago
	Continental shelf 200m
	1000m
32	Surface salinity in parts per 1000 of dissolved salts
	Southern limit of (spring) pack ice

GLOSSARY

abdomen posterior section of body; in insects, spiders, without limbs; in crustaceans often with limbs

acute ending in a point

aerobic in presence of oxygen

alternate leaves placed singly at alternate positions along stem

anaerobic in absence of oxygen

anal fin fin just behind anus

anther part of stamen producing pollen

apex tip or summit

apothecia cup-like structures which produce spores

-ate describing 2-dimensional shape, *eg* ovate

awn in grasses, long, stiff bristle projecting beyond grain

axil angle between leaf and stem

barbel in fish, 'whisker'

basal in plants, at base of stem; in animals, position nearest body

body whorl in gastropods, largest and most recently formed whorl of shell

bract modified leaf, often at base of flower-stalk

byssus threads in bivalves, threads secreted by foot for attachment

calcareous containing or coated with lime (calcium carbonate); of soil, overlying chalk or limestone, therefore alkaline

calyx, calyces (plural) all the sepals, term often used when the sepals are joined to form a tube

carapace in crustaceans, shield covering head and thorax

cilia hair-like projections, usually occurring in large numbers, which beat rhythmically for locomotion, or to create a water current for feeding

columella in gastropods, central pillar of shell

crenulate edged with small, rounded teeth

dorsal in animals, of the back or upper side

dorsal fin fin in mid-line on back

epiphyte plant which grows on another plant but does not derive nourishment from it

exoskeleton hard outer covering of body

filter-feeder animal which filters out food particles suspended in water

flagella long, hair-like projection, usually occurring singly, which performs whip-like movement for locomotion

gills in aquatic animals, membranous structures which extract oxygen from water

gill slits in fish, external openings inside which gills are located

hermaphrodite in plants, having male and female organs in the same flower; in animals, having male and female organs in the same individual

high-water mark the highest point the tide reaches at any given time

holdfast attachment organ of seaweeds

inflorescence flower branch, including bracts, flower-stalks and flowers

lanceolate spear-shaped

lateral line line running along side of body of fish. A row of sensory cells which detect vibrations lie beneath this line

linear thin and narrow

littoral of the upper and middle shore

low-water mark the lowest point the tide reaches at any given time

mantle in molluscs, soft fold of tissue surrounding viscera, lungs, and which secretes the shell

microspecies groups of individuals differing only slightly from other groups, but not interbreeding with them

nerve in plants, strand of strengthening or conducting tissue running through leaf

ob- inverted, with broadest part of structure near apex, *eg* obovate

-oid describing 3-dimensional shape, *eg* ovoid

operculum in gastropods, hard plate which fits across opening of shell; in fan-worms, tentacle enlarged into calcareous plate; in bony fish, largest of several flat bones forming gill cover

opposite leaves paired on opposite sides of stem

ovate, ovoid egg-shaped (see -ate, -oid)

panicle branched inflorescence

palps paired sensory appendages close to the mouth

papilla small, fleshy projection

pectoral fins fins on sides of body, immediately behind head

pelagic living in open water, near the surface

pelvic fins fins on belly; their bony support is situated in front of the anus

perianth all the floral leaves (petals and sepals)

perianth segment one floral leaf; used when petals and sepals are indistinguishable

pharynx region of gut immediately behind mouth

pinnate regular arrangement of leaflets in 2 rows on either side of stalk

preoperculum most anterior bone of gill cover

primaries outermost flight feathers of bird's wing, usually 10

proboscis in insects, tubular mouthparts for sucking; in other invertebrates, trunk-like process of the head

protozoan, protozoa (plural) small to microscopic animal of simple structure

ray-florets in Compositae, elongated florets which form outer ring of 'petals'

rostrum in crustacea, insects, pointed 'snout'

sepals outer ring of floral leaves, usually green and less conspicuous than petals

shore-line water limit at any tide

simple leaf not divided into segments

siphon tube which conducts water into and out of body

species group of similar individuals which can interbreed; cannot usually interbreed with other species to produce fertile offspring

spikelet in grasses, one or more florets enclosed by a pair of stiff bracts

spire in gastropods, shell above most recently formed whorl

sporangium spore-capsule in ferns

spore in plants, minute reproductive body, produced asexually and of simpler structure than a seed

stamen male organ of flower

stigma part of female organ of flower which receives pollen

stipule scale or leaf-like structure at base of leaf-stalk

style female organ of flower

subspecies group of individuals within a species having distinctive features

suture in gastropods, grooves between successive shell whorls; in barnacles, cracks between the 4 plates of the shell

symbiosis individuals of two different species living in a close association which is mutually beneficial

thallus plant body undifferentiated into leaf, stem etc.; often flattened

thorax in insects region between head and abdomen (*qv*) bearing legs and wings; in spiders, crustacea, region between head and abdomen, but usually fused with head

tubercles small, rounded projections

umbel cluster of flowers whose stalks (rays) radiate from top of stem

ventral of the underside

viviparous giving birth to live young

whorls leaves or flowers arising in circles around stem; in gastropods, sections of shell (see also body whorl)

SHORE ZONATION

upper shore	extends from the highest point wetted by spring tides down to the average (mean) high-water level of all tides; uncovered except when tides exceed their average range.
middle shore	extends from the average high-water level of all tides down to the average low-water level.
lower shore	extends from the average low-water level down to the lowest point on the shore ever exposed at low tide; uncovered only when tides exceed their average range.
sublittoral	below the lowest point on the shore ever exposed at low tide; never uncovered.

See also diagram on page 34. These intertidal zones are not clear cut at their limits.

SYMBOLS

♀	female
♂	male
<	up to
>	more than
?	doubtful

ABBREVIATIONS

Distributions are given by seas or by countries, as appropriate.
The ranges are in the order of their listing in the field guide.

W	widespread
T	throughout
Br	Britain (England, Scotland, Wales)
Ir	Ireland
Ic	Iceland
Fr	France, north of the Loire
Lu	Luxembourg
Be	Belgium
Ne	Netherlands
De	Denmark
Ge	Germany
Cz	Czechoslovakia
Po	Poland
Fi	Finland
Sw	Sweden
No	Norway
FS	Fenno-Scandia (Norway, Sweden, Finland)
SC	Scandinavia (Norway, Sweden)
NE	Fenno-Scandia, Denmark, north Germany, north Poland
CE	Czechoslovakia, south Germany, south Poland
WE	Britain, Ireland, France, Luxembourg, Belgium, Netherlands
NoS	North Sea
BaS	Baltic Sea
nBaS	Baltic Sea north of latitude 57°N
EnC	English Channel
AtO	Atlantic Ocean
n, s, e, w, c	north, south, east, west, central

When the species is not native but introduced and naturalized, the countries are put in brackets eg Fr, Ge, (Br, Ir)

c	about
ad	adult
av	average
esp	especially
fl(s)	flower(s)
fl-head	flowerhead
fr(s)	fruit(s)
imm	immature
inflor	inflorescence
juv	juvenile
lf (lvs)	leaf (leaves)
lflet	leaflet
microsp(p)	microspecies
sp	species (singular)
spp	species (plural)
ssp	subspecies
var	variety

MEASUREMENTS

Scale in the plates: the relative sizes of the plants and animals are preserved whenever possible, but the measurements in the entries themselves should be noted.

B	breadth
BL	body length (excludes tentacles, antennae, limbs, filaments in invertebrates, tail fin in fish)
D	diameter
EL	extended length
H	height
L	total length (includes appendages in invertebrates, beak, tail in birds)
LS	limbspan
SD	shell diameter
SH	shell height
SL	shell length (along long axis)
WS	wingspan

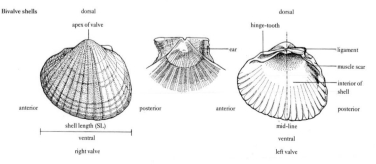

Bivalve shells

dorsal · apex of valve · anterior · posterior · shell length (SL) · ventral · right valve

dorsal · hinge-tooth · ear · ligament · muscle scar · interior of shell · anterior · posterior · mid-line · ventral · left valve

Gastropod shell

shell
height
(SH)

spire

body whorl

teeth

aperture

outer lip

columellar
teeth

siphonal canal

Generalized polychaete worm

antenna palp

eye

tooth

jaw

everted
pharynx

setigerous
segments

tail filament

tentacular cirrus

seta

flap-like
parapodium

parapodial
cirrus

gill

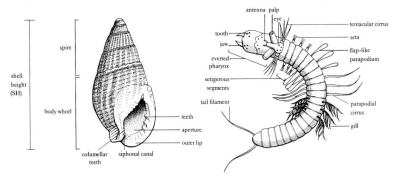

**Malacostracan crustaceans
Prawn**

carapace

rostrum

upper margin

lower margin

inner antenna

abodmen
(folded under
carapace in
most crabs)

tail-
fan

5 pairs of
swimming
limbs

5 pairs of
walking
limbs (crabs)

outer antenna

Oppossum-shrimp

inner antennae

eye

outer antenna

carapace
(absent in isopods,
amphipods)

8 pairs of
thoracic
limbs

abdomen

telson

tail-fan

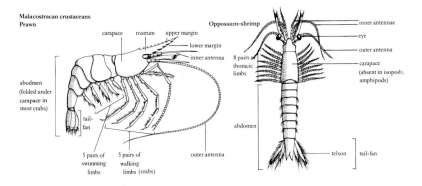

Bony fish

operculum

lateral line

dorsal fin

fleshy fin

tail fin

preoperculum

pectoral fin

pelvic fin

anal fin

Cartilaginous fish

first dorsal fin

second dorsal fin

tail fin

pectoral fin

pelvic fin

gill slits

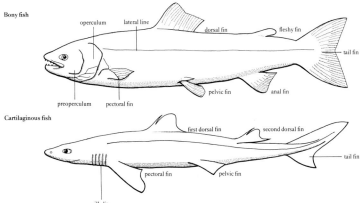

lichen *Lichina pygmaea* LICHINACEAE
Gelatinous, in erect, densely-branched
tufts, < 1 cm; dark brown, black when
dry; looks like seaweed. Spores produced
in swollen tips of somewhat flattened
branches. Crevices in rocks, among
seaweeds and barnacles, middle-shore. Br,
Ir, Ic, Fr, Ge, Fi, No. [1] *L. confinis* only
½ as large with cylindrical branches, just
above mean high-water level. T, ex Lu,
Be, Ne, Cz.

Dog Lichen *Peltigera canina* PELTI-
GERACEAE Spreading; forms large, flat
lobes, < 2·5 cm wide; soft, flexible, bluish-
brown when wet, but brittle, papery, pale
grey when dry; upper surface downy,
lower surface white and felted. Apothecia
oval, chestnut-brown. Sand-dunes, also
inland in sand- and clay-pits. T, ex Lu,
Cz. [2]

Sea Ivory *Ramalina siliquosa* USNEACEAE
Very variable lichen, forming smooth,
shiny, sparsely branched tufts < 10 cm;
pale grey-green, surface covered in
minute white spots. Apothecia raised,
yellow-grey discs. Rocks, walls, near sea;
inland, less frequent, usually infertile. T,
ex Lu, Be, Cz, Po. [3]

lichen *Anaptychia fusca* PHYSCIACEAE
Spreading; forms cushion-like rosettes
< 10 cm across, attached by fine threads.
Thallus leathery, with lobes < 3 mm
wide, growing over one another; light to
dark brown when dry, dark green when
wet. Apothecia abundant blackish discs
with prominent margins. Rocks, trees by
sea, rarely inland. T, ex Ic, Lu, Cz, Po. [4]

Sea Black Shields *Lecanora atra*
LECANORACEAE Crust-like, thick, patchy,
with rough, cracked surface; pale grey,
each patch surrounded by faint blue-
black line. Apothecia ('shields') black
cups with wavy, notched, greyish rims,
dark purple inside when cut open. Rocks
just above mean high-water level, also
inland. T. [5]

lichen *Ochrolechia parella* LECANORACEAE
Crust-like, thick, grey, with concentrically
zoned margin and prominent white edge.

Numerous apothecia, in older, warty,
central part; large, greyish-pink discs
with thick margins. Rocks by sea, also
widespread inland on rocks, walls, trees.
T, ex Ic, Lu, Cz. [6]

lichen *Verrucaria maura* VERRUCARIACEAE
Thallus thin, smooth, dull black; surface
covered with network of fine cracks.
Spores produced in small, dot-like
apothecia sunk in thallus and slightly
protruding. Forms black zone, which
looks like tar, on rocks at top of beach.
T, ex Lu, Be, Cz. [7]

lichen *Caloplaca marina* PYRENULACEAE
Crust-like, dark orange, peppered with
orange to yellow-orange granules.
Apothecia occur among the granules,
smooth discs, same colour as thallus,
inconspicuous. Rocks, about mean high-
water level. T, ex Lu, Be, Cz, Po. [8]

Sand-dune Screw-moss *Tortula
ruraliformis* POTTIALES H 1·5–8 cm. Forms
extensive, loose patches, dull brown when
dry, yellowish-green or golden-brown
when moist. Lvs < 7 mm, ovate-
lanceolate, with long, silvery hair-point ½
as long as lvs. Spore capsules narrowly
cylindrical, < 6 mm, on long, reddish
stalks < 25 mm. Unstable sand-dunes, by
sea and inland. T, ex Lu, Cz, Fi, No. [9]

Sea Cushion-moss *Grimmia maritima*
GRIMMIACEAE H 1–4 cm. Forms neat,
round, olive-green cushions. Lvs < 2 mm,
triangular, with long acute tip, into which
reddish-brown nerve runs. Spore
capsules spherical, on short stalks, hidden
by lvs. Confined to rocks near mean high-
water level. T, ex Lu, Be, Ge, Cz. [10]

Yellow Feather-moss *Camptothecium
lutescens* HYPNACEAE Tufted, much-
branched, yellowish-green, forming
irregular patches. Lvs < 2·5 mm,
lanceolate-triangular, tapering to long,
straight, fine point, with nerve $c\frac{3}{4}$ length.
Spore capsules rare, < 2 mm long,
slightly curved, on stalks < 2 cm. Dunes
of shell–sand; also inland in calcareous
grassland. T. [11]

moss *Trichostomum brachydontium* POTTIACEAE H 1–4 cm. Robust, forming flat, bright green cushions. Lvs <4 mm, tongue-shaped, with wavy margins, nerve running into short point; very curled when dry. Spore capsules elliptical, on yellow stalks; rarely produced. Rocks, about mean high-water level; also on walls and bare soil inland. T, ex Ne, Ge, Cz, Po, Fi. [1]

moss *Ulota phyllantha* ORTHOTRICHACEAE H 5–15 mm. Forms rather loose, yellowish-green cushions. Lvs <3 mm, oblong-lanceolate, with nerve running into short point, curled when dry. Lf-tip develops tiny, brown, rod-shaped 'gemmae', which are reproductive structures. Spore capsules rarely produced. Rocks, near mean high-water level; also on trees inland. T, ex Lu, Cz, Po. [2]

Sea-lettuce *Ulva lactuca* ULVACEAE H 10–40 cm. Large, roundish, translucent fronds with irregular, wavy margins; pale watery-green when young, darkening with age; attached by a short, solid stalk to a small, disc-like holdfast. Estuaries, pools on upper shore esp near a fresh, or even sewage-polluted, water outlet. T, ex Lu, Cz. [3]

Green Laver *Monostroma grevillei* ULVACEAE H 5–15 cm. Delicate, translucent, pale green bladders. Holdfast a tiny, fibrous disc. With age the bladders split and spread out flat like sea-lettuce. Sticks easily to paper when dried which sea-lettuce does not. Annual, on rocks or in pools on lower shore, in spring and summer. T, ex Lu, Cz, Po, Fi, No. [4]

green seaweed *Enteromorpha intestinalis* ULVACEAE H 10–60 cm. Long, unbranched, tubular, grass-green fronds, <2 cm wide, constricted at irregular intervals, attached by very small disc but often free-floating.

Annual, Mar–Aug, estuaries, pools near mean high-water level. T, ex Lu, Cz. [5]

green seaweed *Cladophora rupestris* CLADOPHORACEAE H 7–12 cm. Wiry, filamentous, dark green, moss-like perennial, attached by small holdfast. Spreading by short runners to form large, turf-like patches. Irregularly branched from base upwards. Rocks on middle and lower shore, often forming a sward beneath saw wrack *Fucus serratus*. T, ex Lu, Cz. [6]

green seaweed *Bryopsis plumosa* BRYOPSIDACEAE H 5–10 cm. Delicate, bright green, with stems <1 mm wide at base, tapering upwards. Branches irregular, decreasing in length upwards, producing triangular, plume-like tip. Separate ♂ and ♀ plants; when fertile, ♂ yellowish-green, ♀ dark green. Deep pools on lower shore. Br, Ir, Fr, Be, Ne, SC. [7]

green seaweed *Codium tomentosum* CODIACEAE H 10–25 cm. Velvety, spongy, much-branched, dark green, cylindrical fronds, made up of densely interwoven filaments. Holdfast an irregularly lobed, spongy disc <3 cm. On rocks, in deep pools on middle and lower shore. Br, Ir, Fr, Ne. [8]

Channelled Wrack *Pelvetia canaliculata* FUCACEAE 5–15 cm. Regularly branched fronds, <6 mm wide, inrolled and channelled on one side; yellow-brown when damp, almost black when dry. Fronds end in yellowish-green, divided tips, usually swollen and granular, <25 mm, containing reproductive structures. On rocks, hanging downwards with channelled side inwards, c1 m below mean high-water of spring tides. Br, Ir, Ic, Fr, Ne, SC. [9]

Brush Seaweed *Pilayella littoralis*
ECTOCARPACEAE H 15–45 cm. Filamentous
olive or reddish-brown plants arising
from a creeping base. Plants become
matted and worn at tip. Abundant in
spring and summer, moving down shore
with season: at first attached to
Ascophyllum on middle shore and later to
Fucus on lower shore. T, ex Lu, Be, Cz.
[1]

brown seaweed *Ralfsia verrucosa*
RALFSIACEAE Brittle, encrusting seaweed
forming patches < 10 cm across, firmly
attached to rocks or shells; dark brown.
Young plants smooth, circular, faintly
marked with concentric rings. Older
plants coalesce to form irregular plates.
Shallow pools, upper and middle shore,
occasionally sublittoral. T, ex Lu, Cz,
Po, Fi. [2]

brown seaweed *Chordaria flagelliformis*
CHORDARIACEAE H 20–50 cm. Irregularly
branched, cylindrical, greenish-brown
fronds, < 3 mm across, with disc-like
holdfast. Fringed with tiny, colourless,
jelly-like hairs which give it a slimy feel.
Annual, summer and autumn, attached to
stones and rocks on middle shore. Br, Ir,
Ic, Fr, Ne, Ge, Sw, No. [3]

brown seaweed *Eudesme virescens*
CHORDARIACEAE H 15–30 cm. Alternately
branched, thread-like, limp, yellow-brown
fronds with tiny holdfast. Fringed with
colourless, jelly-like hairs giving it a
slimy feel. Pools, lower or middle shore,
Apr–Sep. Br, Ir, Fr, Ne, Ge, Po, Sw,
No. [4]

brown seaweed *Scytosiphon lomentaria*
SCYTOSIPHONACEAE H 15–40 cm. Hollow,
unbranched fronds with constrictions
every 3–4 cm; olive-brown; slimy to
touch. Short-lived: in winter on middle
shore, later generations moving down
shore as temperature rises. T, ex Lu, Cz,
Fi. [5]

brown seaweed *Sphacelaria cirrosa*
SPHACELARIACEAE H 1–3 cm. Dense, tufted
seaweed of variously branched, stiff
threads. Epiphytic on other species,

attached by holdfast of radiating filaments, some growing out as runners to form new plants. Middle and lower shore. T, ex Lu, Cz, Fi. [6]

brown seaweed *Cladostephus verticillatus* SPHACELARIACEAE H 10–15 cm. Irregularly branched, with stiff, wiry stems; branches clothed in short, curved branchlets in whorls < 1 mm apart; dark greenish-brown. Harsh to touch; disc-like holdfast < 12 mm. Pools on middle shore. Br, Ir, Fr, Ge, Sw. [7]

Spiral Wrack *Fucus spiralis* FUCACEAE H 15–40 cm. Regularly branched 6–8 times into flat segments < 4 cm wide, lacking bladders, attached by short, flattened stalk to disc-like holdfast; olive-brown when wet, green-black when dry. Pale, swollen tips of fronds contain reproductive structures. Below channelled wrack zone on upper shore. Br, Ir, Ic, Fr, Ne, Ge, No. [8]

Horned Wrack *Fucus ceranoides* FUCACEAE H 25–50 cm. Regularly branched into flat segments < 1 cm wide, distinct midrib, attached by long, slender stalk to disc-like holdfast; pale olive-green. Fronds have narrow, fertile branches in fan-shaped groups. Shores of estuaries. Br, Ir, Fr, Be, Ne, Ge, No. [9]

Knotted Wrack *Ascophyllum nodosum* FUCACEAE H < 3 m. Flat, irregularly branched fronds < 1 cm wide, lacking midrib; olive-green when wet, green-black when dry. At intervals of c5 cm, elliptical air-bladders < 3 cm, too tough to 'pop' between fingers; greenish-yellow bodies on side-stems contain reproductive organs. Sheltered, rocky shores. T, ex Lu, Be, Cz, Fi. [10]

Rainbow Bladderweed *Cystoseira tamariscifolia* CYSTOSEIRACEAE H 25–50 cm. Much branched, stiff, leathery fronds, whole plant covered in short lf-like spines < 3 mm; olive-green with beautiful blue-green iridescence under water, almost black when dry. Small air bladders at tips of branches. Rocky pools, lower shore. Br, Ir, Fr. [11]

brown seaweed *Leathesia difformis*
CORYNOPHLOEACEAE H 2–5 cm. Stalkless,
shiny, olive-brown lumps; rounded and
solid when young, becoming lobed and
hollow with age. Attached to rocks, other
seaweeds, on middle and lower shore;
annual. T, ex Lu, Be, Cz, Fi. [1]

Sea Bootlaces *Chorda filum* CHORDACEAE
H 3–7 m. Long, cylindrical, unbranched,
olive-brown 'boot laces', <6 mm
diameter, clothed in short, colourless
hairs, slippery to touch. Attached to rocks
by disc-like holdfast. Become hollow and
extremely tough with age. Annual, lower
shore and sublittoral. T, ex Lu, Be, Cz. [2]

Tangle *Laminaria digitata* LAMINARIACEAE
H 50–150 cm. Large, tough, brown
seaweed with flexible stalk, oval in
section <4 cm across, expanded above
into flat, leathery, oar-shaped frond,
divided lengthways, <60 cm wide.
Strong, thin, root-like growths form dome-
shaped holdfast. Lower shore and below.
T, ex Lu, Cz, Po, Fi. [3]

Cuvie *Laminaria hyperborea* LAMINARIA-
CEAE H 1–2 m. Large, tough, brown
seaweed with rough, stiff stalks <2·5 cm
across, tapering above and then expanded
into flat, leathery, divided frond. Short,
thick, root-like growths form cone-shaped
holdfast. Rough stalks produce foothold
for other seaweeds. Lower shore and
below. Br, Ir, Ic, Fr, Ge, Sw, No. [4]

Sea Belt *Laminaria saccharina*
LAMINARIACEAE H 25–250 cm. Long, flat,
unbranched, olive-yellow fronds with
frilly edges, <15 cm wide, without
midrib. Smooth, slender stalk <25 cm,
attached to rock by several tiers of thick,
root-like growths. Lower shore and below.
Dry fronds produce white deposit sweet
to taste, hence the name *saccharina*.
T, ex Lu, Cz, Po, Fi. [5]

Furbelows *Saccorhiza polyschides*
PHYLLARIACEAE H 3–5 m. One of longest
seaweeds in NE Atlantic although only
living one year. Fan-shaped, brown fronds
<4 m across, divided into broad ribbons;

flattened, twisted stalk with wavy
margins; massive, hollow, knobbly
holdfast <30 cm across. Lower shore,
sublittoral fringe, on rocky coasts. Br, Ir,
Fr, No. [6]

Murlins *Alaria esculenta* ALARIACEAE
H 60–200 cm. Flat, unbranched, olive-
yellow, easily-torn fronds, <15 cm wide,
with wavy edges. Holdfast of branched,
root-like growths; stalk <15 cm long,
flattened above and continued as midrib
of frond. Attached to rocks on lower shore
of exposed coasts. Succulent midribs of
young plants edible. Br, Ir, Ic, Fr, Ne,
No. [7]

Saw Wrack *Fucus serratus* FUCACEAE
H 60–150 cm. Robust, flat, irregularly
branched, olive-brown fronds, <15 mm
wide, with coarse teeth, and well-
developed midrib. In autumn and winter
tips of branches swollen with reproductive
structures. Attached to rocks on middle
shore. T, ex Lu, De, Cz, Po, Fi. [8]

Bladder Wrack *Fucus vesiculosus*
FUCACEAE H 30–150 cm. Robust, branched,
olive-brown, strap-like fronds, <15 mm
wide, with numerous air bladders in pairs
on either side of midrib, which act as
floats. Tips of fronds carry swollen
reproductive structures. Attached to rocks
on middle shore by disc-like holdfast.
T, ex Lu, Cz. [9]

Thong-weed *Himanthalia elongata*
HIMANTHALIACEAE H 1–2·5 m. Long,
leathery, olive-brown, strap-like fronds,
<1 cm wide, mottled with brown spots
when fertile in spring. Fronds develop
from short-stalked, button-like growths,
<4 cm across. Lower shore on exposed
coasts. Br, Ir, Fr, Ne, Ge, No. [10]

Sea Oak *Halidrys siliquosa* CYSTOSEIR-
ACEAE H 30–100 cm. Branched, leathery,
olive-brown fronds with long, pointed
air-bladders <5 cm, at tips of branches,
divided by transverse partitions into <12
compartments. Cone-shaped holdfast.
Lower shore or deep pools on middle
shore. T, ex Ic, Lu, Cz, Fi. [11]

red seaweed *Rhodochorton floridulum*
ACROCHAETIACEAE H 1–3 cm. Forms dense,
velvety, crimson tufts of branched threads
over sand-covered rocks. Middle shore.
Br, Ir, Fr, Ne, Ge, Sw, No. [1]

red seaweed *Furcellaria lumbricalis*
FURCELLARIACEAE H 15–30 cm. Bushy,
erect, rather stiff, regularly forked 6–8
times, purplish-red; developing pod-like
reproductive swellings at tip in summer
which fall in autumn. Attached by
branching, root-like holdfast, <25 mm
across, to rocks in pools low on middle
shore and below. T. [2] Goat tang
Polyides rotundus similar but holdfast
fleshy, reproductive parts well below tip.
T, ex Ic, Lu, Cz, Po, Fi.

red seaweed *Gracilaria verrucosa*
GRACILARIACEAE H 15–30 cm. Irregularly
branched, stringy fronds, ending in
smooth, slender points; spores produced
in rough knobs scattered over fronds.
Fleshy holdfast <5 mm across. Middle
shore. T, ex Ic, Lu, Cz, Po, Fi. [3]

red seaweed *Bostrychia scorpioides*
PHYLLOPHORACEAE H 5–10 cm. Tufts of
irregularly branched and entangled, wavy,
red-brown threads covered with finely-
pointed segments. Grows among stalks
of plants on salt-marshes, or on upper
shore of very sheltered coasts. Br, Ir, Fr,
Be, Ne. [4]

red seaweed *Gigartina stellata*
GIGARTINACEAE H 10–20 cm. Clusters of
flat fronds with inrolled margins,
regularly forked 6–7 times, dark
purplish-red, rarely black. In summer and
autumn frond covered in oval, spore-
bearing projections <1 cm long. Middle
and lower shore. Old plants often over-
grown with sea-mat *Flustrellidra hispida*, a
brownish-grey bryozoan. Br, Ir, Ic, Fr,
Ne, De, No. [5]

Carragheen *Chondrus crispus*
GIGARTINACEAE H 5–15 cm. Clusters of
flat fronds, margins never inrolled,
regularly forked 6–8 times, varying in
colour with increasing light from

purplish-red to green. 2 forms, one with narrow fronds, <5 mm wide, the other broader, <2 cm. Middle shore. Edible, used in making puddings and jellies. T, ex Lu, Cz, Po, Fi. [broad form 6]

red seaweed *Dumontia incrassata* DUMONTIACEAE H 15–35 cm. Delicate, irregularly branched, slimy fronds with jelly-like texture, <6 mm wide; narrow at base, blunt at apex, solid when young, hollow when old; varying from dull red in shade to yellow-green in full sunlight. Middle shore, spring and early summer. T, ex Lu, Cz, Po, Fi. [7]

Common Coralweed *Corallina officinalis* CORALLINACEAE H 2–12 cm. Regularly-branched, tufted plants made up of many bead-like segments, <2 mm, covered in hard deposit of lime, varying from plum-coloured in shade to yellowish-pink or white in bright light. Attached by crusty holdfast <12 mm across, to rocks in pools or shady places on middle shore. T, ex Lu, Cz, Po, Fi. [8]

Common Red Ceramium *Ceramium rubrum* CERAMIACEAE H 8–30 cm. Regularly branched threads ending in pair of hooked points, varying in colour with increasing light from deep red to greenish-yellow. Threads banded with dark and light areas. Attached by minute conical holdfast to rocks, shells, other seaweeds, in pools on middle shore. T, ex Lu, Cz. [9]

red seaweed *Polysiphonia lanosa* RHODOMELACEAE H 3–5 cm. Stiff, reddish-brown plants growing on knotted wrack *Ascophyllum nodosum*; creeping bases send out 'rootlets' into fronds of host. Pear-shaped reproductive structures occur in fan-shaped upper branches. Occasionally on species of *Fucus* or on rocks. Br, Ir, Fr, Ne, No. [10]

red seaweed *Hildenbrandia rubra* HILDENBRANDIACEAE Forms smooth, dark red, paint-like patches over rock surfaces, which lose their lustre when dry. Shaded rocks, moist crevices, on middle shore. T, ex Lu, Be, Cz, Fi. [11]

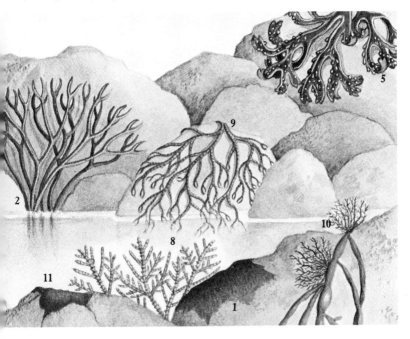

Purple Laver *Porphyra umbilicalis*
BANGIACEAE H 15–50 cm. Irregularly
shaped, thin, flexible, membranous
fronds, rosy-purple when young to olive-
green or dirty-brown when old. Attached
by minute, disc-like holdfast to rocks at all
levels of shore on exposed coasts. Eaten
as 'laver bread' in S Wales and Ireland;
boiled then fried with bacon. T, ex Lu,
Cz, Po, Fi. [1]

red seaweed *Cystoclonium purpureum*
RHODOPHYLLIDACEAE H 15–45 cm. Soft,
bushy, purple-red plant with cylindrical
stems <3 mm, twice as thick as branches.
Spores in small swellings on the
branchlets. Attached by holdfast of
branched, root-like structures to rocks in
pools on middle and lower shore. T, ex
Lu, Cz, Po, Fi. [2]

Cockscomb *Plocamium cartilagineum*
PLOCAMIACEAE H 8–20 cm. Tufted, rose-
red plant with narrow, flattened stems
<1 mm, regularly 4–5 times divided, the
final division one-sided like teeth of a

comb. Attached to stones by small, root-
like holdfast in pools on lower shore, but
often cast up on beach. T, ex Lu, Cz, Po,
Fi. [3]

Red Rags *Dilsea carnosa* DUMONTIACEAE
H 15–50 cm. Tough, thick, flat, opaque,
blood-red fronds, <12 cm wide, smooth
to touch, rounded in outline, but
becoming deeply cut by wave action;
narrowed below into short, cylindrical
stalk. Attached by small, disc-like holdfast
to rocks and stones on middle and lower
shore. Br, Ir, Ic, Fr, De, SC. [4]

red seaweed *Lomentaria articulata*
LOMENTARIACEAE H 3–12 cm. Shiny, pale
crimson or purplish, with stem and
branches constricted at regular intervals
into oval, bead-like segments. Attached by
tiny disc to rocks and other seaweeds, in
pools on middle and lower shore. Br, Ir,
Fr, Be, Ne, No. [5]

Dulse *Palmaria palmata* RHODYMENIACEAE
H 10–30 cm. Tough, thick, translucent,

reddish-purple fronds, <10 cm wide, very variable in shape from scarcely to much divided, but always distinguishable by very short, or absent, stalk joining frond to disc-like holdfast. On rocks or large seaweeds on middle or lower shore. T, ex Lu, Ge, Cz, Po, Fi. [6]

red seaweed *Griffithsia flosculosa*
CERAMIACEAE H 8–15 cm. Delicate threads, regularly branched, bright crimson when young becoming dark red or brownish with age, losing colour in fresh water. Spores occur in tiny, stalked structures. Rock pools on lower shore of exposed coasts. Br, Ir, Fr, Ne. [7]

red seaweed *Delesseria sanguinea*
DELESSERIACEAE H 15–25 cm. Showy, crimson plant having wavy-edged, lanceolate-ovate, leaf-like fronds, with well-developed midrib and pairs of forwardly directed veins. 'Lvs' attached to much-branched, cylindrical stalk. Holdfast a thickened disc <6 mm across. Attached to rocks or other seaweeds in

deep pools on lower shore and below. T, ex Lu, Cz, Po, Fi. [8]

Pepper Dulse *Laurencia pinnatifida*
RHODOMELACEAE H 4–20 cm. Tufted plant with flat thallus. Branches, in one plane only, becoming progressively smaller upwards with narrowly lanceolate terminal segments. Variable in colour: olive-green in full sunlight, dark reddish-purple in shady pools. Strong main stalk attached by root-like structures and disc-shaped holdfast to rocks, middle shore downwards. T, ex Ic, Lu, Ge, Cz, Po, Fi. [9]

red seaweed *Odonthalia dentata*
RHODOMELACEAE H 12–25 cm. Tough, flattened, reddish-purple fronds with distinct peppery smell, much divided into alternately arranged segments with sharply pointed teeth at the tip. Reproductive bodies in tufts between these teeth. Attached to rocks or other seaweeds in sublittoral zone, but often washed up on shore. Br, Ic, Fr, De, SC. [10]

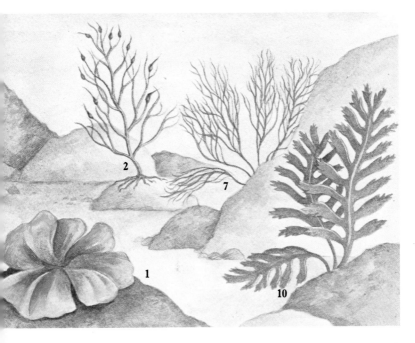

Adder's-tongue *Ophioglossum vulgatum*
OPHIOGLOSSACEAE H <20 cm. Fern. Lvs
usually single, ovate-lanceolate, <20 cm,
sheathing stalk of fertile spike. Sporangia
in 2 rows on margins of spike. Spores
ripe May–Aug. Damp places in dunes,
also inland. T, ex Ic. [1]

Sea Spleenwort *Asplenium marinum*
ASPLENIACEAE H <30 cm. Fern. Lvs linear
in outline, <30 cm, leathery, once-divided.
Sporangia ½-way between midrib and
margin, covered by brownish flap. Spores
ripe Jun–Sep. Caves and crevices in cliffs.
Br, Ir, Fr, No. [2]

Creeping Willow *Salix repens* SALICACEAE
H <150 cm. Erect or creeping shrub with
creeping underground stems. Lvs <45
mm, oval-elliptical, silky beneath and
above when young. Catkins appear before
lvs, Apr–May. Damp places in dunes,
also inland. T, ex Ic, Fi. [3]

Sea Beet *Beta vulgaris* ssp *maritima*
CHENOPODIACEAE H 30–120 cm. Annual or
perennial, rosette-forming herb. Lvs
variable in shape and colour, usually
<10 cm, thick, leathery, rhomboid,
yellowish-green. Fls green, in clusters of
2–3, on branched spike, Jul–Sep. Cliffs,
salt-marshes. Br, Ir, Fr, Be, Ne, De, Ge,
Sw. [4] Cultivated sugar beet, *B. vulgaris*
ssp *vulgaris*, very similar, but with thick
root, sometimes occurs as an escape.

Grass-leaved Orache *Atriplex littoralis*
CHENOPODIACEAE H 50–100 cm. Erect,
mealy, much-branched, annual herb. Lvs
<3 cm, linear-oblong, often toothed,
lower stalked, upper stalkless. Fls green,
in clusters, on branched spike, Jul–Aug.
Frs enclosed in 2 spiny, swollen, lf-like
flaps. Muddy shores, salt-marshes, rarely
inland. T, ex Ic, Lu. [5]

Frosted Orache *Atriplex laciniata*
CHENOPODIACEAE H <30 cm. Silvery,
much-branched, prostrate annual herb.
Lvs <2 cm, rhomboid-ovate, mealy
above and below. Fls green, in short
spikes, Aug–Sep. Frs enclosed in 2
toothed, lf-like flaps. Sandy or gravelly

shores just above high-water mark. Br,
Ir, Fr, Be, Ne, De, Ge, SC. [6]

Babington's Orache *Atriplex glabriuscula*
CHENOPODIACEAE H <20 cm. Slightly
mealy, prostrate, annual herb with
spreading, ridged stems. Lvs <10 cm,
lower deltoid with wedge-shaped bases.
Fls tiny, green, Jul–Sep. Frs enclosed in
2 lf-like flaps joined almost to middle.
Sandy or gravelly shores above high-
water mark. T, ex Lu, Cz, Fi. [7]

Sea-purslane *Halimione portulacoides*
CHENOPODIACEAE H 20–80 cm. Mealy
shrub. Lower lvs opposite, <5 cm,
elliptical, short-stalked; upper lvs sessile,
linear. Fls yellow-green, in compact
spikes, Jul–Sep. Frs enclosed in 2 lf-like,
3-lobed flaps joined almost to top.
Salt-marshes, at edges of pools, dykes. Br,
Ir, Fr, Be, Ne, De, Ge. [8]

Glasswort *Salicornia europaea*
CHENOPODIACEAE H 15–40 cm. Very
variable, fleshy, annual herb; at first dark
green, becoming yellow-green, then pink
or red. Lvs in opposite pairs, completely
surrounding stem. Fls in 3s, in terminal
spike of <10 fertile segments, Aug–Sep.
Salt-marshes. Edible. T, ex Ic, Lu. [9]
Several related spp often grow together.

Annual Sea-blite *Suaeda maritima*
CHENOPODIACEAE H 10–50 cm. Very
variable, fleshy, red-tinged, prostrate or
erect, annual herb. Lvs <5 cm long, *c*1
mm wide, almost cylindrical. Fls tiny,
green, 1–3 together in lf-axils, Jul–Oct.
Frs shining black seeds, <2 mm across.
Salt-marshes, shores, often below high-
water mark. T, ex Ic, Lu. [10]

Prickly Saltwort *Salsola kali* CHENOPO-
DIACEAE H <60 cm. Prostrate, rarely
erect, much-branched, prickly annual
herb. Lvs <4 cm, fleshy, cylindrical,
spine-tipped. Fls green, solitary in lf-
axils, each with 2 lf-like bracts, Jul–Sep.
Frs enclosed in persistent perianth, which
develops broad wing or ridge. Sandy
shores. T, ex Ic, Lu, Cz. [11]

Thyme-leaved Sandwort *Arenaria serpyllifolia* CARYOPHYLLACEAE H 2·5–25 cm. Annual or biennial herb. Lvs <6 mm, ovate–lanceolate, roughly hairy. Fls 3–8 mm across, white, 5 petals shorter than sepals, Jun–Aug. Frs flask-shaped capsules, <5 mm. Dry, sandy places. T, ex Ic. [1]

Sea Sandwort *Honkenya peploides* CARYOPHYLLACEAE H <25 cm. Yellow-green, perennial herb, branches rooting in sand. Lvs <18 mm, very succulent. ♂ and ♀ fls separate, 5 greenish-white petals shorter than sepals in ♀, equalling sepals in ♂, May–Aug. Frs globular capsules, <8 mm. Coastal sand, shingle. T, ex Lu, Cz. [2]

Sea Mouse-ear *Cerastium diffusum* CARYOPHYLLACEAE H 5–30 cm. Hairy, annual herb. Lvs <1 cm, opposite, lower tongue-shaped, upper ovate–elliptical. Fls <6 mm across, white, 4–5 notched petals shorter than sepals, May–Jul. Frs cylindrical capsules, <7·5 mm. Sandy or gravelly places. T, ex Ic, Lu, Fi. [3]

Greater Sea-spurrey *Spergularia media* CARYOPHYLLACEAE H 2–5 cm. Prostrate, perennial herb. Lvs <25 mm, fleshy, flat above, rounded beneath. Fls <12 mm, white or pink, 5 petals longer than sepals, *c*10 stamens, Jun–Sep. Frs capsules, <8 mm, almost all seeds winged. Salt-marshes, muddy shores. T, ex Ic, Lu, Fi. [4] Lesser sea-spurrey *Spergularia marina*, annual; petals shorter than sepals, 4–8 stamens; seeds mainly unwinged. T.

Rock Sea-spurrey *Spergularia rupicola* CARYOPHYLLACEAE H 2–5 cm. Prostrate, glandular-hairy, perennial herb. Lvs <15 mm, opposite, linear, fleshy, with horny tip. Fls <10 mm, deep pink, with 5 petals as long as sepals, 10 stamens, Jun–Sep. Frs capsules, <7 mm, with wingless seeds. Rocky coasts. Br, Ir, Fr. [5]

Sea Campion *Silene maritima* CARYOPHYLLACEAE H 25 cm. Bluish-green, perennial herb. Lvs <2 cm, elliptical-lanceolate. Fls <25 mm across, white, 5 petals divided to ½-way, Jun–Aug. Calyces form bladders surrounding ovoid frs, <9 mm. Rocks, shingle, and rarely in mountains. T, ex Lu, Cz, Po. [6]

Lesser Meadow-rue *Thalictrum minus* RANUNCULACEAE H 15–150 cm. Perennial herb with wiry, furrowed stems. Lvs divided into 3–7 lobed lflets. Fls greenish-yellow, 4–5 petals soon falling, numerous drooping anthers, Jun–Aug. Very variable. Coastal dunes, also inland. T, ex Ic. [7]

Yellow Horned-poppy *Glaucium flavum* PAPAVERACEAE H 30–90 cm. Blue-green, biennial or perennial herb. Basal lvs <35 cm, stalked, lyre-shaped; upper lvs stalkless, half-clasping stem. Fls <9 cm, 4 petals, Jun–Sep. Frs long capsules, <30 cm ('horn'). Sandy or gravelly coasts. Br, Ir, Fr, Be, Ne, De, Ge, SC, (Cz, Po). [8]

Common Scurvy-grass *Cochlearia officinalis* CRUCIFERAE H 5–50 cm. Fleshy, biennial or perennial herb. Basal lvs <15 mm, round to kidney-shaped, long-stalked; stem lvs ovate to oblong, clasping stem. Fls <1 cm, white, rarely lilac, 4 petals 2–3 times as long as sepals, May–Aug. Frs swollen capsules, <7 mm. Rocks, salt-marshes. Once eaten by sailors as source of vitamin C. Br, Ir, Fr, Be, Ne, De, Ge, Po, SC. [9]

Sea Rocket *Cakile maritima* CRUCIFERAE H 15–45 cm. Prostrate or ascending annual herb. Lvs succulent, lower <6 cm, stalked; upper less lobed, unstalked. Fls <3 cm, lilac or white, 4 petals twice as long as sepals, Jun–Aug. Frs of 2 joints, upper larger, <25 mm. Sand, shingle, at high-tide level. T, ex Ic, Lu, Be, (but Cz). [10]

Sea-kale *Crambe maritima* CRUCIFERAE H 40–60 cm. Cabbage-like, perennial herb. Lower lvs lobed, <30 cm, upper narrow. Fls <18 mm, white, 4 petals, Jun–Aug. Frs <14 mm, of 2 segments, lower slender, seedless, upper spherical, one-seeded. Sand, shingle, cliffs. Br, Ir, Fr, Be, Ne, De, Ge, FS, (Cz). [11]

Weld *Reseda luteola* RESEDACEAE H 50–150 cm. Biennial herb. Lvs <8 cm, linear-lanceolate, with wavy margins. Fls <5 mm, yellow-green, 4 petals, all except lower 3-lobed, Jun–Aug. Frs ovoid capsules, <6 mm, with pointed lobes. Calcareous dunes, open places near sea, also inland. T, ex Ic, Fi, No, (but Ge, Po). [1]

English Stonecrop *Sedum anglicum* CRASSULACEAE H 2–15 cm. Creeping, perennial herb with ascending flowering stems. Lvs <5 mm, succulent, ovoid, often pink. Fls <12 mm, white or pink, Jun–Aug. Acid rocks near Atlantic coasts. Br, Ir, Fr, SC. [2]

Burnet Rose *Rosa pimpinellifolia* ROSACEAE H 10–100 cm. Low shrub with prickly and bristly stems, spreading by suckers. Lvs divided into 7–11 toothed lflets <15 mm, hairless or slightly hairy beneath. Fls <4 cm, creamy-white, rarely pink, May–Jul. Frs spherical, purplish-black, <15 mm. Dunes, sandy heaths, esp near sea. T, ex Fi, Sw. [3]

Mountain Avens *Dryas octopetala* ROSACEAE H 2–8 cm. Mat-forming, dwarf shrub. Lvs <4 cm, densely woolly beneath. Fls <4 cm, 7–10 (often 8) petals, Jun–Jul. Frs with long, hairy, persistent styles. Limestone rocks and sands, near sea, also on mountains. T, ex Lu, Be, Ne, De. [4]

Sea Pea *Lathyrus japonicus* LEGUMINOSAE H <30 cm. Creeping, perennial herb with angled stems. Lvs divided into 6–8 lflets <4 cm. Fls <18 mm long, purple to blue, in clusters of 2–12, Jun–Aug. Frs hairless pods, <5 cm, with 4–11 seeds. Sandy or shingly shores. Br, Ir, Ic, De, Ge, Po, FS. [5]

Common Restharrow *Ononis repens* LEGUMINOSAE H 30–60 cm. Perennial herb. Stems usually spineless, with hairs all round. Lvs with 3 toothed, glandular-hairy lflets <2 cm. Fls <2 cm long, pink or purple, solitary or rarely in pairs, Jun–

Sep. Frs pods, <7 mm, with 1–4 seeds. Dunes, rough grassland. T, ex Ic, (but Fi). [6]

Tall Melilot *Melilotus altissima* LEGUMINOSAE H 60–120 cm. Biennial or short-lived perennial herb. Fls <7 mm, yellow, with all petals equal, in clusters <5 cm, lengthening in fr, Jun–Aug. Frs hairy, net-veined, black when ripe, <6 mm. Open grassland near sea, also in waste places inland. T, ex Ic, Fi, (but Br, Ir). [7]

Kidney Vetch *Anthyllis vulneraria* LEGUMINOSAE H 10–60 cm. Hairy, perennial herb. Lvs <15 cm, divided into 1–6 pairs of ovate lflets, terminal one largest. Fls <15 mm, yellow or red, in dense heads <4 cm across, arranged in pairs, Jun–Sep. Frs hairless pods, <3 mm. Coastal grassland, also on calcareous soils inland. T. [8]

Herb-Robert *Geranium robertianum* GERANIACEAE H 10–50 cm. Annual or biennial herb with red-tinged stems, hairy at base; unpleasant smell when crushed. Lvs <8 cm wide, divided into 5 lobed lflets. Fls <25 mm, pink, rarely white, May–Sep. Frs with beak, <2 cm. Shingle, cliffs, walls; also inland in woods, hedges. T, ex Ic. [9]

Common Stork's-bill *Erodium cicutarium* GERANIACEAE H 10–60 cm. Very variable, glandular-hairy, annual herb. Fls <14 mm, rose-pink, rarely white, often with black spot at base of petals, in umbels of <7 fls, May–Sep. Frs with beak, <4 cm. Coastal dunes, also inland on sandy soils. T, ex Ic. [10]

Fairy Flax *Linum catharticum* LINACEAE H 5–25 cm. Hairless, annual herb. Lvs <12 mm, opposite, 1-veined, lower oblong, upper lanceolate. Fls <1 cm, white, 5 petals, nodding in bud, in loose clusters, Jun–Sep. Frs spherical capsules, <3 mm. Coastal dunes, grassland, also inland on calcareous grassland, heaths. T. [11]

Sea Spurge *Euphorbia paralias*
EUPHORBIACEAE H 20–40 cm. Perennial
herb. Lvs <2 cm, fleshy. Fls green, in
clusters, lacking petals and sepals, in
umbels of 3–6 rays, each once- or twice-
divided, Jul–Oct. Frs granular-surfaced
capsules, <4 mm. Coastal sands, dunes.
Br, Ir, Fr, Be, Ne. [1]

Common Milkwort *Polygala vulgaris*
POLYGALACEAE H 7–35 cm. Perennial herb,
woody at base. Lvs alternate, lower <15
mm, elliptical, upper <35 mm,
lanceolate. Fls <8 mm, blue, pink or
white, May–Sep. Frs flattened, oval, 2-
lobed capsules, <5 mm. Sand-dunes, also
inland on grassland, heaths. T, ex Ic. [2]

Marsh-mallow *Althaea officinalis*
MALVACEAE H 60–120 cm. Velvety-hairy,
grey-white, perennial herb. Lvs ovate,
<8 cm across, irregularly toothed. Fls
<4 cm, pale pink, Aug–Sep. Frs hairy
nutlets, brownish-green when ripe.
Salt-marshes, also inland as relic of
cultivation. T, ex Ic, Lu, FS. [3]

Sea-buckthorn *Hippophae rhamnoides*
ELAEAGNACEAE H <3 m. Thorny,
deciduous shrub, spreading by suckers.
Lvs <8 cm, covered in silvery scales
when young. Fls very small, green, ♂ and
♀ on separate plants, before lvs, Mar–
Apr. Frs bright orange berries, <8 mm.
Dunes, sea-cliffs, also on mountain river
gravels. Frs winter food for birds. T, ex
Ic, Lu, (but Ir). [4]

Wild Pansy *Viola tricolor* ssp *curtisii*
VIOLACEAE H 3–15 cm. Perennial herb.
Lvs <3 cm, lower heart-shaped, upper
ovate-lanceolate, all bluntly toothed. Fls
<15 mm, of 5 petals longer than sepals,
blue-violet, yellow, or a mixture of these,
May–Sep. Frs globular capsules, <1 cm.
Dunes, dry grassland. Br, Ir, Fr, Be, Ne,
De, Ge. [5]

Tamarisk *Tamarix gallica* TAMARICACEAE
H <3 m. Blue-green, deciduous shrub.
Lvs <2 mm, triangular, acute, clasping
stem at base. Fls <3 mm, pink or white,
in dense-fld spikes <3 cm, Jul–Sep. Frs

ovoid capsules. Planted near coast for
shelter, ornament. Fr, (Br). [6]

Large-flowered Evening-primrose
Oenothera erythrosepala ONAGRACEAE
H 50–100 cm. Biennial herb; stem covered
in red hairs. Lvs <20 cm, strongly
crinkled. Fls <7 cm, opening suddenly at
dusk, Jun–Sep. Frs capsules, tapering
upwards, <4 cm. Naturalized on coastal
dunes, also inland in waste places. (Br,
Fr, Lu, Be, De, Ge, Cz, Po, from N
America.) [7] Common evening-primrose
O. biennis has stems without red hairs.
(T, ex Ic, Fi, from N America.)

Sea-holly *Eryngium maritimum*
UMBELLIFERAE H 15–60 cm. Spiny,
perennial herb. Lvs <12 cm across, with
thickened margin; lower stalked, upper
stalkless. Fls <8 mm, in compact heads
<25 mm, Jul–Aug. Frs covered with
small hooks. Sand or shingle shores. T,
ex Ic, Lu, Cz, Fi. [8]

Alexanders *Smyrnium olusatrum*
UMBELLIFERAE H 50–150 cm. Perennial
herb with furrowed stems. Lvs <30 cm,
divided into bluntly-toothed lobes. Fls
<1·5 mm, 5 short-pointed petals, in
umbels of 7–15 rays, Apr–Jun. Frs roundish, nearly black, <8 mm. Hedges, waste
places, esp near sea. Fr, (Br, Ir, Ne). [9]

Rock Samphire *Crithmum maritimum*
UMBELLIFERAE H 15–30 cm. Perennial
herb. Lvs triangular in outline, much-
divided into linear segments, <5 cm.
Fls <2 mm, in umbels of 8–20 rays,
Jun–Aug. Frs oval, olive-green to purple,
with thick, vertical ridges, <6 mm. Rocky
places. Br, Ir, Fr, Ne. [10]

Parsley Water-dropwort *Oenanthe
lachenalii* UMBELLIFERAE H 30–100 cm.
Perennial herb. Lower lvs twice-divided
into linear segments <5 mm, soon
withering, upper lvs less divided. Fls <4
mm, 5 petals, in umbels of 5–15 slender
rays, Jun–Sep. Frs ovoid, <3 mm;
persistent style $\frac{1}{3}$–$\frac{1}{2}$ as long as fr.
Salt-marshes, also inland in fens. Br, Ir,
Fr, Be, Ne, De, Cz, Po, Sw. [11]

Scots Lovage *Ligusticum scoticum*
UMBELLIFERAE H 15–90 cm. Perennial herb
with ribbed stem. Lvs < 10 cm, twice-
divided into toothed or lobed segments.
Fls < 2 mm, 5 petals, in umbels of 8–12
rays, Jul–Aug. Frs oblong, with acute
vertical ridges, < 4 mm. Rocky coasts.
Lvs used as herb. Br, Ir, Ic, De, SC. [1]

Wild Carrot *Daucus carota* UMBELLIFERAE
H 30–100 cm. Hairy, biennial herb with
solid, ridged stems. Lvs 3 times divided.
Fls < 5 mm, white, central one of umbel
red or purple, 5 petals, Jun–Aug. Frs oval,
with spiny, vertical ridges, < 4 mm.
Coastal cliffs, dunes, also inland on dry
grassland. T, ex Ic, (but Fi). [2]

Scarlet Pimpernel *Anagallis arvensis*
PRIMULACEAE H 6–30 cm. Creeping, annual
herb with square stems. Lvs < 28 mm,
opposite, stalkless. Fls < 14 mm, scarlet,
sometimes blue, 5 petals, solitary on long
stalks in lf-axils, Jun–Aug. Frs capsules,
< 5 mm across, opening with cap-like
cover. Sand-dunes, also inland on arable
fields. T, ex Ic. [3]

Sea-milkwort *Glaux maritima*
PRIMULACEAE H 5 cm. Succulent, creeping
herb. Lvs < 12 mm, elliptical–ovate, in
alternating pairs. Fls < 5 mm, lacking
petals but with petal-like, 5-lobed calyx,
usually pink, Jun–Aug. Frs 5-valved,
spherical capsules, < 3 mm. Damp places
by sea, also inland on saline soil. T, ex
Lu. [4]

Brookweed *Samolus valerandi*
PRIMULACEAE H 5–45 cm. Perennial herb.
Lvs < 8 cm, obovate, mostly basal. Fls
< 3 mm, 5 petals twice as long as sepals,
in simple or branched spike, Jun–Aug.
Frs 5-valved, spherical capsules, < 3 mm.
Wet places by sea, also inland fens. T, ex
Ic, Lu, No. [5]

Common Sea-lavender *Limonium
vulgare* PLUMBAGINACEAE H 15–70 cm.
Perennial herb with woody stock. Lvs all
basal, < 15 cm, obovate, pinnately veined,
narrowing gradually into slender stalk.
Fls < 8 mm, blue-purple, of 5 petals;

clustered in 2 rows on wiry stems, branched above middle, Jul–Sep; much visited for nectar by bees. Muddy salt-marshes. Br, Fr, Be, Ne, De, Ge, Sw. [6] Lax-flowered sea-lavender *L. humile*, more frequent on Atlantic coasts, has stems branched below middle. Br, Ir, Fr, De, Ge, SC.

Rock Sea-lavender *Limonium binervosum* PLUMBAGINACEAE H 20–30 cm. Very variable, perennial herb. Lvs like *L. vulgare*, but smaller, <5 cm, only 1–3 veined. Fls <8 mm, violet-blue, 5 petals, clustered in pyramidal inflorescence, Jul–Aug. Cliffs, shingle. Br, Ir, Fr. [7]

Thrift *Armeria maritima* PLUMBAGINACEAE H 5–15 cm. Woody-based, perennial herb. Lvs narrow, usually 1-veined. Fls <8 mm, rose-pink or white, 5 petals, in dense heads on erect, lfless stalks, Apr–Oct; fragrant, much visited by insects. Cliffs, salt-marshes, also inland on mountains. T, ex Lu. [8]

Seaside Centaury *Centaurium littorale* GENTIANACEAE H 2–25 cm. Annual herb. Lvs <2 cm, linear, blunt. Fls <1 cm, funnel-shaped, pinkish-purple, of 5 joined petals, Jul–Aug. Frs narrow capsules, <15 mm. Sandy shores, also inland in saline areas. T, ex Ic, Lu. [9] Common centaury *C. erythraea*, found on cliffs, dunes, also grassland, open woods, has broad, ovate basal lvs <5 cm. T, ex Ic, Fi, No.

Yellow-wort *Blackstonia perfoliata* GENTIANACEAE H 10–60 cm. Annual herb. Stem lvs in opposite pairs joined at base to form cup. Fls <15 mm, 6–8 joined petals, Jun–Oct. Calcareous sand-dunes, also widespread inland on calcareous soils. Br, Ir, Fr, Be, Ne, Ge, Cz. [10]

Field Gentian *Gentianella campestris* GENTIANACEAE H 10–30 cm. Annual or biennial herb. Fls <25 mm, bluish-lilac, rarely white, of 4 joined petals and 2 large outer sepals hiding 2 small inner ones, Jul–Oct. Dunes, also inland on dry grassland. T. [11]

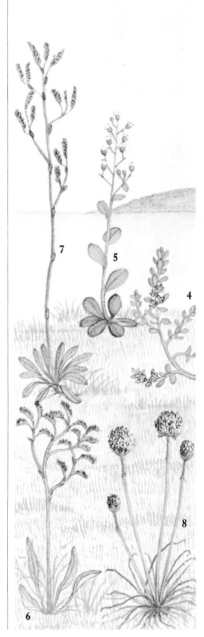

Cleavers *Galium aparine* RUBIACEAE
H 20–180 cm. Prickly, annual herb with
4-angled stems. Lvs <5 cm, in whorls of
6–8. Fls <2 mm, of 4 joined petals, in
clusters of 2–5, Jun–Aug. Frs 2-celled,
olive or purple, covered in white, hooked
bristles, <6 mm; dispersed in animal fur,
clothing. Shingle banks, also inland. T,
ex Ic. [1]

Lady's Bedstraw *Galium verum*
RUBIACEAE H 15–100 cm. Sparsely hairy
perennial with 4-angled stems. Lvs <25
cm, in whorls of 8–12. Fls <4 mm, of 4
joined petals, Jul–Aug. Frs 2-celled,
smooth, becoming black, <1·5 mm.
Sand-dunes, also on dry grassland. Smell
of new-mown hay attracts insects. T. [2]

Sea Bindweed *Calystegia soldanella*
CONVOLVULACEAE H <5 cm. Perennial
herb. Lvs <4 cm across, kidney-shaped,
fleshy. Fls <5 cm, pink or pale purple,
Jun–Aug. Frs ovoid, 2-celled capsules,
<2 cm. Sandy or shingly shores. Br, Ir,
Fr, Be, Ne, De, Ge. [3]

Hound's-tongue *Cynoglossum officinale*
BORAGINACEAE H 30–90 cm. Softly hairy,
biennial herb. Lvs <30 cm, with silky
hairs on both surfaces. Fls <1 cm, of 5
joined petals, in branched clusters
elongating after flowering, Jun–Aug. Frs
4 flattened nutlets covered in short,
barbed spines, <6 mm, (rough like dog's
tongue). Sand-dunes, also inland on dry
grassland. T, ex Ic. [4]

Bugloss *Lycopsis arvensis* BORAGINACEAE
H 15–50 cm. Bristly, annual or biennial
herb. Lvs <15 cm, lanceolate to linear,
lower stalked. Fls <6 mm, curved tube of
5 joined petals, in clusters elongating
after flowering, Jun–Sep. Frs nutlets, <4
mm. Sandy places by sea, also inland on
dry soils. T, ex Ic. [5]

Oysterplant *Mertensia maritima*
BORAGINACEAE H <5 cm. Perennial herb
with purple stems. Lvs <6 cm, oval, in
2 rows, upper surface dotted. Fls <6
mm, pink then bluish, Jun–Aug. Frs

flattened, fleshy nutlets, <6 mm, outer
coat becoming papery. Sandy or shingly
shores. Br, Ir, Ic, De, SC. [6]

Early Forget-me-not *Myosotis
ramosissima* BORAGINACEAE H 2–25 cm.
Annual herb. Fls <2 mm, blue, rarely
white, on stalks shorter than calyx, Apr–
Jun. Frs shiny, pale brown nutlets. Sandy
places by sea, also inland on dry soils. T.
[7] Field forget-me-not *M. arvensis* has
fl-stalks longer than calyx. T, ex Ic.

Common Gromwell *Lithospermum
officinale* BORAGINACEAE H 30–80 cm.
Roughly hairy, perennial herb. Lvs <7
cm, with conspicuous lateral veins
beneath. Fls <6 mm, funnel-shaped, in
terminal and axillary clusters elongating
after flowering, Jun–Jul. Frs shining white
nutlets. Bushy places near sea, also inland.
T, ex Ic, (but Fi). [8]

Viper's-bugloss *Echium vulgare*
BORAGINACEAE H 20–90 cm. Biennial herb.
Lvs <15 cm, elliptical–lanceolate, with
prominent mid-vein, lower stalked, upper
stalkless. Fls <18 mm, pink in bud,
becoming bright blue, Jun–Sep. Cliffs,
dunes, also inland on dry soils. T, ex Ic.
[9]

Wild Thyme *Thymus praecox* LABIATAE
H 2–7 cm. Perennial herb. Lvs <8 mm,
often with hairy margins, conspicuous
veins beneath. Fls <6 mm, 2-lipped
(lower lip 3-lobed), in terminal heads, on
4-angled stems with hairs on opposite
sides, May–Aug. Dunes, rocks by sea,
also inland on dry grassland. T, ex Lu,
De, Fi, Sw. [10]

Henbane *Hyoscyamus niger* SOLANACEAE
H 30–80 cm. Sticky, hairy, strong-
smelling, annual or biennial herb. Lvs
<20 cm, with few, coarse teeth, lower
stalked, upper clasping stem. Fls <3
cm, funnel-shaped, irregularly 5-lobed,
yellow veined with purple, in lfy clusters,
Jun–Aug. Frs many-seeded, spherical
capsules, enclosed in calyces, <2 cm.
Sandy places by sea, also inland in waste
places. Poisonous, narcotic. T, ex Ic. [11]

Bittersweet *Solanum dulcamara*
SOLANACEAE H 30–200 cm. Perennial herb.
Lvs <8 cm, ovate, with 1–4 deep lobes or
stalked segments at base. Fls <1 cm,
Jun–Sep. Frs red berries, many-seeded,
<1 cm. Shingle beaches, also inland in
wet woods, hedges. T, ex Ic. [1]

Wall Speedwell *Veronica arvensis*
SCROPHULARIACEAE H 5–25 cm. Hairy,
annual herb. Lvs <15 mm, coarsely
toothed, lower stalked, upper stalkless.
Fls <3 mm, blue, 4 joined petals, in long,
loose, lfy spikes, Mar–Oct. Frs flattened,
2-celled capsules, <3 mm. Sand-dunes,
cliffs, also inland on arable, grassland,
heaths. T, (but Ic). [2]

Red Bartsia *Odontites verna* SCROPH-
ULARIACEAE H 10–50 cm. Hairy, annual
herb; stems often purple-tinted. Fls <9
mm long, 2-lipped, lower lip 3-lobed,
purplish-pink, Jun–Aug. Frs hairy,
oblong capsules equalling calyx, <8 mm.
Sandy grassland by sea, also inland on
dry grassland, waste ground. T, ex Ic. [3]

Eyebright *Euphrasia officinalis*
SCROPHULARIACEAE H 15–35 cm. Annual
herb, semi-parasitic on grasses, other
herbs. Lvs <12 mm, elliptical or oblong,
with 3–5 pairs of blunt teeth. Fls <1 cm
long, 2-lipped, upper lip 2-lobed, lower
3-lobed, white to lilac, May–Sep. Frs
oblong capsules, <6 mm. Sand-dunes,
short cliff-top turf. T. [4] Many closely
related spp inland on grassland, heaths,
moors.

Yellow Rattle *Rhinanthus minor*
SCROPHULARIACEAE H 5–50 cm. Annual
herb with small black spots on stem,
semi-parasitic on grasses, other herbs.
Fls <15 mm, 2-lipped, upper lip with 2
violet teeth, lower 3-lobed, May–Aug.
Frs flattened capsules, <1 mm, with
seeds that rattle inside. Sand-dunes, also
inland in grassland. T. [5]

Buck's-horn Plantain *Plantago coronopus*
PLANTAGINACEAE H <10 cm. Somewhat
hairy, biennial or perennial herb. Lvs <6
cm, variable, from narrow and slightly
toothed to 2–3 times divided. Fls <3 mm,
yellowish, 4 petals, in spike <4 cm, on
long stalk curved below, May–Jul. Dunes,
cliffs, also inland on dry sand. Br, Ir, Fr,
Be, Ne, De, Ge, Po, Sw. [6]

Sea Plantain *Plantago maritima*
PLANTAGINACEAE H 2–7 cm. Perennial
herb with stout, woody base. Lvs <25
cm, fleshy, faintly 3–5 veined. Fls <3
mm, brownish, 4 petals, in spike <7 cm,
on stalks equalling or exceeding lvs, Jun–
Aug. Salt-marshes, grassland by sea, also
mountains. T, ex Lu. [7]

Common Cornsalad *Valerianella locusta*
VALERIANACEAE H 7–40 cm. Annual herb
with brittle stems. Fls <2 mm, whitish-
lilac, Apr–Jun. Frs rounded, corky on
back, <2·5 mm. Sand-dunes, also inland
on arable, rocks. Edible in salad. T, ex
Ic. [8]

Harebell *Campanula rotundifolia*
CAMPANULACEAE H 15–40 cm. Perennial
herb producing underground runners.
Basal lvs rounded, <15 mm across,
toothed, long-stalked; upper stem lvs
linear, stalkless. Fls <15 mm, in loose,
terminal clusters or solitary, Jul–Sep. Frs
erect, ovoid capsules, <3 mm. Dunes,
also inland on dry grassland, heaths. T. [9]

Sheep's-bit *Jasione montana* CAMPANUL-
ACEAE H 5–50 cm. Hairy, biennial herb.
Lvs <5 cm, with wavy or toothed
margins, basal short-stalked, upper
stalkless. Fls <5 mm, blue, 5 petals, in
compact, terminal head <35 mm across,
May–Aug. Cliffs, rocks by sea, also inland
in open, arid areas. T, ex Ic. [10]

Sea Aster *Aster tripolium* COMPOSITAE
H 15–100 mm. Perennial herb. Lvs <12
cm, fleshy, faintly 3-veined. Fl-heads
<2 cm, with blue-purple ray-florets,
sometimes absent, and yellow central
florets, in terminal clusters, Jul–Oct.
Salt-marshes, sea-cliffs, also inland in
saline places. T, ex Ic, Lu. [11]

Ox-eye Daisy *Chrysanthemum leucanthemum* COMPOSITAE H 20–70 cm. Perennial herb. Lower lvs <10 cm, rounded, toothed, long-stalked; upper smaller, stalkless. Fl-heads <5 cm, with white ray-florets, yellow central florets, May–Aug. Sand-dunes, cliffs, also inland in dry grassland. T, (but Ic). [1]

Scentless Mayweed *Matricaria maritima* COMPOSITAE H 10–60 cm. Biennial or perennial herb. Lvs fleshy. Fl-heads <5 cm, with 20–30 white ray-florets, yellow central florets, Jun–Sep. Abundant at top of many beaches, also inland in waste places. T, ex Lu, Cz. [2]

Sea Wormwood *Artemisia maritima* COMPOSITAE H 10–50 cm. Hairy, aromatic, perennial herb. Lvs <5 cm, once- or twice-divided, woolly. Fl-heads ovoid, <2 mm, yellow or reddish, Aug–Sep. Drier salt-marshes, sea-walls, also inland in saline areas. Br, Ir, Fr, Be, Ne, De, Ge, SC. [3]

Sticky Groundsel *Senecio viscosus* COMPOSITAE H 10–60 cm. Very sticky, annual herb with unpleasant smell. Fl-heads <12 mm, yellow, with <13 ray-florets, Jul–Sep. Sands, gravels by sea, also inland in disturbed areas, esp railway lines. Br, Fr, Lu, Be, Ne, Ge, Cz, Po, (Ir, De, FS). [4]

Carline Thistle *Carlina vulgaris* COMPOSITAE H 10–60 cm. Spiny, biennial herb with purplish, cottony stems. Rosette lvs 7–13 cm, cottony beneath, dying before flowering; stem lvs shorter, half-clasping stem, almost hairless. Fl-heads <4 cm, lacking ray-florets but with spreading, straw-yellow bracts surrounding yellow central florets, Jul–Oct. Dry grassland by sea, also inland. T, ex Ic. [5]

Slender Thistle *Carduus tenuiflorus* COMPOSITAE H 15–75 cm. Cottony, annual or biennial herb; stems with spiny wings. Basal lvs <20 cm, very woolly beneath; stem lvs all spiny-margined. Fl-heads <15 mm, in dense, terminal clusters of 3–10, Jun–Aug. Waste ground near sea, rarely inland. Br, Ir, Fr, Be, Ne, (SC). [6]

Cotton Thistle *Onopordum acanthium*
COMPOSITAE H 45–150 cm. Cottony,
biennial herb; stems with spiny wings.
Fl-heads <5 cm, pale purple, rarely
white, Jul–Sep. Roadsides, waste ground
near sea, also inland. Br, Fr, Lu, Be, Ne,
De, Ge, Cz, Sw. [7]

Common Knapweed *Centaurea nigra*
COMPOSITAE H 15–100 cm. Hairy,
perennial herb. Lower lvs <15 cm,
ovate–lanceolate, toothed or lobed; upper
lvs with few or no basal teeth. Fl-heads
<4 cm, solitary, blackish-brown with red-
purple florets, ray-florets rarely present,
Jun–Sep. Cliffs, dunes, also inland on
grassland. Br, Ir, Fr, Lu, Be, Ne, Ge,
SC, (De, Cz). [8]

Autumn Hawkbit *Leontodon autumnalis*
COMPOSITAE H 5–60 cm. Perennial herb.
Lvs <20 cm, deeply divided into linear
segments, hairless or sparsely hairy. Fl-
heads <35 mm, outer florets with red
streaks beneath, solitary on branched
stems, Jun–Oct. Dunes, waste ground by
sea, also inland on grassland, roadsides.
T. [9]

Goat's-beard *Tragopogon pratensis*
COMPOSITAE H 30–70 cm. Annual or
perennial herb. Lvs <50 cm, grass-like,
sheathing stem at base. Fl-heads conical,
<3 cm, of 8 bracts surrounding shorter
yellow florets, Jun–Jul. Frs develop into
large, hairy ball. Called 'Jack-go-to-bed-
at-noon', as fl-heads close about midday.
Sand-dunes, also inland on rough
grassland. T, ex Ic. [10]

Lesser Dandelion *Taraxacum laevigatum*
COMPOSITAE H 4–15 cm. Variable,
perennial herb; aggregate of similar
microspp, difficult to separate. Lvs <15
cm, variously lobed, in basal rosette. Fl-
heads <35 mm, pale yellow, solitary,
terminal on slender stalk <15 cm, Apr–
Jun. Frs produce small 'clocks'. Sand-
dunes, also inland on dry grassland. T.
[11]

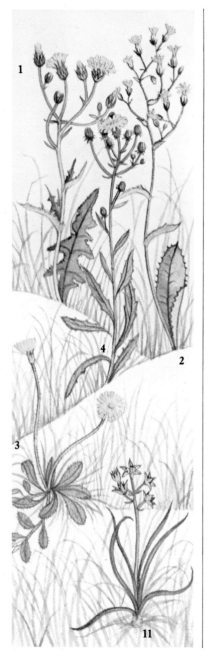

Perennial Sow-thistle *Sonchus arvensis*
COMPOSITAE H 60–150 cm. Perennial herb
with creeping, underground stems. Lvs
<50 cm, lower with ear-like flaps at base.
Fl-heads <5 cm, in glandular-hairy
clusters, Jul–Oct. Frs 5-ribbed, dark
brown, <3·5 mm. Sand-dunes, also
inland on arable, waste ground. T, ex Ic.
[1]

Great Lettuce *Lactuca virosa* COMPOSITAE
H 60–200 cm. Annual or biennial herb
with white or reddish stems, hairless or
prickly below. Lvs <20 cm, spiny on
midrib, undivided or variously divided.
Fl-heads <1 cm, pale greenish-yellow, in
pyramidal cluster, Jul–Sep. Sand-dunes,
also inland on waste ground. Br, Fr, Lu,
Be, Ge, (Po). [2]

Mouse-ear Hawkweed *Hieracium
pilosella* COMPOSITAE H 5–30 cm. Hairy,
perennial herb, spreading by creeping
runners. Basal lvs in rosettes, stem lvs
absent or scale-like. Fl-heads <11 mm,
May–Aug. Sand-dunes, also inland on dry
grassland, heaths. T, ex Ic. [3]

Hawkweed *Hieracium umbellatum*
COMPOSITAE H 30–80 cm. Hairy,
perennial herb. Fl-heads <11 mm,
yellow, with blunt, blackish-green bracts
in umbel-like, terminal cluster, Aug–Sep.
Sand-dunes, also inland in open woods,
hedge-banks, heaths. T, ex Ic. [4]

Sea Arrowgrass *Triglochin maritima*
JUNCAGINACEAE H 15–70 cm. Perennial
herb. Lvs semi-cylindrical, <3 mm
across, not furrowed. Fls <3 mm, of 2
whorls of 3 perianth segments, in slender
spikes, Jul–Sep. Frs oblong, <4 mm.
Salt-marshes, rocky shores. T, ex Lu. [5]

Fennel Pondweed *Potamogeton pectinatus*
POTAMOGETONACEAE H 40–200 cm.
Aquatic, perennial herb with creeping
root-system. Lvs all submerged, <20
cm × 2 mm, with 3–5 longitudinal veins.
Fls of 4 perianth segments, in spike <5
cm of 4–8 whorls, May–Sep. Brackish
pools, also inland. T, ex Ic. [6]

Spiral Tasselweed *Ruppia cirrhosa*
RUPPIACEAE H 10–30 cm. Aquatic,
perennial herb with thread-like stems.
Lvs grass-like, <1 mm wide, with
swollen basal sheaths. Fls lacking
perianth, of 2 stamens and 4 styles, in
pairs on stalk elongating well above
surface after flowering, often spirally
coiled, Jul–Sep. Salt or brackish pools.
T, ex Ic, Lu, Cz. [7]

Eelgrass *Zostera marina* ZOSTERACEAE
H 20–50 cm. Marine, perennial herb with
creeping, tuberous, underground stems.
Lvs <50 cm, linear, rounded, with point
at tip, <1 cm wide. ♂ and ♀ fls separate,
reduced to 1 anther (♂) or 2 stigmas (♀),
in spike <12 cm, enclosed by lf-sheath
with membranous border, Jun–Sep.
Shores and shallow seas, rarely in
estuaries. T, ex Lu, Cz. [8]

Narrow-leaved Eelgrass *Zostera
angustifolia* ZOSTERACEAE H 15–30 cm.
Marine, perennial herb. Lvs <30 cm,
narrow, <2 mm wide, tip rounded when
young, later notched. Fl-spikes <11 cm,
enclosed by lf-sheaths with membranous
border, Jun–Nov. Mud in shallow seas,
estuaries. Br, Ir, De, Sw. [9] Dwarf
eelgrass *Z. noltii*, has lvs <1 mm wide.
T, ex Ic, Lu, Cz, Po, Fi.

Horned Pondweed *Zannichellia palustris*
ZANNICHELLIACEAE H <50 cm. Aquatic,
perennial herb with slender, creeping
underground stems. Lvs <5 cm, narrow,
<2 mm wide, mostly opposite, tapering
to fine point. Separate ♂ and ♀ fls,
reduced to 1 anther (♂) or 1 stigma (♀),
occur together in transparent cup in lf-
axils, May–Aug. Brackish water, also
inland in fresh water. T. [10]

Spring Squill *Scilla verna* LILIACEAE
H 3–20 cm. Bulbous, perennial herb. Lvs
<20 cm, 3–6, produced before fls. Fls
<1 cm, 6 perianth segments, in spikes of
2–12, Apr–May. Frs rounded, triangular
capsules, <4 mm. Cliffs, dry grassland.
Br, Ir, Fr, No. [11]

Saltmarsh Rush *Juncus gerardii*
JUNCACEAE H 10–30 cm. Perennial herb.
Fls <4 mm, dark brown to blackish, of 6
perianth segments, in branched clusters,
on stiff, wavy stems, Jun–Jul. Frs pointed
capsules. Salt-marshes, occasionally inland
in saline areas. T, ex Lu. [1]

Sea Rush *Juncus maritimus* JUNCACEAE
H 30–100 cm. Perennial herb. Lvs rigid,
sharply pointed. Fls <6 mm, straw-
coloured, of 6 perianth segments, in
many-fld heads, overtopped by sharp-
pointed bracts, Jul–Aug. Frs triangular
capsules. Salt-marshes, also inland on
saline soils. Br, Ir, Fr, Be, Ne, De, Ge,
Sw. [2]

Sand Couch *Agropyron junceiforme*
GRAMINEAE H 25–60 cm. Perennial herb,
spreading by far-creeping, underground
stems. Lvs <6 mm wide, often rolled,
smooth below, with minutely hairy ribs
above. Fls awnless, in stalkless spikelets
of 3–8, <28 mm, Jun–Aug. Young dunes.
Br, Ir, Fr, Be, Ne, De, Ge, FS, ?Po. [3]

Sea Couch *Agropyron pungens* GRAMINEAE
H 30–90 cm. Grey-green perennial herb,
spreading by underground stems. Lvs
<6 mm wide, often tightly rolled, smooth
below, with rough ribs above. Fls
awnless, in stalkless spikelets of 3–10, <2
cm, Jun–Aug. Margins of salt-marshes,
mature dunes. Br, Ir, Fr, Be, Ne, De,
Ge. [4]

Lyme-grass *Elymus arenarius* GRAMINEAE
H 60–200 cm. Stout, blue-green perennial
herb, with long underground stems,
forming large tufts or mats. Lvs <2
cm wide, flat or rolled, smooth beneath,
rough ribs above. Fls awnless, in stalkless
spikelets of 3–6, <32 mm, Jul–Aug.
Sand-dunes. T, ex Lu, Po, (but Cz). [5]

Squirreltail Fescue *Vulpia bromoides*
GRAMINEAE H 5–60 cm. Erect or ascending,
annual herb. Lvs flat or rolled, <3 mm
wide, rough near tip and on margins. Fls
long-awned, in spikelets of 5–10, <14
mm (excluding awns), in erect or slightly
nodding, 1-sided panicles, on ribbed stems,

1   9   4   3   5   11

May–Jul. Sandy or rocky coasts, also inland in dry, open areas. T, ex Ic, Fi, No. [6]

Common Saltmarsh-grass *Puccinellia maritima* GRAMINEAE H 10–80 cm. Grey-green, perennial herb, spreading by rooting, overground stems. Lvs folded or rolled, <3 mm wide if opened out. Fls awnless, in spikelets of 3–10, <13 mm, in erect panicles with branches upright, or few spreading, Jun–Jul. Salt-marshes, more rarely sand or shingle, also inland in brackish areas. T, ex Lu, Cz, Fi. [7] Reflexed saltmarsh-grass *P. distans*, more widespread inland, has all branches of panicles finally spreading. T.

Hard-grass *Parapholis strigosa* GRAMINEAE H 15–40 cm. Grey-green, annual herb. Lvs flat or rolled, <2·5 mm wide, rough on nerves above, and on margins. Fls awnless, in 1-fld spikelets, embedded in hollows in stem, forming stiff, cylindrical spike, Jun–Aug. Salt-marshes. Br, Ir, Fr, Be, Ne, De, Ge, Sw. [8]

Crested Hair-grass *Koeleria cristata* GRAMINEAE H 10–60 cm. Hairy, perennial herb. Lvs rolled or flat, <2·5 mm wide. Fls awnless, in spikelets of 2–3, <6 mm, on short branches in spike-like panicles <65 mm, Jun–Jul. Dunes, also inland on dry grassland. T, ex Ic, Fi, No. [9]

Marram *Ammophila arenaria* GRAMINEAE H 50–120 cm. Perennial herb, spreading by underground stems. Lvs tightly inrolled, <6 mm when spread out, upper surface ribbed and densely hairy. Fls awnless, in 1-fld spikelets, <16 mm, on short branches in spike-like panicles <22 cm, Jun–Aug. Sand-dunes; planted as sand-binder. T, ex Ic, Lu, Cz. [10]

Sand Cat's-tail *Phleum arenarium* GRAMINEAE H 3–15 cm. Whitish-green, annual herb. Lvs flat, <4 mm wide. Fls awnless, in flattened 1-fld spikelets, <4 mm, almost stalkless in spike-like panicles <5 cm, May–Jul. Sand-dunes, also inland on sandy fields. Br, Ir, Fr, Be, Ne, De, Ge, Sw, No. [11]

8   10   7   6   2

Townsend's Cord-grass *Spartina anglica*
GRAMINEAE H 40–130 cm. Perennial herb,
forming circular patches or extensive
'meadows'. Lvs flat or inrolled, <15 mm
wide, densely ribbed above. Fls awnless,
in 1-fld spikelets <2 cm, sessile on spikes
<23 cm, in panicles of 3–6 spikes, Jul–
Nov. Tidal mud-flats; planted as mud-
binder. Br, Ir, Fr, Be, Ne, Ge. [1]

Sea Club-rush *Scirpus maritimus*
CYPERACEAE H 30–100 cm. Perennial herb
with 3-angled stems. Lvs keeled, <1 cm
wide, with rough margins. Fls
hermaphrodite, in many-fld, red-brown
spikelets <2 cm, in groups of 2–5, Jul–
Aug. Salt-marshes, ditches near sea,
occasionally inland. T, ex Ic. [2]

Sand Sedge *Carex arenaria* CYPERACEAE
H 10–40 cm. Perennial herb, spreading by
underground runners. Lvs keeled or
channelled, <3·5 mm, tough, with brown
sheaths. Fls in many-fld spikes <14 mm,
5–15 spikes in dense, terminal head, upper
all ♂, lower all ♀, hermaphrodite between,
Jun–Jul. Sand-dunes, also inland in areas
of blown sand. T, ex Ic, Lu, Cz. [3]

Distant Sedge *Carex distans* CYPERACEAE
H 15–100 cm. Perennial herb with smooth,
3-angled stems. Lvs almost flat, grey-
green, <5 mm wide, with persistent,
brown sheaths. Fls in 4–5 stalked spikes,
single ♂ spike above, <3 cm, ♀ spikes
below, <2 cm, May–Jun. Marshes, wet
rocks by sea, also inland in mineral-rich
marshes. T, ex Ic. [4]

Long-bracted Sedge *Carex extensa*
CYPERACEAE H 10–40 cm. Perennial herb
with smooth, 3-angled stems. Lvs
channelled, <3 mm wide, with red-
brown sheaths; bracts below fl-spikes may
be reflexed. Fls in 4–5 mainly stalkless
spikes, single ♂ spike above, <25 mm, ♀
spikes below, <2 cm, Jun–Jul.
Salt-marshes, damp cliffs, rocks. T, ex Ic,
Lu, Cz. [5]

Early Marsh-orchid *Dactylorhiza
incarnata* ORCHIDACEAE H 5–50 cm.
Yellow-green perennial herb. Lower lvs

<20 cm, keeled, with narrow, hooded tip; upper lvs bract-like. Fls <1 cm across, flesh-pink to deep magenta, sides of lower lip strongly turned back with conical spur <8·5 mm, May–Jul. Sand-dunes (when small, compact, with magenta fls), also inland in marshes. T, ex Ic. [6]

Pyramidal Orchid *Anacamptis pyramidalis* ORCHIDACEAE H 20–50 cm. Perennial herb. Lvs <15 cm, acute, keeled; upper bract-like. Fls <6 mm across, lower lip deeply 3-lobed with thread-like spur <12 mm, in pyramidal cluster, with foxy smell, Jun–Aug. Sand-dunes, also inland on calcareous grassland. Pollinated by butterflies and moths. T, ex Ic, No. [7]

Marsh Helleborine *Epipactis palustris* ORCHIDACEAE H 15–50 cm. Hairy, perennial herb. Lvs <15 cm, often purple beneath; upper bract-like. Fls <12 mm across, brown and white, lower lip white with yellow spot and frilly margin, no spur, Jun–Aug. Damp dunes, also inland in calcareous marshes. T, ex Ic. [8]

Autumn Lady's-tresses *Spiranthes spiralis* ORCHIDACEAE H 7–20 cm. Hairy, perennial herb. Fls <5 mm, greenish-white, lower lip with fringed margin, arranged spirally on stem, with scale-like bracts below, Aug–Sep. Calcareous sand-dunes, also inland on dry grassland. T, ex Ic, FS. [9]

Common Twayblade *Listera ovata* ORCHIDACEAE H 20–60 cm. Perennial herb, somewhat hairy above. Lvs 2, <20 cm, broadly ovate, stalkless. Fls <15 mm, yellow-green, central lobe of lower lip deeply divided into 2 narrow segments, in long, loose spike <25 cm, Jun–Jul. Damp dunes, also inland woods, pastures. T. [10]

Bee Orchid *Ophrys apifera* ORCHIDACEAE H 15–45 cm. Perennial herb. Lvs <8 cm, elliptical-oblong, upper smaller, bract-like. Fls <15 mm, resembling bumble-bees, in loose spikes of 2–7, Jun–Jul. Calcareous dunes, and inland on calcareous grassland. Br, Ir, Fr, Lu, Be, Ne, Ge, Cz. [11]

Sponges (Porifera) have internal cavity connected to outside water by numerous small inhalent apertures (ostia) and larger exhalent apertures (oscula). Flagella create currents of water bearing food particles.

sponge *Leucosolenia complicata* HOMOCOELIDAE H <2·5 cm, B <5 cm. Lower parts branching; upright parts tubular with conspicuous osculum; surface rough; dirty-white. On stones, weeds; middle shore to sublittoral. T, ex nBaS. [1]

sponge *Sycon coronatum* SYCETTIDAE H <3 cm. Surface rough; conspicuous spicules around apical osculum; yellowish-white. On solid surfaces; lower shore to sublittoral. T, ex nBaS. [2]

Purse Sponge *Grantia compressa* GRANTIIDAE H <5 cm. Purse-like out of water, rounded when immersed; apical osculum conspicuous; yellow-white. Under overhangs; lower shore. T, ex nBaS. [3]

Sulphur Sponge *Suberites domuncula* CLAVULIDAE D <30 cm. Massive, rounded surface smooth with prominent oscula; firm dough-like texture; grey or sulphur-yellow. On mollusc shells occupied by hermit-crabs. Occasionally solid objects; sublittoral. T, ex nBaS. [4]

Boring Sponge *Cliona celata* CLAVULIDAE D *c*2 mm (littoral form), B <1 m (massive form). Littoral form bores into dead bivalve shells, is visible as rounded projections through holes in shell surface. Sublittoral form massive, tough, lobed, dough-like; surface covered with soft papillate projections bearing oscula. Sulphur-yellow, green or bluish; lower shore to sublittoral. T, ex nBaS. [5]

sponge *Hymeniacidon perlevis* AXINELLIDAE H <3 cm, B often >30 cm. Smooth encrustation; oscula numerous, small; orange to scarlet. In rock fissures; amongst holdfasts of large seaweeds; middle shore to sublittoral. T, ex nBaS. [6]

sponge *Haliclona oculata* HAPLOSCLERIDAE H <30 cm. Upright with slender branches, narrow base; oscula in rows along 1

side of main branch; yellow or pale olive-green. On solid objects; lower shore to sublittoral. T, ex nBaS. [7]

Breadcrumb Sponge *Halichondria panicea* DESMACIDONIDAE H <3 cm, B <25 cm. Smooth encrustation; oscula on volcano-like protuberances; green, yellow, orange or brown. On rocks, holdfasts; middle shore to sublittoral. T, ex nBaS. [8]

Hydroids, jellyfish, sea-anemones, corals (Cnidaria) have body-wall enclosing vase-like digestive cavity. Tentacles with stinging cells. Each animal is a polyp.

hydroid *Tubularia indivisa* TUBULARIIDAE H *c*15 cm. Basal part root-like; upright part sheathed in horny, pale brown, skeletal sleeve; polyp globular, pink or red and white. On boulders and in gullies, where strong flow of water; lower shore to sublittoral. T, ex nBaS. [9]

hydroid *Arum cocksi* MYRIOTHELIDAE H <6 cm. Basal part branched, elongated, brown; upright part grey-white, club-shaped, covered with short brownish-purple-tipped tentacles except at tip. Under boulders; lower shore. T, ex nBaS. [10]

hydroid *Hydractinia echinata* HYDRACTINIIDAE H <1·5 cm, B <5 cm. Basal part spreading; straw-coloured; stalked polyps numerous (look furry), tinged pink or brown. On mollusc shells inhabited by hermit-crabs, rarely on stones; lower shore to sublittoral. T, ex nBaS. [11]

hydroid *Obelia geniculata* CAMPANULARIIDAE H <5 cm. Upright stems zigzagged, branched, arise from root-like base; polyp-cups wine-glass shaped; straw-coloured. On weeds; lower shore to sublittoral. T, ex nBaS. [12]

hydroid *Dynamena pumila* SERTULARIIDAE H <5 cm. Upright stems with unequal branches; polyp-cups paired, each pair triangular in outline; dirty-white. On weeds, rocks, in crevices; middle to lower shore. T, ex nBaS. [13]

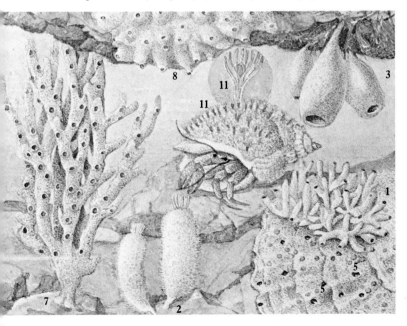

stalked jellyfish *Lucernariopsis campanulata* ELEUTHEROCARPIDAE H <4 cm. Body trumpet-shaped; bell-margin extended into 8 short arms each with cluster of knobbed tentacles; mouth square; pink, plum-red or olive-green. Attached by short stalk to weeds, eelgrasses; often in rock pools, lower shore. T, ex nBaS, but rare far north. [1]

stalked jellyfish *Haliclystus auricula* ELEUTHEROCARPIDAE H <1 cm. Similar to *Lucernariopsis*, but has obvious granular lump or 'anchor' between each pair of arms; pink or dull green. On weeds, eelgrasses; lower shore. Probably only s of arca. [2]

stalked jellyfish *Depastrum cyathiforme* CLEISTOCARPIDAE H <1 cm. Similar to *Lucanariopsis*, but with 4 horseshoe-shaped 'anchors' between each pair of arms; dull brown or brownish-pink. On weeds, underneath boulders; lower shore. Probably only s of area. [3]

jellyfish *Pelagia noctiluca* PELAGIIDAE D <15 cm. Umbrella dome-shaped; margin lobed and bearing 8 long slender tentacles (longer than the 4 slightly frilled mouth lobes); surface spotted all over; transparent or 'milky', purple-pink or reddish-brown, phosphorescent. Pelagic. Only s of area. [4]

Compass Jellyfish *Chrysaora hysoscella* PELAGIIDAE D <30 cm. Umbrella bowl-shaped; margin with 32 lobes and 24 long slender tentacles (shorter than the 4 frilled mouth lobes); centre of umbrella brown, with 24 brown triangular areas radiating towards margin; biscuit-coloured and brown. Pelagic. Only s of area. [5]

jellyfish *Cyanaea lamarcki* CYANEIDAE D c30 cm. Umbrella saucer-shaped; margin with 32 lobes and numerous tentacles grouped into 8 clusters (longer than the 4 highly frilled mouth lobes);

vivid blue and violet with white areas. Pelagic. T, ex nBaS. [6]

Common Jellyfish *Aurelia aurita* AURELIIDAE D <25 cm. Umbrella saucer-shaped, shallow; marginal tentacles numerous, short; mouth surrounded by 4 long, frilled lobes; 4 conspicuous, horse-shoe-shaped sexual organs within body; transparent to grey-blue, sexual organs blue or purplish. Pelagic. T, ex nBaS. [7]

jellyfish *Rhizostoma pulmo* RHIZOSTOMIDAE D c60 cm. Umbrella deeply dome-shaped; margin with 96 lobes, no tentacles; umbrella rather leathery; no central mouth; 8 mouth lobes fused into bunched mass, containing numerous tiny openings into digestive cavity; milky-white and blue or yellow, with purple areas, red markings on mouth lobes. Pelagic. T, ex nBaS. [8]

Dead Man's Fingers *Alcyonium digitatum* ALCYONIDAE H <20 cm (colony), L <1 cm (polyp). Tough rounded branching colonies of coral; polyps transparent with 8 feathery tentacles; white, pink, flesh-coloured or orange. On solid objects; lower shore to sublittoral. T, ex nBaS. [9]

Sea Fan *Eunicella verrucosa* PLEXAURIDAE H <30 cm. Irregularly branching colony; central horny support clothed in soft tissue from which polyps protrude on slight swellings; pink, polyps paler pink. On rocks; sublittoral. Br, Ir, Fr. [10]

Cylinder Anemone *Cerianthus lloydi* CERIANTHIDAE BL <20 cm. Body with pointed hind end; 2 whorls of <60 slender tapering tentacles, outer whorl long, inner whorl short; tube thick, slimy inside; body yellowish, tentacles various shades of brown, often patterned, tube dark brown. Tube buried in muddy sand; sublittoral. T, ex nBaS. [11]

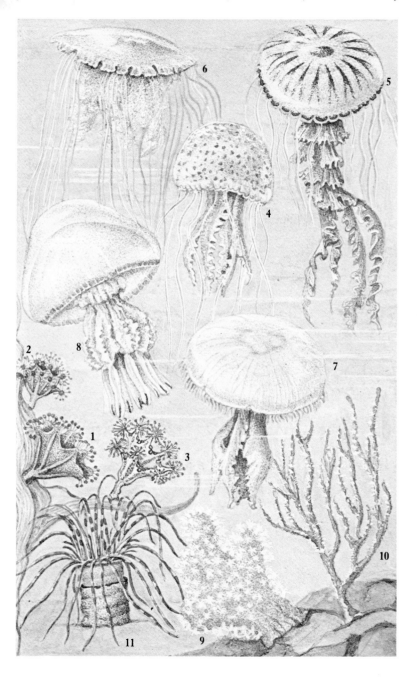

burrowing anemone *Fagesia carnea*
EDWARDSIIDAE H <2 cm. Body worm-like,
lacks adhesive basal disc; c28 pink
tapering tentacles; mouth and gut red. In
crevices in rocks; lower shore. T, ex
nBaS. [1]

burrowing anemone *Halcampa chrysanthellum* HALCAMPIDAE H <5 cm.
Body worm-like, lacks adhesive basal disc;
12 stubby tentacles; translucent body-
wall; body biscuit-coloured, brown bands
on tentacles. Burrows in sand, muddy
sand, esp amongst roots of eelgrasses;
lower shore to sublittoral. T, ex nBaS. [2]

burrowing anemone *Peachia hastata*
HALOCLAVIDAE H <10 cm. Body worm-
like, lacks adhesive basal disc; usually 12
tapering tentacles; pinkish-brown.
Burrows in sand, mud, gravel; lower
shore to sublittoral. T, ex nBaS. [3]

Devonshire Cup Coral *Caryophyllia smithi* TURBINOLIDAE H <2 cm, D <1·5
cm. Limy skeleton cup-shaped; polyp
anemone-like when expanded, with
flattened oral disc and <50 transparent,
knobbed tentacles; skeleton whitish, or
pale brown, polyps white, pink, pale green
or shades of brown. On rocks; lower shore
to sublittoral. T, ex nBaS. [4] [skeleton 5]

Scarlet-and-gold Star Coral
Balanophyllia regia EUPSAMMIDAE H <2
cm, D <1·5 cm. Limy skeleton cup-
shaped, white, with longitudinal ridges;
polyp anemone-like, with flattened oral
disc and <50 transparent, pointed
tentacles; polyp unable to retract fully;
polyp scarlet or orange, tentacles with
yellow patches. On rocks, in deep rock
pools; lower shore to sublittoral. Br. [6]

Jewel Anemone *Corynactis viridis*
CORALLIMORPHIDAE H <1 cm. Polyp
anemone-like, with <100 knobbed
tentacles in 3 circles; mouth elevated on
tiny cone; colours brilliant, often appear
fluorescent, usually bright green or orange
but may be red, magenta or grey. On
rocks, in crevices and under overhangs;
lower shore to sublittoral. Br, Ir, Fr. [7]

compound coral *Lophelia pertusa*
OCULINIDAE H <50 cm. Colonial; skeleton
irregularly branched; polyps arise from
cups; skeleton yellowish-white, polyps
pink. On rocks; sublittoral. nBr, SC. [8]

Beadlet Anemone *Actinia equina*
ACTINIIDAE H <8 cm. Column smooth;
adhesive base with narrow blue line round
margin; oral disc with c200 tentacles in 6
circles, and 24 bright blue spots; red, dull
green, brown or orange, sometimes clear
red speckled pale green. On rocks, in
crevices; upper/middle shore to
sublittoral. T, ex nBaS. [9]

Snakelocks Anemone *Anemonia sulcata*
ACTINIIDAE H <10 cm. Column smooth,
basal disc weakly adhesive; <6 circles of
c200 long, sticky, sinuous, violet-tipped
non-retractile tentacles; grey, green or
light brown. On rocks and large weeds,
often in pools, along ledges; middle shore
to sublittoral. Br, Ir, Fr. [10]

Dahlia Anemone *Tealia felina* ACTINIIDAE
H <15 cm, D <7 cm (base). Column
warty, sticky, often covered with gravel;
oral disc flattish with 80 (sometimes more)
short, stubby, retractile tentacles; colour
variable, usually pink, red, blue, green or
grey, tentacles translucent and banded.
Often in crevices; middle shore to
sublittoral. T, ex nBaS. [11]

Wartlet or **Gem Anemone** *Bunodactis verrucosa* ACTINIIDAE H <5 cm. Column
with 6 longitudinal rows of white warts
and rows of smaller greyish warts, basal
disc adhesive; <50 tentacles in c6 circles;
column usually pink, may be mottled with
grey-green, tentacles banded. Under
boulders, in crevices, rock pools; middle
to lower shore. Br, Ir, Fr. [12]

anemone *Anthopleura balli* ACTINIIDAE
H <5 cm. Column with c50 vertical rows
of warts, larger at top, basal disc adhesive;
50 tapering, slowly retractile tentacles;
reddish-pink or yellowish shades of olive-
green, tentacles often mottled brown and
green. In rocky crevices, under overhangs;
lower shore to sublittoral. Br, Ir, Fr. [13]

Plumose Anemone *Metridium senile*
METRIDIIDAE H <10 cm. Column smooth
and slimy; wide oral lobe deeply curved
into <8 lobes; conspicuous collar beneath
oral lobe; tentacles numerous, giving a
feathery effect; white, fawn, orange, pink
or brown. On solid objects, usually under
overhangs; lower shore to sublittoral. T,
ex nBAS. [1]

parasitic anemone *Calliactis parasitica*
HORMATHIIDAE H <10 cm. Column tough,
stiff, with numerous pale vertical lines,
basal disc strongly adhesive; c300
translucent tentacles; column buff to
brown, often spotted. Usually on shell of
common whelk *Buccinum undatum*
occupied by hermit-crab *Pagurus bernhardus*; sublittoral. Br, Ir, Fr. [2]

Strawberry Anemone *Adamsia palliata*
HORMATHIIDAE D <5 cm. Column and
base wrapped around gastropod shell
occupied by hermit-crab *Pagurus prideauxi*
(older specimens may replace shell); c500
tentacles clustered around shell aperture,
often on underside; creamy-fawn or
yellowish with magenta or purple spots,
tentacles white; purple threads ejected
when disturbed. On sandy and muddy
bottoms; sublittoral. T, ex nBaS. [3]

anemone *Sagartia elegans* SAGARTIIDAE
H <6 cm. Column smooth with scattered
warts, basal disc strongly adhesive; <200
slender tentacles; colour variable, column
usually orange or orange-brown, tentacles
and oral disc orange, white, pink or
patterned brown; discharges white threads
when disturbed. On solid objects, often in
crevices; lower shore to sublittoral. T, ex
nBaS. [4]

Daisy Anemone *Cereus pedunculatus*
SAGARTIIDAE H <10 cm. Column trumpet-
shaped, smooth with scattered warts,
basal disc adhesive; often >700 short
tentacles; cream, pale grey or orange,
tentacles and oral disc often patterned
brown. In crevices, sheltered rock pools,
on solid objects buried in soft mud, often
in estuaries; lower shore to sublittoral.
Br, Ir, Fr. [5]

Comb-jellies (Ctenophora) resemble
jellyfish but lack stinging cells. Move by
beating of cilia in comb-like rows.

Sea-gooseberry *Pleurobrachia pileus*
PLEUROBRACHIIDAE BL <3 cm. Globular
with 8 longitudinal rows of 'comb-plates',
1 pair of long fringed tentacles; transparent,
gut may be pinkish. Pelagic, trapped in
rock pools. T, ex nBaS. [6]

comb-jelly *Beroe cucumis* BEROIDAE
BL <10 cm. Tulip-shaped body, wide
mouth, large internal cavity; 8 conspicuous
rows of 'comb-plates', no tentacles;
transparent, pale pink. Pelagic, trapped in
rock pools. T, ex nBaS. [7]

Flatworms (Platyhelminthes) are flattened,
worm-like. Often without gut. Glide by
beating of cilia on underside.

flatworm *Convoluta convoluta*
CONVOLUTIDAE EL <6 mm. Body broadens
slightly at head end; no tentacles, eyes, or
gut; leaf-green due to symbiotic algae.
Amongst weeds, in tide-pools; lower
shore to sublittoral. T, ex nBaS. [8]

flatworm *Procerodes littoralis* PROCERO-
DIDAE EL <5 mm. Body rounded at
posterior, narrowing towards head; 2
tentacles, 2 eyes; dull brown or blackish,
often with longitudinal streaks. Under
stones, esp near sources of fresh water;
upper and middle shore. T, ex nBaS. [9]

flatworm *Prostheceraeus vittatus*
EURYLEPTIDAE EL <7 cm. Body broad with
wavy edges; head blunt, 2 tentacles,
numerous eyes in 2 groups; creamy-white
with dark grey or black longitudinal
stripes, outermost continuous around
body. Under boulders, amongst weeds;
lower shore to sublittoral. T, ex nBaS.
[10]

flatworm *Oligocladus sanguinolentus*
EURYLEPTIDAE EL <1·5 cm. Body leaf-
shaped with smooth margin; 2 tentacles,
numerous eyes; gut visible through body
wall; cream with reddish brown spots.
Under weeds, stones; middle shore to
sublittoral. T, ex nBaS. [11]

Ribbonworms (Nemertea) are elongated, worm-like. Feed using eversible tubular proboscis (lying above gut); trap small invertebrates. Head often with eyes.

ribbonworm *Tubulanus annulatus* TUBULANIDAE BL *c*20 cm. Body rounded above, flattened below, smooth; head rounded with lateral slits, lacks eyes; brick-red with longitudinal white stripes, white annulations. Under boulders in sand, in crevices, holdfasts; lower shore to sublittoral. T, ex nBaS. [1]

ribbonworm *Cephalothrix rufifrons* CEPHALOTHRICHIDAE BL < 10 cm. Body rounded, tapering at each end; head lacks eyes, slits; changes dramatically from thread to thick 'blob'; cream with orange patch at head end, pale line along part of dorsal surface. Under boulders, weeds in muddy gravel, in shell gravel, sand; lower shore to sublittoral. T, ex nBaS. [2]

Bootlace Worm *Lineus longissimus* LINEIDAE BL < 5 m, rarely > 30 m. Body rounded, slimy, usually coiled when uncovered; head spoon-shaped, deeply cleft on each side, numerous eyes in 2 groups; blackish-brown with blue or purple reflections, head paler, striped longitudinally. Under boulders and weeds; lower shore to sublittoral. T, ex BaS. [3]

priapulid *Priapulus caudatus* PRIAPU-LOIDEA:PRIAPULIDAE BL < 7 cm. Body round, plump, rubbery; body-wall annulated; anterior, voluminous, eversible proboscis armed with spines in longitudinal rows; 1 posterior bunch of finger-like papillae; grey-fawn, proboscis lighter. In thick mud; lower shore to sublittoral. T, ex nBaS. [4]

entoproct *Pedicellina cernua* ENTOPROCTA H < 5 mm. Individual animals wine-glass-shaped, on contractile stems arising from delicate branched 'roots'; gut U-shaped, mouth and anus surrounded by rings of ciliated tentacles; transparent, colourless. Cilia create current, bearing food particles. On solid objects, coralline algae; lower shore. T, ex nBaS. [5]

Moss-animals (Bryozoa or Ectoprocta) are small, colonial; each animal enclosed within horny calcareous or gelatinous sleeve (zooecium). Feed using ring of ciliated tentacles enclosing mouth.

bryozoan *Crisia eburnea* CRISIIDAE H <3 cm (colony). Resembles fibrous weed, but horny to touch; highly branched; zooecia tubular, slightly flattened; openings round, each with long spine; fawn or dirty white. Attached to weeds; lower shore to sublittoral. T, ex nBaS. [6]

Sea-mat *Membranipora membranacea* MEMBRANIPORIDAE Size variable. Thin lacy, encrusting; zooecia rectangular, with pair of short blunt 'horns' at front corners; some zooecia have central, blunt, upright peg; edges of colony usually wavy; white or very pale grey. On *Laminaria* and other seaweeds; middle shore to sublittoral. T, ex nBaS. [7]

Hairy Sea-mat *Electra pilosa* MEMBRANI-PORIDAE Size variable. As *Membranipora membranacea*, but zooecia slightly rounded, with 2 blunt anterior 'horns' and 1 long posterior spine; other spines may occur; appears hairy; off-white. On weeds; middle shore to sublittoral. T, ex nBaS. [8]

Hornwrack *Flustra foliacea* FLUSTRIDAE H < 20 cm (colony). Leaf-like, branching, upright, fairly tough, horny; zooecia rectangular, slightly rounded at corners, with 2 pairs of small blunt 'horns' at front corners; golden-brown, paler when dead and dry. On solid objects; sublittoral, often washed up. T, ex nBaS. [9]

Hard Sea-mat *Umbonula littoralis* UMBONULIDAE D <7 cm (colony). Thin encrustation; hard, brittle; zooecia vase-shaped; orange-red. On stones, holdfasts; lower shore to sublittoral. T, ex nBaS. [10]

bryozoan *Bowerbankia imbricata* VESICULARIIDAE H <7 cm (colony). Branched, tufty; animals in groups along stems; zooecia pear-shaped; greyish-fawn. On seaweeds, esp *Fucus*, *Corallina*, *Ascophyllum*; middle to lower shore. T, ex nBaS. [11]

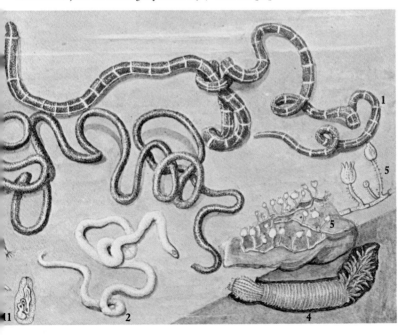

Molluscs are muscular-bodied with well-developed head bearing sense organs; powerful muscular foot. Often with shell.

Chitons (Amphineura). Oval in outline; shell of 8 calcareous plates articulating with each other. Use rasping tongue (radula) to scrape vegetation.

chiton *Lepidochiton cinerea* LEPIDOCHITO-NIDAE SL <2 cm. Transverse plates arched, lightly granulated; margin with minute granules; 16-19 pairs of gills; grey, olive-green or dull reddish-brown. On rocks; middle to lower shore. T, ex nBaS. [1]

chiton *Acanthochitona crinitus* CRYPTO-PLACIDAE SL <1·5 cm. Transverse plates with coarse granules, rough to touch; central crest conspicuous; margin wide with 9 pairs of groups of bristles; greyish- or yellowish-brown. On rocks; lower shore. T, ex nBaS. [2]

Snails, slugs (Gastropoda). Head with sensory tentacles and eyes; mouth with rasping tongue (radula). Foot broad and flat. Shell single; varies in form from simple curved plate to highly ornamented spiral; reduced or absent in some. Feed as chitons on vegetation or flesh, or with acid glands bore holes in other organisms.

Ormer *Haliotis tuberculata* HALIOTIDAE SL <8 cm. Spiral very reduced, body whorl large, flattened; round holes along 1 side; outer surface furrowed, brown inner surface of green-shot mother-of-pearl. Under stones; lower shore to sublittoral. Channel Is. [3]

Slit Limpet *Emarginula reticulata* FISSURELLIDAE SL <1 cm. Shell with anterior slit; apex curved backwards; ribs radiate from apex; off-white. On boulders, often in muddy conditions; lower shore to sublittoral. T, ex nBaS. [4]

Keyhole Limpet *Diodora apertura* FISSURELLIDAE SL <3 cm. Shell apex with hole, radiating ribs and cross-ridges; fawn. Under stones; lower shore to sublittoral. T, ex nBaS. [5]

Common Limpet *Patella vulgata* PATELLIDAE SL *c*6 cm. Shell conical; outer surface coarsely sculptured, grey, inner surface with silvery lustre. On rocks; upper to lower shore. T, ex nBaS. [6]

Blue-rayed Limpet *Patina pellucida* PATELLIDAE SL <1·5 cm (old specimens <2·5 cm). Apex of shell off-centre; dark brown with rows of electric-blue spots, old specimens horn-coloured with traces of blue rays. On *Laminaria*; lower shore to sublittoral. T, ex nBaS. [7]

White Tortoiseshell Limpet *Acmaea virginea* ACMAEIDAE SL <1·2 cm. Apex of shell pointed; off-white or pale pink, with rays from apex. On stones; lower shore to sublittoral. T, ex nBaS. [8]

Painted Top-shell *Calliostoma zizyphinum* TROCHIDAE SH <3 cm. Shell resembles a whipping top; greyish-green with red, brown, sometimes purple markings. Under boulders; lower shore to sublittoral. T, ex nBaS. [9]

Thick Top-shell *Monodonta lineata* TROCHIDAE SH <3 cm. Shell solid with pronounced spire; whorls slightly inflated, unsculptured except for growth lines; tooth near base of columella; dark greyish-green or grey with zigzags of purplish-red, base and aperture white with mother-of-pearl. On rocks; upper to middle shore. Br. [10]

Giant Top-shell *Gibbula magus* TROCHIDAE SH <2 cm. Shell broader than high, spired; each whorl straight-sided with a basal keel and bulges on upper side; greyish-white with reddish spots and bands. On sandy gravel; lower shore to sublittoral. Br. [11]

Purple Top-shell *Gibbula umbilicalis* TROCHIDAE SH <1·5 cm. Shell rounded, body whorl often bulged; grey-green with broad wavy purplish-red stripes. Under stones; middle to lower shore. Br, Ir, Fr. [12]. Grey top-shell *G. cineraria* similar, but greyish-white with narrow wavy greyish-violet marks. Middle shore to sublittoral. T, ex nBaS. [13]

Pheasant Shell *Tricolia pullus* TURBINIDAE
SH <7 mm. Shell spired; operculum
massive, white; shell off-white with
reddish-brown smudges. Amongst
encrusting organisms on rocks; lower
shore to sublittoral. Br, Ir, Fr. [1]

Small Periwinkle *Littorina neritoides*
LITTORINIDAE SH <5 mm. Shell with sharp
spire, smooth; dark brown with bluish
sheen. In crevices and dead barnacles;
extreme upper shore. T, ex nBaS. [2]

Rough Periwinkle *Littorina saxatilis*
LITTORINIDAE SH <1 cm. Shell spired;
whorls deeply grooved; outer lip of
aperture meets body whorl at right angles;
brown to dark brown. In crevices; upper
to middle shore. T, ex nBaS. [3]

Edible Winkle *Littorina littorea*
LITTORINIDAE SH <3cm. Shell spired;
outer lip of aperture meets body whorl at
acute angle; whorls with some
sculpturing; dull browns, greys and black,
with darker bands. On rocks and weeds;
middle to lower shore. T, ex nBaS. [4]

Flat Periwinkle *Littorina littoralis*
LITTORINIDAE SH <1 cm. Shell with
flattened spire; dark brown, yellows or
green. On brown algae; middle to lower
shore. T, ex nBaS. [5]

Laver Spire Shell *Hydrobia ulvae*
HYDROBIIDAE SH <6 mm. Shell with blunt
spire; shades of brown. On mud, usually
in estuaries; middle to lower shore. T. [6]
H. ventrosa (SH <5 mm) similar, but
whorls rounded, sutures deep.

Common Wentletrap *Clathrus clathrus*
SCALIDAE SH <4 cm. Shell with round
ribbed whorls; cream or pale fawn. On
solid substrates; sublittoral but to lower
shore in spring. T, ex nBaS. [7]

Necklace Shell *Natica alderi* NATICIDAE
SH <1·5 cm. Shell with short spire; body
whorl large; cream or fawn with red-
brown spots. In surface layers of sand;
lower shore to sublittoral. T, ex nBaS. [8]
Large necklace shell *N. catena* (H <3·5

cm) similar, but nut-brown with spots
around upper margins of whorls.

Slipper Limpet *Crepidula fornicata*
CALYPTRAEIDAE SL <5 cm. Shell oval,
curved at apex; smooth, but with clear
growth lines; $c\frac{1}{2}$ of aperture occupied by
shelf; pink and brown. Normally occurs
in chains of individuals. On oyster beds;
lower shore to sublittoral. Br. [9]

European Cowrie *Trivia monacha*
ERATOIDAE SL <1·2 cm. Body-whorl
envelops other whorls; ridged; pinkish-
white with 3 black spots. Under stones,
esp amongst sea-squirts; lower shore to
sublittoral. T, ex nBaS. [10] *T. arctica*
similar, but lacks spots.

Dog-whelk *Nucella lapillus* MURICIDAE SH
<3·5 cm. Shell thick; body whorl large
with spiral marks, not ribbed; aperture
flared, outer lip with row of teeth,
siphonal canal; yellowish-white to grey;
aperture may have purple area inside. On
rocks; middle shore to sublittoral. T, ex
nBaS. [11]

Sting Winkle *Ocenebra erinacea*
MURICIDAE SH <6 cm. Shell heavily
sculptured; body whorl large; ridges
flared around aperture; siphonal canal
open in juv, closed in adult; fawn and
yellow. On rocks; lower shore to sublittoral. T, ex nBaS, but rare in north. [12]

Common Whelk *Buccinum undatum*
BUCCINIDAE SH <8 cm. Shell thick;
whorls clear, with wavy ribs and shallow
longitudinal ridges; dirty-white or greyish-
fawn. On rocks; lower shore to sublittoral.
T, ex nBaS. [13]

Netted Dog-whelk *Nassarius reticulatus*
NASSIDAE SH <2·5 cm. Whorls flat-sided
with criss-crossing ridges; greyish-brown.
Under stones, often on sand; lower shore
to sublittoral. T, ex nBaS. [14]

Thick-lipped Dog-whelk *Nassarius
incrassatus* NASSIDAE SH <1 cm. Whorls
distinct with deep sutures and criss-
crossing ridges; light brown with black
smudge on siphonal canal. Under stones;
lower shore to sublittoral. T, ex nBaS. [15]

parasitic snail *Turbonilla elegantissima*
PYRAMIDELLIDAE SH <1 cm. Shell slender,
steeply tapering; whorls with light
longitudinal sculpturing; pure white,
glossy. Parasitic on worms *Cirriformia*,
Amphitrite; lower shore. T, ex nBaS. [1]

Sea-hare *Aplysia punctata* APLYSIIDAE
BL <20 cm. Body elongated, flabby; head
with 2 eyes and 4 tentacles; shell internal,
fragile, in mid-dorsal position, flanked by
2 large flaps (parapodia); young specimens
reddish, older specimens brown, often
blotched; exudes bright purple slime
when irritated. Amongst weeds; lower
shore to sublittoral. T, ex nBaS. [2]

sea-slug *Elysia viridis* ELYSIIDAE BL <4
cm. Body elongated, flattened; head with 2
eyes and 2 tentacles; 2 elongated wing-
like flaps (parapodia) may be carried
upright or flat, thus radically altering
appearance; green or red (depending upon
food-source) but always with tiny red,
blue and green spots. On weeds, esp
Codium and *Cladophora*; middle shore to
sublittoral. T, ex nBaS. [3]

sea-slug *Berthella plumula* PLEURO-
BRANCHIDAE BL <6 cm. Body rounded,
plump; mantle overhangs foot except at
rear; single feathery gill appears from
under mantle on right side; head with 1
pair of tentacles and broad veil; shell
internal, fragile; yellow, often with orange
central area. Under stones; lower shore to
sublittoral. T, ex nBaS. [4]

Sea-lemon *Archidoris pseudoargus*
ARCHIDORIDIDAE BL <12 cm. Body
elongated, humped, leathery, conceals
foot; head with 2 stout, pleated tentacles;
anus surrounded by 8–9 feathery gills;
commonly dull yellow, blotched all over
with brown, green, pink, red and white.
On boulders, grazes encrusting sponges;
middle shore to sublittoral. T, ex nBaS.
[5] 2 similar spp. *Onchidoris bilamellata*
(BL <4 cm) with club-shaped tubercles
covering mantle; 7–9 gills; cream with
brown patches; feeds mainly upon acorn-
barnacles [6] *Cadlina laevis* (BL <3·5 cm)
with flattened semi-transparent body;

usually 5 gills; white, with yellow
glandular areas around mantle margin. [7]

sea-slug *Polycera quadrilineata*
POLYCERIDAE BL <4 cm. Body narrow,
elongated; dorsal surface with 1 finger-
like, pointed tubercle projecting backward
on each side of ring of <11 gills; head
with 2 eyes, 2 pleated tentacles, 2 pairs of
pointed tubercles; white blotched yellow
or black, gills and projections tipped
yellow or orange. Amongst encrusting
organisms; lower shore to sublittoral. T,
ex nBaS. [8]

sea-slug *Limacia clavigera* POLYCERIDAE
BL <2 cm. Dorsal surface with short,
stout papillae; mantle margin drawn out
into series of finger-like projections, finely
papillate on anterior margin; 3 feathery
gills; white, with papillae, tentacles and
gills tipped bright yellow. Amongst
encrusting organisms; lower shore to
sublittoral. T, ex nBaS. [9]

sea-slug *Doto coronata* DOTOIDAE
BL <1·5 cm. Dorsal surface with <8
pairs of finger-like projections, each with 1
red dot; head with pleated tentacles
surrounded by collar-like sheaths,
anterior margin drawn out into peak on
each side; creamy-white with scattered
patches of rosy pigment. Amongst
hydroids; lower shore to sublittoral. T, ex
nBaS. [10]

sea-slug *Facelina auriculata* FACELINIDAE
BL <5 cm. Body elongated, tapering
posteriorly, narrow; dorsal surface with
about 8 groups of slender finger-like
projections each side; head with 1 pair of
long tentacles; white with pink or red
projections. Amongst hydroids; lower
shore to sublittoral. T, ex nBaS. [11]

Common Grey Sea-slug *Aeolidia
papillosa* AEOLIDIIDAE BL <12 cm. Body
broad, tapering; dorsal surface with
numerous finger-like projections in *c*25
rows; head with 2 curved and 2 pleated
tentacles; shades of pinkish-grey, lilac or
pale brown. Amongst rocks; lower shore
to sublittoral. T, ex nBaS. [12]

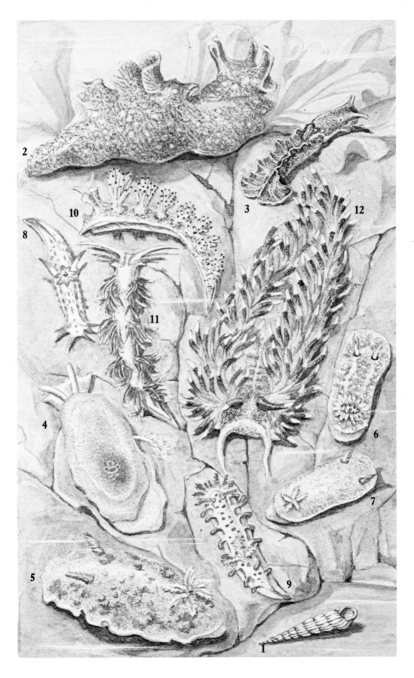

Tusk shells (Scaphopoda). Elongated slender shells, modified feet, and tentacles trapping food particles.

Tusk Shell *Dentalium entalis* DENTALIIDAE SL <5 cm. Shell tubular, elongated, gradually tapering, open at both ends; off-white to pale fawn. In sand and mud; sublittoral. T, ex nBaS. [1]

Bivalves (Lamellibranchiata). Laterally-flattened bodies covered by pair of hinged shell valves, joined by ligament. Foot usually powerful, muscular, digging organ. Ciliated gills create currents of water, drawn in and out through 2 siphons. Gills filter out food particles.

Common Nut-shell *Nucula turgida* NUCULANIDAE SL <1·25 cm. Margin of valves with minute crenulations; many hinge-teeth, more in front of than behind mid-line; shades of brown or off-white, often tinged with blue, ligament dark brown. In sand, gravel and mud; sublittoral. T, ex nBaS. [2]

Dog Cockle *Glycymeris glycymeris* GLYCYMERIDAE SL <6 cm. Shell almost circular in outline with crenulate margins and many hinge-teeth; light fawn with characteristic zigzag brown markings. In muddy sand and gravel; lower shore to sublittoral. T, ex nBaS. [3]

Common Mussel *Mytilus edulis* MYTILIDAE SL <10 cm. Shell elongated; attached to substrate by tough byssus threads; blue-black, sometimes shaded purple, sometimes with brown markings. On solid substrates, often in estuaries; middle shore to sublittoral. T, ex nBaS. [4]

Horse Mussel *Modiolus modiolus* MYTILIDAE SL < or > 15 cm. Shell more rounded and bulky than *Mytilus edulis*, growth lines coarser; brownish-purple. Attached to rocks, holdfasts of *Laminaria*; lower shore to sublittoral. T, ex nBaS. [5] Bearded horse mussel *Modiolus barbatus* (L <6 cm) similar but outer shell layer produced into 'whiskery' filaments. [6]

Native or **European Oyster** *Ostrea edulis* OSTREIDAE SL <10 cm. Shell almost circular in outline, but often irregular; left (lower) valve saucer-shaped, often cemented to substrate; right (upper) valve flat, crenulate, with layered, pleated appearance; dirty-fawn, inside pearly, single muscle scar white or dirty-white. On solid substrates, often in estuaries; lower shore to sublittoral. T, ex nBaS. [7] American oyster *Crassostrea virginica* (L <18 cm) has purple or red-brown muscle scar. Imported.

Common Saddle Oyster *Anomia ephippium* ANOMIIDAE SL <6 cm. Shell round in outline although often distorted due to association with substrate; left (upper) valve slightly domed; right (lower) valve much smaller, with large aperture somewhat off-centre; light fawn, inside pearly. On rocks; lower shore to sublittoral. T, ex nBaS. [right valve 8]

Great Scallop, Clam *Pecten maximus* PECTINIDAE SL <15 cm. Shell fan-shaped; right (lower) valve bowl-shaped, left (upper) valve flat, conspicuously ridged; ears equal, squared-off; shades of reddish-brown with white and brown markings. On sand and gravel; sublittoral. T, ex nBaS. [9]

Queen Scallop *Chlamys opercularis* PECTINIDAE SL <9 cm. As *Pecten maximus*, but left valve more curved than right, anterior ear longer and more rounded than posterior; colour very variable, white to yellow, brown and red, sometimes striped. On sand and gravel; lower shore to sublittoral. T, ex nBaS. [10]

Variegated Scallop *Chlamys varia* PECTINIDAE SL <6 cm. As *Pecten maximus*, but narrower; both valves shallowly curved; anterior ear long, wing-shaped, posterior ear reduced; ribs often with small, blunt spines; colours very variable, usually yellow, brown, red or purple. Attached to solid objects by byssus threads; lower shore to sublittoral. T, ex nBaS. [11]

Gaping File-shell *Lima hians* LIMIDAE
SL <4 cm. Shell narrow, outline irregular,
asymmetrical; ears reduced, unequal;
sculpture of spiny ribs; mantle of animal
with numerous non-retractile tentacles;
shell dirty-fawn, animal bright orange-
red. Amongst rocks and holdfasts; lower
shore to sublittoral. Br, Ir, Fr. [1]

bivalve *Astarte sulcata* ASTARTIDAE
SL <2·5 cm. Shell solid with apex of
valves anterior to mid-line; ligament
external and prominent; shell white or
pale pink; outer shell layer thick with very
delicate pattern of concentric grooves,
shades of brown. In muddy gravel or
shingly sand; sublittoral. T, ex nBaS. [2]

Iceland Cyprina *Arctica islandica*
ARCTICIDAE SL <13 cm. Shell solid, thick,
heavy, usually broadly oval in outline;
ligament long, conspicuous; shell light to
dark brown; outer shell layer thick, glossy,
greenish-brown, chesnut or black. In

muddy sand; lower shore to sublittoral.
T, ex nBaS. [3]

bivalve *Montacuta ferruginosa* MONTACU-
TIDAE SL <1 cm. Shell distinctly oval,
bean-like; apex of valve markedly off-
centre; shell white, but thin outer shell
layer usually deep rust-red due to a
deposit. In burrow of sea-potato *Echinocardium cordatum*, in clean sand; lower
shore to sublittoral. T, ex nBaS. [4]

Common Cockle *Cerastoderma* (*Cardium*)
edule CARDIIDAE SL <5 cm. Shell broadly
oval in outline, solid, with conspicuous
ribs ornamented with scale-like spines;
yellow, fawn or light brown. In sand;
middle shore to sublittoral. T, ex nBaS. [5]

Prickly Cockle *Acanthocardia echinata*
CARDIIDAE SL <7·5 cm. Shell broadly oval
in outline, solid; sculpture of conspicuous
radiating ribs with sharp spines connected
to each other by low ridges; margin

crenulate; off-white or fawn. In sandy or muddy substrates; sublittoral. T, ex nBaS. [6]

Rayed Artemis *Dosinia exoleta* VENERIDAE SL <5·5 cm. Shell solid, almost circular in outline, with sculpture of clear concentric ridges; heart-shaped depressed area in front of apex of valve; off-white with various irregular patterns of light brown. In shelly gravel, often where mud; lower shore to sublittoral. T, ex nBaS. [7]

Banded Venus *Venus fasciata* VENERIDAE SL <2·5 cm. Shell triangular in outline, solid, with sculpture of few broad-angled ridges; colour variable, shades of off-white, yellow, pink, violet and brown with brown patterning. In sandy gravel or muddy sand; lower shore to sublittoral. T, ex nBaS. [8]

Striped Venus *Venus striatula* VENERIDAE SL <4·5 cm. Shell triangular in outline,

solid, with sculpture of numerous fine, but prominent, concentric ridges; off-white, cream or fawn, often with rayed pattern in shades of brown. In sand; lower shore to sublittoral. T, ex nBaS. [9]

Ridged Venus *Venus casina* VENERIDAE SL <5 cm. Shell rounder in outline than other *Venus*, with sculpture of numerous prominent concentric ridges more pronounced near posterior margin; off-white or shades of cream and fawn, sometimes glossy, often with brown rays. In sand and muddy sand; lower shore to sublittoral. Br, Ir, Fr. [10]

Carpet Shell *Venerupis decussata* VENERIDAE SL <7·5 cm. Shell solid, oval to rectangular in outline, with sculpture of concentric ridges cross-hatched by radiating lines; light fawn, brown or grey with rayed, blotched or zigzagged brown patterns. In sand and mud; lower shore to sublittoral. Br, Ir, Fr. [11]

Thick Trough-shell *Spisula subtruncata*
MACTRIDAE SL <2·5 cm. Shell broadly
triangular in outline, with sculpture of
numerous distinct close concentric ridges;
triangular pit inside apex of valve (where
ligaments attach); off-white, outer shell
layer light brown. In sand; lower shore to
sublittoral. T, ex nBaS. [1]

Rayed Trough-shell *Mactra corallina*
MACTRIDAE SL <5 cm. Shell broadly
triangular in outline, brittle; sculpture of
delicate concentric marks; cream with
radiating streaks and purple tinting near
apex of valve, glossy. In sand; lower
shore to sublittoral. T, ex nBaS. [2]

Common Otter Shell *Lutraria lutraria*
LUTRARIIDAE SL <13 cm. Shell broadly
oval in outline, solid, with sculpture of
fine concentric lines; off-white or
yellowish-fawn, outer shell layer olive-
brown. In muddy sand or gravel; lower
shore to sublittoral. T, ex nBaS. [3]

Peppery Furrow Shell *Scrobicularia
plana* SCROBICULARIIDAE SL <6 cm. Shell
rather thin but not fragile, broadly oval in
outline; sculpture of fine irregular lines
and ridges; off-white, pale grey, light
brown or yellow. In mud; middle shore
to sublittoral. T, ex nBaS. [4]

Baltic Tellin *Macoma balthica* TELLINIDAE
SL <2·5 cm. Shell solid, rounded, except
posteriorly where triangular; sculpture
slight, of delicate concentric lines;
ligament prominent, long; off-white,
yellow, pink, pale brown or purple,
usually in concentric bands, interior
tinted pink. In mud or muddy sand;
middle shore to sublittoral, often in
estuaries. T. [5]

Blunt Tellin *Tellina crassa* TELLINIDAE
SL <6 cm. Shell broadly oval in outline,
solid, with sculpture of distinct concentric
grooves; depressed area in front of apex

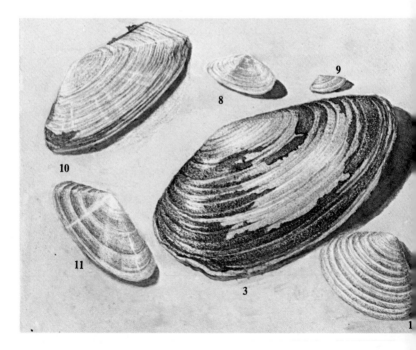

of valves narrow, elongated, in groove; ligament external; off-white or fawn, apex of valves slightly orange, interior of shell glossy white with central bright orange region. In muddy sand and gravel; sublittoral. T, ex nBaS. [6]

Thin Tellin *Tellina tenuis* TELLINIDAE SL <2 cm. Shell oval in outline, fragile, slim; sculpture of delicate concentric lines; all shades of pink, rose, orange and yellow. In sand; middle shore to sublittoral. T, ex nBaS. [7]

tellinid shell *Tellina fabula* TELLINIDAE SL <2 cm. As *Tellina tenuis*, but shell elongated posteriorly; sculpture of fine concentric lines, cross-hatched by radiating lines on right valve only; very pale pink with yellow or orange. In sand; lower shore to sublittoral. T, ex nBaS. [8]

Small Tellin *Tellina pygmaea* TELLINIDAE SL <1 cm. As *Tellina tenuis*, but shell very

fragile, rather narrow elongated oval; both valves slightly twisted to right near posterior margin; sculpture of delicate concentric ridges; shades of pink. In coarse sand; lower shore to sublittoral. T, ex nBaS. [9]

Faroe Sunset Shell *Gari fervensis* GARIIDAE SL <5 cm. Shell thin, elongated, angled posteriorly and slightly twisted to right; sculpture of concentric and radiating ridges; off-white with shades of pink or light brown, radiating bands of paler tints. In sand or gravel; lower shore to sublittoral. T, ex nBaS. [10]

Banded Wedge Shell *Donax vittatus* DONACIDAE SL <4 cm. Shell wedge-shaped, solid, with sculpture of fine radiating lines; margin crenulate, rough; off-white, yellow, pale brown or violet, outer shell layer brown or purple, glossy, interior of shell white or purple. In sand; lower shore to sublittoral. T, ex nBaS. [11]

bivalve *Pharus legumen* SOLECURTIDAE
SL <13 cm. Shell elongated, narrow,
rounded at each end; hinge almost
central; light fawn, outer shell layer
greenish, glossy. In sand; lower shore to
sublittoral. Br, Ir, Fr. [1]

Curved Razor-shell *Ensis ensis* SOLENIDAE
SL <13 cm. Shell thin, elongated, narrow,
curved; both ends shallowly rounded;
creamy-fawn with reddish streaks and
blotches, outer shell layer greenish, glossy.
In sand; lower shore to sublittoral. T, ex
nBaS. [2]

Pod Razor-shell *Ensis siliqua* SOLENIDAE
SL <20 cm. As *E. ensis*, but shell almost
rectangular in outline, anterior and
posterior margins straight with rounded
corners; creamy-fawn with reddish
blotches and lines, outer shell layer olive-
green or brown. T, ex nBaS. [3]

razor-shell *Ensis arcuatus* SOLENIDAE
SL <15 cm. As *E. ensis*, but shell curved
only along ventral margins; creamy-fawn
with reddish or orange markings, outer
shell layer shades of green and grey. In
sand and gravel; lower shore to sublittoral.
T, ex nBaS. [4]

Grooved Razor-shell *Solen marginatus*
SOLENIDAE SL <12·5 cm. As *E. ensis*, but
shell rectangular in outline with straight
ends, posterior end at right angles to long
axis, anterior end angled; deep vertical
groove in each valve just behind anterior
margin and parallel to it; fawn and yellow,
outer shell layer light brown. In muddy
sand; lower shore to sublittoral. T, ex
nBaS. [5]

boring shell *Hiatella arctica* HIATELLIDAE
SL <4 cm. Shell solid, irregular in outline
but broadly rectangular with posterior
gape, often twisted; sculpture of irregular
concentric ridges; off-white. Bores in soft

rock, under stones, in crevices, attached
by byssus threads; lower shore to
sublittoral. T, ex nBaS. [6]

Sand Gaper, Soft-shelled Clam *Mya
arenaria* MYACIDAE SL <15 cm. Shell solid,
broadly oval in outline, tapering slightly
toward gaping posterior margin; interior
of left valve, where ligament attaches,
conspicuous, projecting, shelf-like; off-
white or fawn, outer shell layer fawn,
often stained black. In mud or muddy
sand; lower shore to sublittoral. Often in
estuaries. T, ex nBaS. [7] Blunt gaper
Mya truncata (SL <7·5 cm) similar, but
posterior margin truncated and widely
gaping. [8]

Common Piddock *Pholas dactylus*
PHOLADIDAE SL <15 cm. Shell thin,
brittle, elongated, posterior tapering,
rounded, anterior almost triangular; gapes
along antero-ventral margin; accessory
plates present; sculpture of well-defined
ridges posteriorly and linear ranges of
spines anteriorly; white, interior glossy
and showing traces of external sculpture.
Bores into solid materials; middle shore to
sublittoral. Br, Ir, Fr. [9]

Oval Piddock *Zirfaea crispata* PHOLADIDAE
SL <9 cm. Shell solid, inflated; posterior
rounded, anterior triangular; large gapes
along anterior and posterior margins;
sculpture of concentric ridges, exaggerated
anteriorly; accessory plate small; white,
with outer shell layer brown. Bores into
soft rock and hard clay; lower shore to
sublittoral. T, ex nBaS. [10]

Shipworm *Teredo navalis* TEREDINIDAE
SL <1 cm. Shell brittle, rounded,
globular; outline irregular, notched and
grooved; white; animal elongated,
superficially worm-like, secretes hard,
white, calcareous tube. Burrows into
submerged wood. T, ex nBaS. [11]

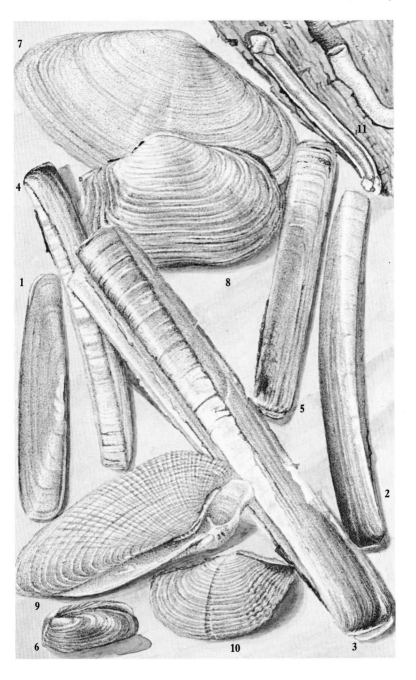

Octopuses, cuttlefish, squids (Cephalopoda). Body sac-like; head with large well-developed eyes; mouth with pair of horny jaws, also rasping tongue (radula). Front part of foot fused with head, extending into circlet of suckered tentacles surrounding mouth. Shell internal, reduced. See prey and seize it in tentacles.

Common Cuttlefish *Sepia officinalis* SEPIIDAE BL < 30 cm. Body flattened, oval, tough; lateral fins extend along right and left body-margins; 10 tentacles, 2 longest ending in leaf-shaped pads; shell the leaf-shaped 'cuttlebone'; cream, but capable of rapid colour-changes (reddish to black). Pelagic, occasionally near shore. T, ex nBaS. [1]

Little Cuttle *Sepiola atlantica* SEPIOLIDAE BL < 5 cm. Body goblet-shaped; lateral fins rounded, $c\frac{1}{2}$ length of body, in middle region; head slightly bulbous; 10 tentacles as *Sepia officinalis*; capable of rapid colour-changes. Over sand and burrowing into surface layers along water's edge. Br, Ir, Fr. [2]

Common Squid *Loligo forbesi* LOLIGINIDAE BL < 60 cm. Body rounded in cross-section; lateral fins triangular, confined to tapering posterior region; shell horny, feather-shaped. Pelagic. T, ex nBaS. [3]

Common Octopus *Octopus vulgaris* OCTOPODIDAE BL < 1 m. Body bag-like; 8 tentacles, each with 2 rows of suckers; grey-brown or greenish, can change to match background colour. In crevices, or constructed lair; sublittoral. Br, Ir, Fr, [4]

Curled or **Lesser Octopus** *Eledone cirrhosa* OCTOPODIDAE BL < 50 cm. As *Octopus vulgaris* but tentacles with 1 row of suckers and thin membrane joining them near bases. Sublittoral, sometimes amongst rocks on lower shore. T, ex nBaS. [5]

Peanutworms (Sipuncula). Worm-like, muscular, cylindrical. Mouth at tip of elongated retractile suctorial proboscis. Feed on microscopic organisms, detritus.

peanutworm *Sipunculus nudus* SIPUNCULIDAE EL < 30 cm. Body sausage-shaped, tapers each end; tough, leathery, with square pattern; proboscis with papillate skin, mouth at tip surrounded by circle of tentacles; greyish-yellow or greyish-pink. In mud, sand; middle shore to sublittoral. T, ex nBaS. [6]

peanutworm *Golfingia elongata* SIPUNCULIDAE EL < 10 cm. Body rounded, tapers each end, wrinkled; proboscis $c\frac{1}{2}$ body length; light fawn, with grey-brown cap-like areas at each end. In muddy areas, often under stones; lower shore to sublittoral. T, ex nBaS. [7]

peanutworm *Phascolion strombi* SIPUNCULIDAE EL < 6 cm. Body gherkin-like, with crescent of adhesive papillae around middle; proboscis slender, swollen at tip; grey-fawn. In mud inside shells of dead molluscs (usually only searching proboscis seen); on sandy, muddy bottoms; sublittoral. T, ex nBaS. [8]

Echiurid worms (Echiurida). Worm-like with soft cylindrical body; may have small hook-like bristles. Anterior proboscis not completely retractile. Feed as peanutworms; also use mucus nets.

echiurid worm *Echiurus echiurus* ECHIURIDAE EL < 15 cm. Body sausage-like, plump, soft; skin warty, semi-transparent; posterior rounded, with 2 rows of bristles; anterior tapering; grooved proboscis with 2 tiny hooks just below its base; greyish-yellow to pink or orange. In membranous U-shaped gallery, in mud, muddy sand; middle shore to sublittoral. T, ex nBaS. [9]

echiurid worm *Thalassema neptuni* ECHIURIDAE EL < 7 cm. Body swollen, plump, soft; skin wrinkled in regular pattern, slimy; posterior pointed, anterior rounded; tapering channelled flesh-coloured proboscis with 2 tiny hooks buried in body-wall just below its base; highly contractile; body pink to purplish with brown tints. In muddy rock crevices; lower shore. Br, Fr. [10]

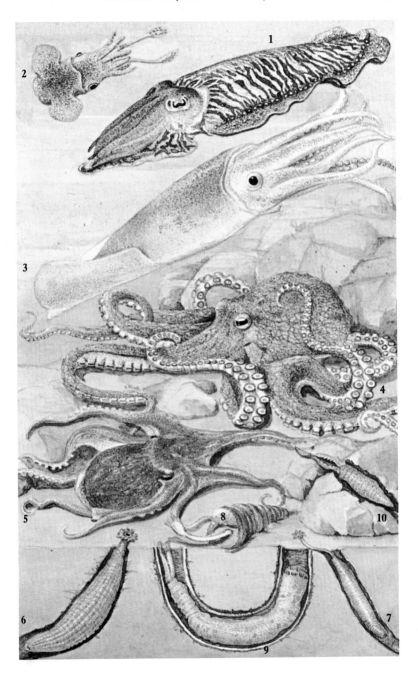

Polychaete worms (Polychaeta). Body segmented, elongated; segments bear lateral flaps (parapodia) with bristles (setae), and finger-like appendages (cirri). Head with well-developed sense organs. Protrusible muscular pharynx: in free-moving spp either suctorial or eversible with jaws. Tube-living worms have fans of ciliated tentacles which either collect suspended particles or secrete mucus and grope along substrate.

Sea-mouse *Aphrodita aculeate* APHRODITIDAE BL <12 cm. Dorsal scales hidden beneath felt of long, grey or brown, tangled setae; parapodia hidden by hair-like mass of iridescent green and gold setae. In soft mud; sublittoral. T, ex nBaS. [1]

scale-worm *Hermonia hystrix* APHRODITIDAE BL <7 cm. Large brown overlapping scales; parapodial cirri long, setae long, brown to golden, numerous; 1 median antenna, 2 tentacular cirri visible. In mud, sand, shell debris; sublittoral. T, ex nBaS. [2]

scale-worm *Lepidonotus squamatus* POLYNOIDAE BL <3 mm. Body flattened; 12 pairs of overlapping scales; parapodial cirri hidden, head appendages visible; yellow and brown. Under stones; middle shore to sublittoral. T, ex nBaS. [3]

scale-worm *Harmothoe impar* POLYNOIDAE BL <3 cm. Body flattened, tapering posteriorly; 15 pairs of overlapping scales, fringed, with club-shaped knobs; conspicuous palps on head; grey and brown with mottled patterns, ventral surface iridescent. Under stones, amongst weeds; middle shore to sublittoral. T, ex nBaS. [4]

scale-worm *Lagisca extenuata* POLYNOIDAE BL <4 cm. Body flattened, leaf-shaped, tapering posteriorly; scales overlapping, absent from last 10 segments; reddish-brown with marbled scales, ventral surface iridescent. Under stones; lower shore to sublittoral. T, ex nBaS. [5]

scale-worm *Polynoe scolopendrina* POLYNOIDAE BL <12 cm. Body narrow,

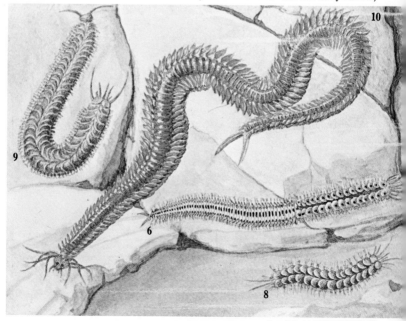

tapering, with 15 oval, overlapping scales covering front half; brown with marbled scales, some red on head. Under stones; lower shore to sublittoral. T, ex nBaS. [6]

scale-worm *Alentia gelatinosa* POLYNOIDAE BL <10 cm. Body almost obscured by 18 pairs of large, irregularly shaped, overlapping, gelatinous grey, mauve or brown scales, body yellow. Under boulders, lower shore to sublittoral. T, ex nBaS. [7]

scale-worm *Gattyana cirrosa* POLYNOIDAE BL <6 cm. Body thick, tapering posteriorly, covered by 15 pairs of large kidney-shaped scales; head concealed but palps visible; sand-coloured. In worm tubes; lower shore to sublittoral. T, ex nBaS. [8]

scale-worm *Sthenelais boa* SIGALIONIDAE BL <30 cm. Dorsal surface of body convex, covered by overlapping pairs of kidney-shaped scales; grey, light brown or dull yellow, scales with metallic iridescence. Under stones, amongst weeds; lower shore to sublittoral. T, ex nBaS. [9]

paddle-worm *Phyllodoce laminosa*
PHYLLODOCIDAE BL <75 cm. Body slender with several 100 segments; parapodia with green paddles; head heart-shaped with small knob in indentation, 2 eyes, 4 small antennae, 4 pairs of tentacular cirri; iridescent steel-blue, banded green or brown, ventral surface often pink. Under boulders, in crevices; lower shore to sublittoral. T, ex nBaS. [10]

paddle-worm *Anaitides maculata*
PHYLLODOCIDAE BL <15 cm. Body thin, flattened; parapodia with brown paddles; head heart-shaped with small knob in indentation, 2 eyes, 4 small antennae, 4 short and 4 long tentacular cirri; sandy-brown. In sand, under stones; lower shore to sublittoral. T, ex nBaS. [11]

paddle-worm *Eulalia viridis* PHYLLODOCIDAE BL <15 cm. Body rounded, narrow; parapodia with paddles; head rounded with 2 eyes, 5 antennae, 4 at tip and 1 between eyes; green, sometimes with small black markings. Amongst encrustations on stones; middle shore to sublittoral. T, ex nBaS. [12]

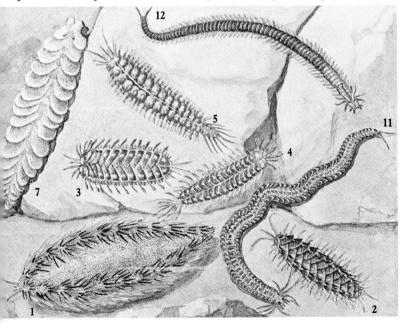

syllid worm *Typosyllis hyalina* SYLLIDAE
BL <3·5 cm. Parapodia with long cirri
like strings of beads; head with 4 large,
2 small eyes, 2 fleshy palps, 3 long
antennae; transparent, tinged pale yellow
or pink, some brown banding. Amongst
fine algae, sponges, hydroids on stones;
middle shore to sublittoral. T, ex nBaS.
[1]

syllid worm *Autolytus prolifer* SYLLIDAE
BL <1·5 cm. Parapodia with cirri, those
of first setigerous segment longer; head
with 4 eyes, 3 smooth antennae; yellowish,
sometimes orange-speckled. In holdfasts,
amongst encrusting organisms; lower
shore to sublittoral. T, ex nBaS. [2]

King Rag-worm *Neanthes* (*Nereis*) *virens*
NEREIDAE BL <50 cm. Parapodia large,
paddle-like; head appendages and sickle-
like jaws in readily protruded pharynx
distinct; green, sheened iridescent purple,
bases of parapodia often pink, margins
fawn. Burrows in mud, muddy sand;
lower shore to sublittoral. T, ex nBaS. [3]

Rag-worm *Neanthes* (*Nereis*) *diversicolor*
NEREIDAE BL <12 cm. Body flattened;
parapodia conspicuous; head appendages
distinct; greenish parapodia, pink or pale
orange along back with conspicuous dorsal
blood vessel. Burrows making galleries in
thick mud; mucus lining often protrudes
from opening as flimsy 'net'; lower shore
to sublittoral. T, ex nBaS. [4] [head 5]
Nereis pelagica (BL <20 cm) distinguished
by position of teeth on pharynx; makes
membranous tube; under boulders,
amongst holdfasts. [6] *Perinereis cultrifera*
(BL <25 cm) with some teeth on pharynx
fused into 2 solid bars (like eyebrows);
last pair of tentacular cirri long. [7]
Platynereis dumerilii (BL <6 cm) groups of
teeth reduced in number and size, teeth
pale; anterior and posterior tentacular
cirri long. [8] *Neanthes* (*Nereis*) *fucata*
(BL <20 cm) distinguished by habitat: in
shells of common whelk *Buccinum
undatum* occupied by hermit-crabs. [9]

cat-worm *Nephtys caeca* NEPHTYIDAE
BL <25 cm. Body rectangular in cross-

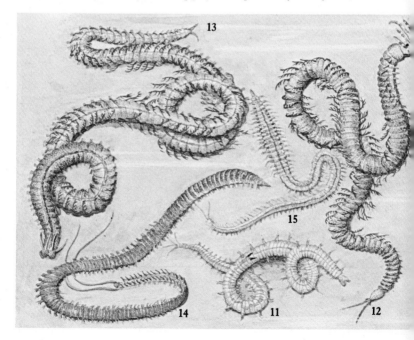

section; parapodia with long silky golden setae; head rounded, small, with 4 tiny antennae and 2 microscopic eyes; pharynx with 22 rows of 5–6 papillae, no large single papilla; tail with 1 filament; silvery-white with pearly sheen. In sand; lower shore to sublittoral. T, ex nBaS. [10]

glycerid worm *Glycera lapidum*
GLYCERIDAE BL <8 cm. Body round, ringed, tapers each end; head reduced to conical snout, 4 tiny antennae at tip; pharynx large, pear-shaped, armed with sickle-shaped black jaws; pale tinged pink or brown. Burrows in sand, gravel; lower shore to sublittoral. T, ex nBaS. [11]

eunicid worm *Eunice harassii* EUNICIDAE BL <25 cm. Segments after 4th with pair of red gills; head with 5 antennae, middle one longest; first segment with pair of dorsal cirri; tail with 2 filaments, sometimes 2 other tiny filaments; purplish-red or brown, each segment with 3 white patches. Under stones, in crevices; lower shore to sublittoral. Br, Ir, Fr. [12]

eunicid worm *Marphysa sanguinea*
EUNICIDAE BL <60 cm. Body thick, flattened; gills red, arise as tuft of 4–7 filaments after first 16–30 segments; head with 5 short antennae; greenish-brown. In gravelly sand, amongst eelgrass roots, occasionally in rock crevices; lower shore to sublittoral. T, ex nBaS. [13]

orbinid worm *Orbinia latreillii*
ORBINIIDAE BL <40 cm. Body massive, rounded, flattened dorsally, fragile; lower parapodial lobe of anterior segments edged with pointed papillae; setae long, thick; spear-shaped gills on all segments after 5th; head small, pointed; anterior pink, posterior yellowish-orange. In sand; lower shore to sublittoral. T, ex nBaS. [14]

orbinid worm *Scoloplos armiger*
ORBINIIDAE BL <12 cm. Anterior flattened, broad, posterior rounded, slender; narrow leaf-shaped red gills from c9th segment. Head pointed, structures not easily seen; rose or orange-pink. In sand; lower shore to sublittoral. T, ex nBaS. [15]

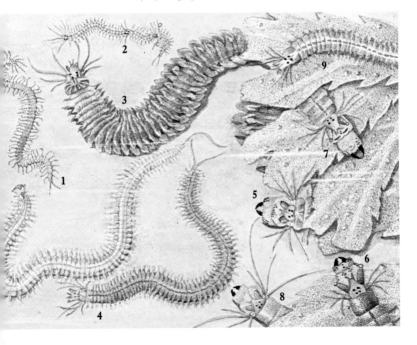

spionid worm *Scolelepis fuliginosa*
SPIONIDAE BL <6 cm. Body slender,
flattened; finger-like gills on segments
after first; head indented, with 2 short
antennae, 4 eyes, 2 long tentacle-like
palps; orange-red, tinted brown, white
patch on head. In sand, under stones;
lower shore to sublittoral. T, ex nBaS. [1]

spionid worm *Nerine cirratulus*
SPIONIDAE BL <8 cm. Body flattened;
gills on all segments except last 7 or 8;
head tapering, 4 small eyes arranged in a
square, 2 long tentacle-like palps; blue-
green, gills red. In sand, gravel; lower
shore to sublittoral. T, ex nBaS. [2]

spionid worm *Spio filicornis* SPIONIDAE
BL <3 cm. Body slender, fragile; finger-
like gills after first segment; head blunt,
4 eyes, 2 short palps; salmon-pink, gut
golden-brown, cream-coloured spots on
parapodia. In sand; lower shore to
sublittoral. T, ex nBaS. [3]

spionid worm *Polydora ciliata* SPIONIDAE
BL <3 cm. Body slender; 5th segment
larger, bears stout setae; finger-like gills
from 7th segment to tail; anus surrounded
by collar-like palps; yellowish-brown,
gills red. In U-shaped galleries bored into
limestone and shells; lower shore to
sublittoral. T, ex nBaS. [4]

magelonid worm *Magelona papillicornis*
MAGELONIDAE BL <17 cm. First 8
segments square in cross-section; 9th
segment with large dorsal, slightly smaller
ventral lobes, specialized setae; head
spoon-shaped, 2 long palps bearing
papillae; anterior pink, posterior greyish-
green. In sand; sublittoral. T, ex nBaS. [5]

chaetopterid worm *Chaetopterus
variopedatus* CHAETOPTERIDAE BL <25 cm.
Body with distinct regions: segments 1–9
with triangular parapodia, bundles of
setae; segment 10 with wing-like
parapodia; segment 11 with cup-like
structure; segments 12–14 semi-circular
paddles; remainder with elongated
parapodia containing bundles of slender
setae internally; head flat with long palps,

large mouth; off-white or light yellow. In
membranous, U-shaped tube (L <75 cm)
in sand; 'paddles' generate current, mucus
filters out food particles; lower shore to
sublittoral. T, ex nBaS. [6]

cirratulid worm *Cirriformia tentaculata*
CIRRATULIDAE BL <20 cm. Body round,
tapering towards tail; first 3 segments lack
setae; filamentous red gills on almost all
remaining segments; tuft of long, grooved
tentacles on fused segments 4 and 5, or 6
and 7; head conical, no obvious eyes;
orange-yellow, brownish or bronze-green.
In muddy sand, under stones; lower shore
to sublittoral. T, ex nBaS. [7]

flabelligerid worm *Flabelligera affinis*
FLABELLIGERIDAE BL <6 cm. Body
rounded tapering towards tail, entirely
sheathed in thick gelatinous mucus sleeve
with long protruding setae tipped with
brown hooks; head flat with finger-like
palps, 2 groups of slender gills, all encased
in 'cage' of long setae; green, parts of
gut orange, mucus coat colourless,
transparent. Under boulders; lower shore
to sublittoral. T, ex nBaS. [8]

opheliid worm *Ophelia bicornis*
OPHELIIDAE BL <7 cm. Body divided into
2 distinct regions: first 9 segments
inflated, round; posterior region
narrower, deeply grooved ventrally,
bearing c15 pairs of slender gills; head
smaller, pointed; pink with brown and
purple tints, iridescent; ♂ green, ♀ white
at sexual maturity. In coarse sand,
restricted locations; lower shore to
sublittoral. Br, Fr. [9]

capitellid worm *Notomastus latericeus*
CAPITELLIDAE BL <30 cm. Earthworm-
like; first 12 segments (all except first bear
setae) different from posterior; head small,
conical, 2 groups of tiny eye-spots;
pharynx voluminous; anterior red, paler
towards transparent posterior. In sand,
amongst eelgrasses; lower shore to
sublittoral. T, ex nBaS. [10] *Capitella
capitata* (BL <10 cm) similar, but with first
9 segments (1–7 have setae) different from
posterior; blood red. In muddy areas. [11]

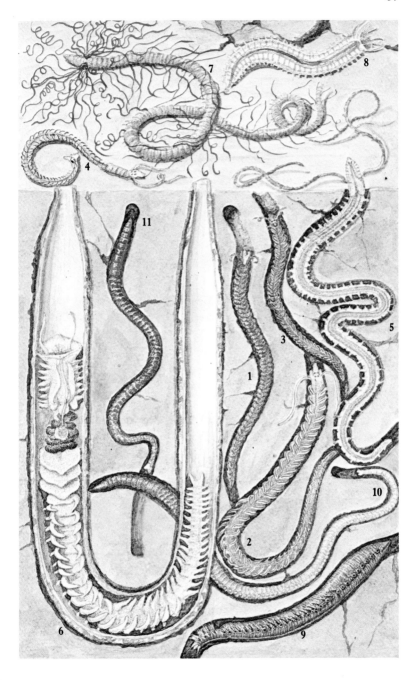

Lug-worm *Arenicola marina* ARENICOLIDAE BL <20 cm. Body round, 13 pairs of red branched gills from segment 7, terminal segments lack setae, gills; head reduced, pharynx voluminous, papillate, eversible; greenish-brown with black shading. In U-shaped burrows in sand; middle shore to sublittoral. T, ex nBaS. [1] [cast 2]

lug-worm *Arenicolides ecaudata* ARENICOL-IDAE BL <25 cm. Body rounded, tapering each end; each segment from c17th with 1 pair of branched gills, 7 terminal segments without gills; head reduced, no appendages; brownish-red with tints of green. Burrows in sand, mud; lower shore to sublittoral. T, ex nBaS. [3]

bamboo-worm *Clymenura clypeata* MALDANIDAE BL <20 cm. Large segments, front end of each often with annular ridge (like bamboo); head pointed, flattened; dorsal surface an inclined plate of tissue; tail blunt, conical; yellowish with pink bands. In brittle temporary tubes in sand; lower shore to sublittoral. T, ex nBaS, but ? far north. [4]

oweniid worm *Owenia fusiformis* OWENIIDAE BL <10 cm. Body round, tapering slightly to round posterior; segments few, long; parapodia reduced, setae slender; head with 2 leaf-like, folded lobes; pink with shades of green or yellow, pale transverse bands; tube of mucus covered with sand grains, flexible, longer than worm. In sand mixed with mud; lower shore to sublittoral. T, ex nBaS. [5]

Honeycomb Worm *Sabellaria alveolata* SABELLARIIDAE BL <4 cm. Anterior almost rectangular in cross-section with conspicuous parapodia, finger-like gills, setae; tail region tubular, recurved; head flattened, with 3 circles of large trowel-like setae, tuft of tentacles; pink, shading to brown; tube of cemented sand grains. Tubes aggregated into reefs on rocks; lower shore. T, ex nBaS. [6]

pectinariid worm *Lagis koreni* PECTINA-RIIDAE BL <5 cm. Body plump, tapering gradually; 15 setigerous segments; 2 pairs of red feathery gills anteriorly; tail region short, curved; head with tuft of knobbed papillae, 2 fans of large dagger-like setae; pink; tube conical, gently curved, of cemented sand grains. In sand, lower shore to sublittoral. T, ex nBaS. [7]
Amphictene auricoma similar, but with 17 setigerous segments; tube very curved.

ampharetid worm *Ampharete acutifrons* AMPHARETIDAE BL <4 cm. First 14 segments rounded, plump, with distinct parapodia and setae, posterior segments with epaulette-like parapodia edged with hooked setae; head elongated, rounded, 2 eyes, 2 tufts of strong golden setae, 2 groups each of 4 green tapering gills; ♀ salmon-pink, ♂ greenish-white, gut terra-cotta; tube membranous, covered with sand grains. In sand, amongst eelgrasses; lower shore to sublittoral. T, ex nBaS. [8]

terebellid worm *Amphitrite edwardsi* TEREBELLIDAE BL <30 cm. Body massive, rounded, anterior swollen; 17 setigerous segments; 3 pairs of red tufted gills; head with numerous yellow elongated tentacles; salmon-pink or pale brown; tube of mucus encrusted with gravel, often protrudes from sand. In sand; lower shore to sublittoral. Br, Fr. [9] Several similar spp. *Neoamphitrite figulus* (BL <25 cm) has first 24 segments with distinct setae; tube only gallery in sand. T, ex nBaS. *Amphitritides gracilis* (BL <12 cm) with first 17, 18 or 19 segments setigerous; 2 pairs of branched gills. T, ex nBaS.

terebellid worm *Nicolea zostericola* TEREBELLIDAE BL <2·5 cm. Body rounded, gently tapering; 2 pairs of branched gills; first 15 segments with distinct setae, segments 3 and 4 with pair of delicate tubes; head with numerous eye-spots, slender tentacles; pink or pale brown, gut red; tube of mucus, flimsy, encrusted with sand. Amongst encrusting organisms; lower shore to sublittoral. T, ex nBaS. [10]
Nicolea venustula (BL <6 cm) similar, but first 17 segments setigerous; gills more elongated; brick red with numerous white spots, tentacles violet.

terebellid worm *Eupolymnia nebulosa*
TEREBELLIDAE BL <15 cm. Body round,
soft, fleshy, fragile, flattening and
narrowing towards posterior; first 17
segments with distinct setae; 3 pairs of
tufted gills; head with numerous eye-
spots and long tentacles; orange-red, pink
or brown with conspicuous white spots,
tentacles pink or white with chalky
markings, gills red with white spots; tube
of gravel and shell debris. Under stones;
lower shore to sublittoral. T, ex nBaS. [1]

Sand Mason *Lanice conchilega* TEREBEL-
LIDAE BL <30 cm. First 17 segments
swollen, with distinct setae; remainder of
body long, slender, fragile; 3 pairs of red
tufted gills; head with long slender pale
pink tentacles; tube characteristic, of sand
gravel and shell debris, top with tuft of
sandy filaments resembling stiff paint
brush; pink or off-white. Tube upright,
protruding from sand; lower shore to
sublittoral. T, ex nBaS. [2]

Peacock Worm *Sabella penicillus*
SABELLIDAE BL <25 cm. Body slightly
flattened; head with 2 fans, each of <45
long flexible tentacles which fan out when
extended from tube; 2 moderately long
palps; body yellowish with orange or
brown tints, tentacles fawn with bands of
brown, violet or black; tube of mud-
reinforced mucus. In muddy sand, tube
protrudes <15 cm; lower shore to
sublittoral. T, ex nBaS. [3]

fan-worm *Bispira volutacornis* SABELLIDAE
BL <15 cm. Body slightly flattened,
plump; 2 fans rolled <4 times around
central axis, tentacles numerous, each
with 3 pairs of small eye-spots; greenish-
brown, often with purple tints, tentacles
pale, sometimes violet; tube of mud-
reinforced mucus, transparent at base.
Attached to rocks, in crevices; lower shore
to sublittoral. Br, Ir, Fr. [4]

fan-worm *Potamilla reniformis* SABELLIDAE
BL <10 cm. Body slender, flattened,
fragile; first 9–12 segments with distinct
setae; head with 2 fans, each of 10–15
feathery tentacles, some having <8 eye-

9 3

8

2

spots; orange or brick red, anterior grey or green, tentacles off-white or pink, banded brown or purple; tube horny, encrusted with sand, open end folds over or rolls up when not supported by worm. In crevices, amongst encrusting organisms; lower shore to sublittoral. T, ex nBaS. [5] *Potamilla torelli* (BL <6 cm) similar, but usually no more than 9 tentacles per fan; no eye-spots on tentacles; tube does not roll up when unsupported.

fan-worm *Branchiomma bombyx*
SABELLIDAE BL <5 cm. Body massive, plump, posterior tapering abruptly; 2 fans each of <25 tentacles with series of eye-spots and paired triangular projections; shades of brown with purple tints; tube of mud-impregnated mucus. Attached to rocks, in crevices; lower shore to sublittoral. T, ex nBaS. [6]

fan-worm *Amphiglena mediterranea*
SABELLIDAE BL <1·5 cm. Body rounded, tapering posteriorly; head with 2 fans, each of 5 feathery tentacles, and 2 palps, each with 'eyebrow-shaped' structure at base; off-white or pale yellow, tentacles pale green; tube of mucus, flimsy, temporary. Amongst encrusting organisms on rocks; lower shore to sublittoral. T, ex nBaS. [7]

fan-worm *Myxicola infundibulum*
SABELLIDAE BL <20 cm. Body plump, flattened; head with 2 semi-circular fans, each of <40 tentacles with membrane attaching one to another except at tip; predominantly yellowish-orange, tentacles brown with violet tints; tube voluminous, thick, gelatinous, transparent. In sand and mud; sublittoral. T, ex nBaS. [8]

fan-worm *Megalomma vesiculosum*
SABELLIDAE BL <15 cm. Body rounded, flattened posteriorly; head with 2 fans, each of 30 tentacles, united at bases; each tentacle with large eye at tip; yellowish, pink or shades of brown, sometimes spotted white; tube horny, encrusted with sand and shell debris. In sand, often amongst eelgrasses; lower shore to sublittoral. Br, Ir, Fr. [9]

tube-worm *Hydroides norvegica*
SERPULIDAE BL < 3 cm. 7 anterior
segments with distinct setae covered by
thin membrane recurved forward into
collar; head with 2 fans, each of <20
tentacles, 1 tentacle enlarged and stiffened
with calcareous material into operculum
crowned by circle of complex spiny
projections; shades of orange, pink and
green, tentacles banded white, yellow and
orange; tube calcareous, round in cross-
section. Under boulders; lower shore to
sublittoral. T, ex nBaS. [1]

serpulid worm *Mercierella enigmatica*
SERPULIDAE BL <3 cm. As *Hydroides
norvegica*, but operculum club-shaped, top
bearing numerous short curved black
spines; tube round with flared lip, similar
flares along length. Commonest in
brackish water. Br, Fr. [2]

serpulid worm *Serpula vermicularis*
SERPULIDAE BL <7 cm. As *Hydroides
norvegica*, but operculum conical, tipped
by daisy-like circle of small teeth; tube
thick-walled, round in cross-section,
ridged and ringed. On stones, shells;
sublittoral. T, ex nBaS. [3]

serpulid worm *Pomatoceros triqueter*
SERPULIDAE BL <3 cm. As *Hydroides
norvegica*, but operculum massive, winged,
club-shaped, sometimes 2 or more
projections from tip; tube triangular in
cross-section. T, ex nBaS. [4]

serpulid worm *Apomatus similis*
SERPULIDAE BL <3 cm. First 7 segments
with distinct setae covered by thin
membrane recurved forward into collar;
head with 2 fans, each of <20 tentacles,
tip of 1 tentacle inflated into bladder-like
operculum; shades of red or orange,
tentacles white with orange bands, repeated
red eye-spots; tube calcareous, circular in
cross-section. On boulders; lower shore to
sublittoral. T, ex nBaS. [5]

serpulid worm *Protula tubularia*
SERPULIDAE BL *c*5 cm. As *Apomatus similis*,
but <45 tentacles per fan; no operculum;
mainly orange and red; tube smooth,
attached at posterior end only. Br, Ir, Fr. [6]

serpulid worm *Filograna dysteri*
SERPULIDAE BL <7 mm. First 7–9
segments with distinct setae, separated
from slightly swollen posterior setigerous
segments by 'waist' without segments or
setae; head with 2 fans, each of 4
tentacles; pink or pale orange, tentacles
colourless or pale pink; tube calcareous,
massed, linked into lacy pattern. Under
stones; lower shore to sublittoral. T, ex
nBaS. [7]

spirorbid worm *Spirorbis spirorbis*
SERPULIDAE D <4 mm (tube). Details of
setation visible only with strong
magnification; 2 fans, each of 5 tentacles,
1 tentacle is modified into flattened club-
shaped operculum; pale green, pink and
pale orange; calcareous tube coiled
clockwise into tight flat spiral. On brown
algae, esp saw wrack *Fucus serratus*;
middle to lower shore. T, ex nBaS. [8]

spirorbid worm *Janua pagenstecheri*
SERPULIDAE D <3 mm (tube). As
Spirorbis spirorbis, but with hollow, wine-
glass-shaped operculum used for
incubation of embryos; tube ridged,
coiled anti-clockwise. On stones and
shells; middle to lower shore. T, ex nBaS.
[9]

parasitic worm *Myzostomum cirriferum*
MYZOSTOMIDAE D <5 mm. Almost
circular in outline; 10 marginal papillae
on each side, 5 conical parapodia with few
setae; 4 suckers on ventral side; yellow or
pale brown; parasitic on feather star
Antedon bifida; lower shore to sublittoral.
T, ex nBaS. [10]

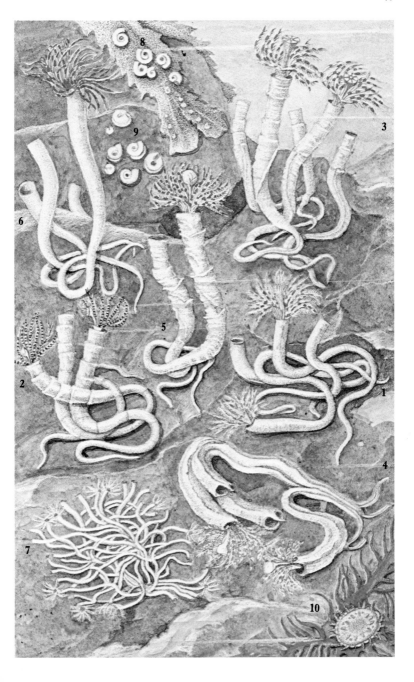

Sea-spiders (Pycnogonida). Resemble spiders, with short slender bodies, 4 pairs of elongated legs; jointed exoskeleton and head with complex biting and sucking mouthparts. Prey on soft parts of hydroids, sea-anemones.

sea-spider *Nymphon gracile* NYMPHONIDAE LS < 5 cm. Body elongated; walking legs slender, tipped with claws; reddish-brown. Amongst encrusting organisms; middle shore to sublittoral. T, ex nBaS. [1]

sea-spider *Pycnogonum littorale* PYCNOGONIDAE BL < 2 cm. Body short, thick; legs short-jointed, tipped with claws; sandy-fawn. Under stones or associated with sea-anemones; lower shore to sublittoral. T, ex nBaS. [2]

Crabs, lobsters and others (Crustacea). Hard exoskeleton, jointed appendages. Head usually with compound eyes, 4 sensory antennae, complex mouthparts. Abdomen often ends with fan-shaped telson. Feeding dependent on specially modified limbs. On barnacles (Cirripedia), except parasitic spp, all limbs are feathery and 'kick' food into the mouth. On free-moving crustaceans (Malacostraca), some walking limbs may be modified into pincers to grasp food, others into mouthparts for shredding food and sieving suspended particles.

Goose Barnacle *Lepas anatifera* LAPADIDAE SL < 5 cm. Body covered by 5 delicate white plates, supported on tubular muscular stalk; animal dark greyish-brown or black. Pelagic, attached to floating objects. T, ex nBaS. [3]

warty barnacle *Verruca stroemia* VERRUCIDAE D < 1 cm. Shell flattened, of 4 deeply grooved plates overlapping asymmetrically; wart-like; off-white, grey or pale brown. On rocks, stones; lower shore to sublittoral. T, ex nBaS. [4]

Acorn-barnacle *Balanus balanoides* BALANIDAE D < 1·5 cm. Shell conical, of 6 grooved plates overlapping at edges; central aperture diamond-shaped; lateral

sutures of central plates oblique; dirty-white or fawn. On rocks; upper to lower shore. T, ex nBaS. [5]

acorn-barnacle *Balanus improvisus* BALANIDAE D < 2 cm. Shell tall, slightly conical, of 6 plates with tapered tips all slightly curved anteriorly; greyish-white. On solid objects, rocks, shells, often in estuaries; middle shore to sublittoral. T, ex nBaS. [6]

acorn-barnacle *Balanus crenatus* BALANIDAE D < 2 cm. As *B. improvisus*, but more conical, tips of plates less tapered. Lower shore to sublittoral. T, ex nBaS. [7]

acorn-barnacle *Balanus perforatus* BALANIDAE D < 3 cm. Shell steeply conical, of 6 solid finely grooved plates; central aperture rounded, edges often jagged; central plates several mm below aperture; reddish-purple-brown. On rocks; lower shore to sublittoral. Br, Ir, Fr. [8]

acorn-barnacle *Elminius modestus* BALANIDAE D < 1 cm. Shell rather flattened, with 4 more-or-less smooth, cross-shaped plates; white. On rocks; middle to lower shore. Probably T. [9]

Star Barnacle *Chthamalus stellatus* CHTHAMALIDAE D < 1·5 cm. As *Balanus balanoides*, but central opening kite-shaped; lateral sutures of central plates straight. Br, Ir, Fr. [10]

parasitic barnacle *Sacculina carcini* SACCULINIDAE D < 4 cm (external part). Body highly modified: thread-like within body of host crab, smooth, sponge-like mass on underside of host's abdomen; yellow-fawn. Parasitic in crabs, *eg Carcinus maenas*; middle shore to sublittoral. T, ex nBaS. [11]

parasitic barnacle *Peltogaster paguri* PELTOGASTRIDAE L < 1·5 cm (external part). As *Sacculina carcini*, but external part compact, on side of host's abdomen; greyish-fawn. Parasitic in hermit-crabs, esp *Pagurus bernhardus*; lower shore to sublittoral. T, ex nBaS. [12]

malacostracan *Nebalia bipes* NEBALIIDAE
BL < 1 cm. Carapace rounded, inflated,
with prominent rostral spine between
stalked eyes; abdomen slender; white to
colourless. Amongst weeds, often on
surface of rock pools; middle to lower
shore. T, ex nBaS. [1]

isopod *Gnathia maxillaris* GNATHIIDAE
BL < 6 mm. Body narrow, oval; eyes
small, antennae tiny; ♀ with elongated
oval thoracic region and slender abdomen,
usually with mass of green eggs visible
through body wall, no jaws; ♂ with broad,
more obviously segmented thorax and
very large pair of jaws; pale grey. Under
stones, in crevices, amongst encrusting
organisms; middle shore to sublittoral. T,
ex nBaS. [♂ 2] [♀ 3]

isopod *Eurydice pulchra* CIROLANIDAE
BL ♂ < 8 mm (♀ smaller). Body broad,
oval, woodlouse-like; first antennae short,
2nd antennae long; breadth of abdominal
segments narrower than thoracic; telson

broad, triangular; pale grey. In pools and
sand; lower shore. T, ex nBaS. [4]

Gribble *Limnoria lignorum* LIMNORIIDAE
BL < 4 mm. Body narrow, oval, woodlouse-
like; antennae tiny; telson oval; greyish-
fawn. Bores into submerged wood; lower
shore to sublittoral. T, ex nBaS. [5]

isopod *Sphaeroma rugicauda* SPHAERO-
MIDAE BL < 1 cm. Body broad, oval,
woodlouse-like, rolling readily into ball
when disturbed; antennae short, 2nd pair
longer than first; telson triangular, broad,
tail-limbs broad, leaf-like; greyish-white,
often with reddish tint on abdomen. In
estuarine and salt-marsh pools, swimming
on back; middle to lower shore. T, ex
nBaS. [6]

isopod *Dynamene bidentata* SPHAEROMIDAE
BL < 5 mm. As *Sphaeroma rugicauda* but
does not roll into ball when disturbed; ♂
with 2 conspicuous curved horn-like
projections from last limb-bearing
segment, bluish-grey with reddish

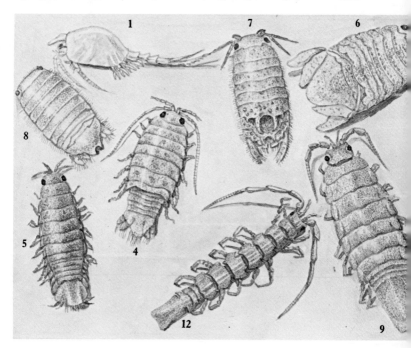

markings; ♀ with broad triangular telson deeply notched at tip; reddish. Under stones, amongst weeds; middle shore to sublittoral. Br, Ir, Fr. [♂ 7] [♀ 8]

isopod *Idotea baltica* IDOTEIDAE BL <3 cm. Body elongated, oval, somewhat flattened; telson long with median point flanked by angular 'shoulders'; 2nd antennae no more than ⅕ body-length; colour variable, usually reddish-brown or green. Amongst weeds; lower shore to sublittoral. T, ex nBaS. [9]

isopod *Idotea neglecta* IDOTEIDAE BL <1·5 cm. As *Idotea baltica*, but 'shoulders' of telson rounded, sloping. In brackish localities, estuaries; upper shore. T. [10]

isopod *Idotea granulosa* IDOTEIDAE BL <2 cm. As *Idotea baltica*, but telson long and narrow, median spine long, pointed, 'shoulders' rounded. Amongst weeds; middle to lower shore. T, ex nBaS. [11]

isopod *Idotea linearis* IDOTEIDAE BL <4 cm. Body slender, elongated; segments rounded; antennae long, at least ½ body-length; eyes small; telson rectangular with straight margin; brown or green with pale longitudinal stripes. Amongst weeds; sublittoral. Br, Fr, De. [12]

isopod *Jaera albifrons* JANIRIDAE BL ♀ <5 mm (♂ smaller). Body woodlouse-like; segments clearly separated at their margins; first antennae very short, 2nd antennae long; telson shield-shaped; ♂ broadens posteriorly; greyish-fawn. Under stones; upper to lower shore. T, ex nBaS. [13]

Sea-slater *Ligia oceanica* LIGIIDAE BL <4 cm. Body typically woodlouse-like, flattened, broad; first antennae much reduced, 2nd antennae conspicuous, stout; tail-limbs narrow, clearly divided into 2 finger-like sections; greyish-brown. Under stones and weed, in crevices, hiding during day; upper shore. T, ex nBaS. [14]

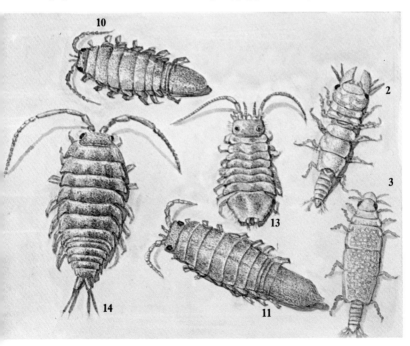

amphipod *Gammarus locusta* GAMMARIDAE BL <2 cm. Body laterally flattened, curved; antennae of nearly equal, moderate length; upper antennae with small branch; appendages of telson and last 3 segments divided into 2; limbs increase in length towards posterior; greenish-brown. Under stones; middle to lower shore. T, ex nBaS. [1] *G. duebeni, G. chevreuxi* and *G. zaddachi* distinguishable from *G. locusta* only with great difficulty; occur chiefly in estuarine conditions.

amphipod *Amphithoe rubricata* AMPHITHOIDAE BL <1·3 cm. As *Gammarus locusta*, but upper antennae rather longer than lower and without branch; colour variable, matching background. Amongst weeds, under stones; middle to lower shore. T, ex nBaS. [2]

sand-hopper *Talitrus saltator* TALITRIDAE BL <1·6 cm. As *Gammarus locusta*, but upper antennae much shorter than lower and without branch; tips of lower antennae of many small segments; grey-green or greenish-fawn with longitudinal dark stripe. In sand, under rotting weeds; upper shore. T, ex nBaS. [3]

sand-hopper *Orchestia gammarella* TALITRIDAE BL <2 cm. As *Gammarus locusta*, but upper antennae much shorter than lower and without branch; tips of lower antennae of many small segments; 3rd limbs terminate in large claw; greenish-brown with red markings. Under stones, amongst weed; upper to middle shore. T, ex nBaS. [4]

amphipod *Jassa falcata* ISCHYROCERIDAE BL <8 mm. As *Gammarus locusta*, but upper antennae lack branch, are shorter than stouter lower antennae; 2nd limbs with large curved pincer, different on ♂ and ♀; colour variable. Amongst weeds, often on buoys, floating objects; lower shore to sublittoral. T, ex nBaS. [♂ 5] [♀ 6]

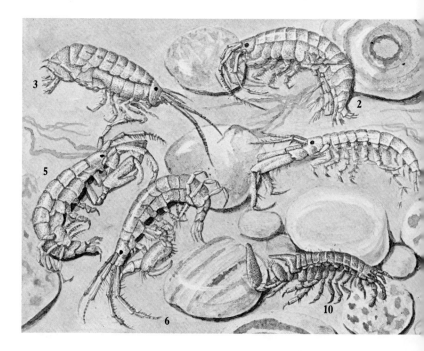

amphipod *Bathyporeia pelagica*
HAUSTORIIDAE BL <5 mm. As *Gammarus
locusta*, but upper antennae with
conspicuous basal joints and very short
branch, lower antennae much longer than
upper, esp on ♂; colourless, translucent;
eyes red. In sand; middle to lower shore.
T, ex nBaS. [7]

amphipod *Haustorius arenarius*
HAUSTORIIDAE BL <1·5 cm. Body thick,
somewhat flattened; head small; antennae
equal, short, stout; limb-bases large, leaf-
like; sand-coloured. In sand; lower shore
to sublittoral. T, ex nBaS. [8]

amphipod *Corophium volutator* CORO-
PHIIDAE BL <1·5 cm. Body elongated,
flattened, oval in cross-section; upper
antennae slender, lack branch, lower
antennae almost body-length, very stout,
tapering from broad base; greyish. In U-
shaped burrows in mud, estuaries; middle
to lower shore. T, ex nBaS. [9] *C.
arenarium* (BL <6 mm) similar, but in sand;
lower shore. Br, Fr.

boring amphipod *Chelura terebrans*
CHELURIDAE BL <6 mm. Body not
flattened laterally; upper antennae with
tiny branch halfway along, lower antennae
longer, with flattened, hairy joints;
posterior segment with spine, telson
upright; last abdominal segments with
elongated paddle-shaped limbs; pale
brown. Burrows into submerged wood;
lower shore to sublittoral. T, ex nBaS. [10]

Ghost Shrimp *Caprella linearis*
CAPRELLIDAE BL <2 cm. Body elongated,
very thin, looks like knotted thread; head
triangular; upper antennae longer than
lower; forelimbs with pincers; 3 pairs of
walking hindlimbs; ♀ with brood-pouch
beneath 3rd and 4th segments; pale brown
or deep red. Amongst encrustations,
weeds; middle shore to sublittoral. T, ex
nBaS. [♀ 11] *Phtisica marina* (BL <1·5 cm)
similar, but 5 pairs of walking
limbs.

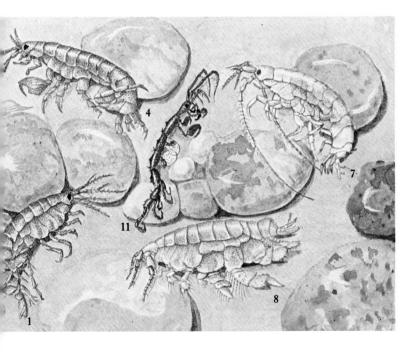

opossum-shrimp *Leptomysis gracilis*
MYSIDAE $<$1·3 cm. Body slender,
carapace scarcely broader than abdomen;
exoskeleton covered with tiny, rectangular
scales; antennae of equal length; rostrum
triangular; tail-fan with conspicuous,
round statocysts (organs sensing position of
shrimp in water); telson undivided at tip;
transparent, faintly tinged yellowish-red.
Amongst weed-bases; lower shore to
sublittoral. T, ex nBaS. [1]

Chameleon Shrimp *Praunus flexuosus*
MYSIDAE BL $<$2·5 cm. As *Leptomysis
gracilis*, but exoskeleton without scales;
telson V-notched at tip; transparent, but
able to change colour. In rock pools,
amongst eelgrasses; lower shore to
sublittoral. T, ex nBaS. [2]

opossum-shrimp *Siriella armata*
MYSIDAE BL $<$2 cm. As *Leptomysis
gracilis*, but carapace very short, leaving 3
thoracic segments uncovered; rostrum
very long, sharply pointed; transparent
with faint reddish tinge on abdomen. In
rock pools, amongst weeds; lower shore to
sublittoral. T, ex nBaS. [3]

Aesop Prawn *Pandalus montagui*
PANDALIDAE BL $<$4 cm. Elongated
abdomen, well-formed tail-fan; carapace
with long rostrum ending in 2 small teeth,
upper margin with 10–12 teeth, lower
margin with 5–6 teeth; inner antennae
scarcely longer than rostrum, outer
antennae almost as long as body; 2nd
walking limbs with small pincer; semi-
transparent, reddish-grey with darker
markings. Amongst weeds in pools and at
water's edge; lower shore. T, ex nBaS [4]

Common Prawn *Palaemon serratus*
PALAEMONIDAE BL $<$6·5 cm. As *Pandalus
montagui*, but rostrum with 6–8 teeth on
upper margin, 2 at tip and 4–5 on lower
margin; first and 2nd walking limbs with
pincers, larger in 2nd; semi-transparent,
pale grey with lilac dots and lines. Br, Ir,
Fr. [5] *Palaemon elegans* (BL $<$5 cm)
similar, but rostrum with 7–10 teeth on
upper margin, 1 at tip, 3 on lower margin.
T, ex nBaS. [6]

Chameleon Prawn *Hippolyte varians*
HIPPOLYTIDAE BL $<$2·5 cm. As *Palaemon
serratus*, but inner antennae scarcely longer
than rostrum; rostrum with 2 widely-
separated teeth on upper margin, 1 at tip
and 2 on lower margin; abdomen sharply
humped; colour varies with time of day,
reddish-brown or green in daylight,
transparent blue by night. Amongst weeds;
lower shore to sublittoral. T, ex nBaS. [7]
H. prideauxiana (BL $<$4 cm) similar, but
rostrum with no teeth on upper margin, 1
at tip and 2 on lower margin. Amongst
weeds, eelgrasses; lower shore to
sublittoral. Br, Ir, Fr.

prawn *Palaemonetes varians* PALAEMONIDAE
BL $<$2·5 cm. As *Pandalus montagui*, but
rostrum with 4–6 teeth on upper margin,
2 at tip and 2 (rarely 1) on lower margin;
first and 2nd walking limbs with pincers,
larger in 2nd; semi-transparent with
brownish-orange lines and dots. In
brackish pools. Only in south? [8]

snapping prawn *Alpheus glaber*
ALPHEIDAE BL $<$4 cm. As *Pandalus montagui*, but inner antennae short, outer
antennae equal body-length; rostrum
smooth, pointed, no teeth; pincers of first
walking limbs large, modified joints make
snapping sound; pinkish-red. Amongst
weeds in muddy habitats; sublittoral,
sometimes lower shore. Br, Ir, Fr. [9]

snapping prawn *Athanas nitescens*
ALPHEIDAE BL $<$3 cm. As *Pandalus
montagui*, but both pairs of antennae of
moderate length; rostrum smooth,
pointed, no teeth; pincers of first walking
limbs large; pink or reddish, with white
dorsal stripe. Amongst weeds; lower shore
to sublittoral. T, ex nBaS. [10]

Common Shrimp *Crangon crangon*
CRANGONIDAE BL $<$5 cm. As *Pandalus
montagui*, but inner antennae short;
rostrum merely point at front of carapace;
carapace with 1 central and 2 lateral
spines; large pincer on first walking limbs
different from that of prawns, tiny pincer
on 2nd; brown or grey with red dots. In
sandy localities, often in pools; lower
shore to sublittoral. T, ex nBaS. [11]

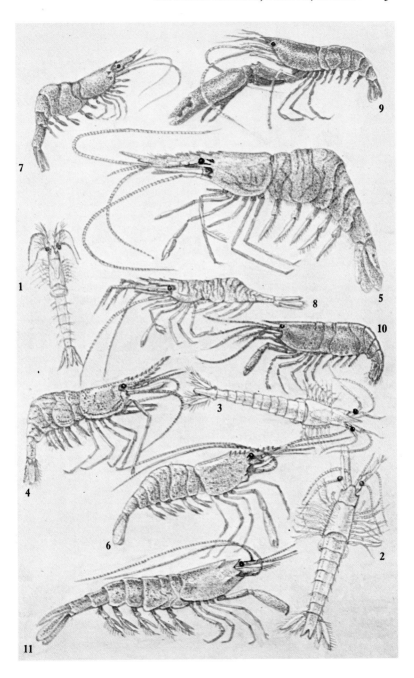

Spiny Lobster, Crawfish *Palinurus elephas* PALINURIDAE BL < 50 cm. Lacks pincers except 5th pair on ♀; outer antennae longer than body, whip-like, strong, basal regions very spiny; carapace box-like, spiny; margins of abdominal segments sharply pointed; shades of brown or rust. In sheltered places; sublittoral. Br, Ir, Fr. [♂ 1]

Common Lobster *Homarus gammarus* NEPHROPSIDAE BL < 50 cm. Body broad, slightly flattened; inner antennae short, outer antennae longer than body; pincers of first walking limbs massive, those of 2nd and 3rd small; blue with reddish touches. In sheltered places, caves, crevices; sublittoral. T, ex nBaS. [2]

Norway Lobster, Scampo, Dublin Bay Prawn *Nephrops norvegicus* NEPHROPSIDAE BL < 30 cm. As *Homarus gammarus*, but more slender; pincers of first walking limbs sculptured; sandy-red. On mud, sand; sublittoral. T, ex nBaS. [3]

squat-lobster *Galathea squamifera* GALATHEIDAE BL < 5 cm. Abdomen permanently carried tucked under thorax; first walking limbs scaly, first with elongated pincers, 5th reduced; rostrum triangular, pointed, with 4 teeth on each lateral margin, the posterior pair smallest; green-brown or blue-brown, sometimes with red flecks. Under boulders; lower shore to sublittoral. T, ex nBaS. [4]

squat-lobster *Galathea strigosa* GALATHEIDAE BL < 15 cm. As *Galathea squamifera*, but rostrum with 3 teeth on each lateral margin; brick or bright red with bright blue transverse bands. [5]

Long-clawed Porcelain-crab *Porcellana longicornis* PORCELLANIDAE BL < 2 cm. Body rounded; eyes tiny; antennae long; first walking limbs with long slender pincers, 2nd, 3rd and 4th with terminal claw, 5th very reduced; hairless, glossy; brown, sometimes with lighter markings. Under stones; lower shore to sublittoral. T, ex nBaS. [6] Broad-clawed porcelain-crab *P. platycheles* (BL < 3·5 cm) similar,

but more massive; pincers broad, flattened, very hairy; greyish-brown with red tints. [7]

burrowing prawn *Callianassa subterranea* CALLIANASSIDAE BL < 4 cm. Abdomen slender, broadening toward spreading tail-fan; rostrum very reduced; first walking limbs with pincers of unequal size, curved hook on 3rd joint; remaining legs end in claws, sometimes paddle-shaped; reddish-orange. Burrows in mud; lower shore to sublittoral. T, ex nBaS. [8]

burrowing prawn *Upogebia deltaura* CALLIANASSIDAE BL < 10 cm. Carapace rather thin-walled; abdomen slender, tail-fan large, spreading; rostrum with conspicuous tubercles in lines; eyes small; first walking limbs with pincers of equal size, moving finger longer than fixed one; greyish-fawn or pink, with green tints. Burrows in mud beneath stones; lower shore to sublittoral. T, ex nBaS. [9] *U. stellata* similar, but moving finger of pincers twice length of fixed one.

Common Hermit-crab *Pagurus bernhardus* PAGURIDAE BL < 10 cm. Pincers massive, sculptured with coarse, granular tubercles, right pincer larger than left; 2nd and 3rd walking limbs spiny, clawed, 4th and 5th very reduced; shades of red, orange, yellow, greyish-white, abdomen darker. In gastropod shells, large individuals in *Buccinum undatum*; lower shore to sublittoral. T, ex nBaS. [10]

hermit-crab *Pagurus prideauxi* PAGURIDAE BL < 6 cm. As *Pagurus bernhardus*, but granulations on pincers more delicate, more scattered; 2nd and 3rd walking limbs ridged but not spiny; reddish-brown. In gastropod shells, often with strawberry anemone *Adamsia palliata*. Usually sublittoral. T, ex nBaS. [11]

hermit-crab *Anapagurus laevis* PAGURIDAE BL < 2 cm. As *Pagurus bernhardus*, but pincers slender, delicate, right pincer much larger than left, delicately granulated; 2nd and 3rd walking limbs slender; white with cream touches. Lower shore. T, ex nBaS. [12]

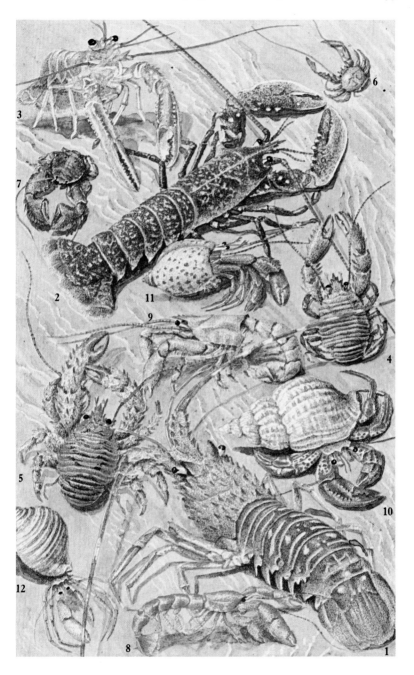

Masked Crab *Corystes cassivelaunus*
CORYSTIDAE L <4 cm (carapace). Carapace
oval, longer than broad, anterior margin
with 2 spines on each side of eyes, 2 blunt
projections between them; first walking
limbs very long with pincers; antennae
very long, hairy, together form a tube;
sand-coloured. Burrows into clean sand;
lower shore to sublittoral. T, ex nBaS. [1]

crab *Pirimela denticulata* PIRIMELIDAE
B <3·5 cm (carapace). Carapace almost
diamond shaped, anterior margin with 7
sharp teeth on each side of eyes, 3 teeth
between them, sometimes a few smaller
teeth; pincers small; sandy-fawn, often
blotched. Amongst stones, weed; lower
shore to sublittoral. T, ex nBaS. [2]

Edible Crab *Cancer pagurus* CANCRIDAE
B <25 cm (carapace). Carapace broader
than long, front margin like 'pie-crust', 3
blunt teeth between eyes; pincers massive;
brick red, tips of pincers dark brown or
black. In sheltered places, crevices; lower
shore to sublittoral. T, ex nBaS. [3]

Shore Crab *Carcinus maenas* PORTUNIDAE
B <10 cm (carapace). Carapace with
rounded front margin, 5 'saw' teeth on
each side of eyes, 3 blunt teeth between
them; first walking limbs with massive
pincers, others end in claws, claw on 5th
limb flattened; dark green, mottled black;
juv may be sand-coloured with darker
patterns. Amongst weeds; middle shore to
lower shore. T, ex nBaS. [4]

Velvet Swimming-crab *Macropipus
puber* PORTUNIDAE B <12 cm (carapace).
As *Carcinus maenas*, but 8–10 teeth
between eyes; pincers grooved; 5th
walking limbs with oval paddle; covered
with short hair; dark brown with bright
blue bands, eyes red. Under stones; lower
shore to sublittoral. T, ex nBaS. [5]

Swimming-crab *Macropipus depurator*
PORTUNIDAE B <5 cm (carapace). As
Carcinus maenas, but 3 sharp teeth between
eyes; 5th walking limbs with oval paddle;
scaly. Pelagic, sometimes amongst stones;
lower shore to sublittoral. T, ex nBaS. [6]

crab *Xantho incisus* XANTHIDAE B <7 cm
(carapace). Carapace solid; anterior
margin with blunt projections; pincers
massive, tips chocolate-brown. Under
stones; lower shore to sublittoral. T, ex
nBaS. [7]

Hairy Crab *Pilumnus hirtellus* XANTHIDAE
B <4 cm (carapace). Carapace rounded,
solid, 5 teeth on each side of eyes, 2
flattish lobes between them; hairy, esp
when young; brown or reddish-brown,
tips of pincers chocolate-brown. Under
stones; lower shore to sublittoral. Br, Ir,
Fr. [8]

Pea Crab *Pinnotheres pisum* PINNOTHERIDAE
D <1·5 cm (carapace). Carapace almost
spherical, margins smooth; limbs
including pincers small, slender; looks
inflated; creamy-yellow, often with dark
yellow blotches, glossy. Within mantle
cavity of bivalve molluscs, often common
mussel *Mytilus edulis*. T, ex nBaS. [9]

Spiny Spider-crab *Maja squinado*
MAJIDAE L <30 cm (carapace). Carapace
pear-shaped, spiny; 2 spines between
eyes; first walking limbs long with
elongated pincers, remaining limbs long,
hairy; pink and terracotta. Amongst
stones, over sand; usually sublittoral. Br,
Ir, Fr. [10]

spider-crab *Inachus dorsettensis* MAJIDAE
L <3 cm (carapace). Carapace pear-
shaped, patterned with spines; 2
divergent spines between eyes; eyes
retractible into sockets; first walking limbs
with massive claws, 2nd limbs longest,
broader, hairy. Usually covered with weed
or sponge, amongst weeds; lower shore
to sublittoral. T, ex nBaS. [11]

spider-crab *Macropodia longirostris*
MAJIDAE L <2 cm (carapace). Carapace
pear-shaped, with short spines, 2 long
projections between eyes; eyes on stalks;
first walking limbs long, with slender
pincers, other limbs slender, spiny at
joints; reddish-fawn. Usually covered with
weed or sponge, amongst weeds; lower
shore to sublittoral. T, ex nBaS. [12]

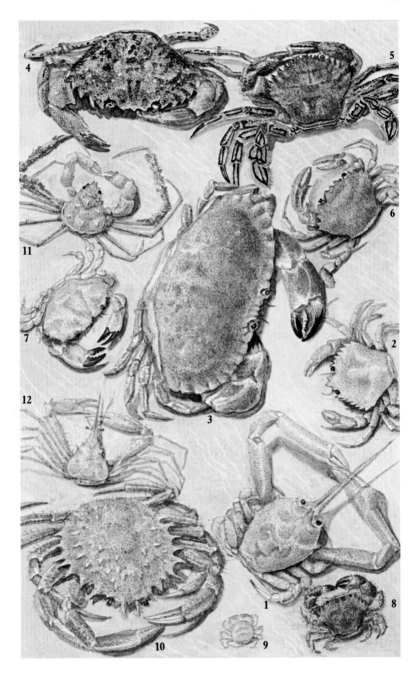

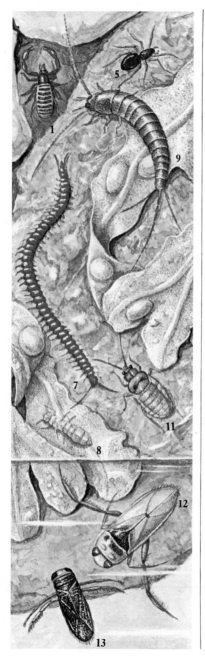

pseudoscorpion *Neobisium maritimum*
NEOBISIIDAE BL < 5 mm. Looks very much
like a scorpion without the long sting-
bearing tail-region; massive pair of
pincers; chestnut-brown, varnished
appearance; young olive-green. Feeds
largely on springtails. Tolerates tidal
floods. In deep narrow crevices; upper
shore. wBr, Ir, wFr. [1]

crab-spider *Tibellus maritimus* THOMISIDAE
BL 8–10 mm. Straw-coloured, sometimes
greyish, with darker central band and
spots on abdomen. On grasses around
sandhills, rough ground. Runs up grass
stems when disturbed and stops with
extended legs, thus becoming inconspicuous. T, ex Ic, Sw, No. [2] *T. oblongus*
similar, but more widespread. T, ex Ic.

wolf-spider *Pardosa purbeckensis*
LYCOSIDAE BL 6–9 mm. Dark brown,
white abdominal spots. Salt-marshes,
mud-flats, estuarine shores. Survives tidal
flooding by breathing air trapped in bubble
retained by hairy body. Br, Ir, De. [3]

wolf-spider *Arctosa perita* LYCOSIDAE
BL 6–9 mm. Mottled black, yellow and
red-brown with annulated legs. Sandy
places and heaths. Well camouflaged on
sand; lives in burrow, often active in
sunshine, May–Oct. T, ex Ic. [4]

money-spider *Erigone arctica* LINYPHI-
IDAE BL 2–3 mm. Small, blackish. Amongst
litter, seaweed and stones, by tidal
estuaries and on coasts. T, ex Cz. [5]
E. longipalpis similar; ubiquitous.

millipede *Schizophyllum sabulosum*
IULIDAE BL 15–47 mm. Orange-red dorsal
stripes distinctive. Usually in sandy soils,
in litter and under moss, but often feeds
on aerial vegetation; frequent in conifer
woods, coastal areas in old dunes. T, ex
Ic. [6]

centipede *Strigamia maritima* GEOPHILIDAE
BL 20–40 mm. Red. Active at night; has
been recorded feeding on barnacles and
periwinkles. In shingle, crevices, seaweed;
upper shore. T, ex Ic, Cz. [7]

springtail *Anurida maritima* COLLEMBOLA
BL <4 mm. Wingless insect; body
elongated, plump; head small with short
beaded antennae; bright blue-grey.
Scavenges in detritus. Floats on surface
of water in pools, crevices, dead barnacle
shells; upper to middle shore. T. [8]

bristletail *Petrobius maritimus* ARCHAE-
OGNATHA BL <15 mm. Wingless insect;
body elongated, tapering; antennae
slender, long; 3 posterior filaments, middle
one longest; sandy-grey. Feeds on lichen,
organic debris. In rocky fissures and
crevices; upper shore. T. [9]

bug *Halosalda lateralis* SALDIDAE BL <4
mm. Forewings brown with darker
markings; body covered with fine hairs.
Adults run rapidly, generally flightless.
Salt-marshes, often submerged by tide.
Feeds on various salt-marsh plants, esp
Chenopodiaceae. T, ex Ic, Cz, Po. [10]

marine bug *Aepophilus bonnairei*
SALDIDAE BL 2–3 cm. Forewings short,
abdomen exposed; all covered with fine
hairs. In cracks in rocks, amongst fully
marine animals. Hunts prey around
crevices at low water; middle shore. Br,
Ir, Fr. [11]

water-boatman, backswimmer
Notonecta marmorea NOTONECTIDAE
BL 13–15 mm. Legs fringed with hairs for
swimming, hindlegs longest. Swims under
water on back with legs uppermost in
rapid, rowing motion; surfaces with tip
of abdomen to take air; flies from pool to
pool. Adult can produce chirping sound.
Forelegs used to seize prey. Brackish
coastal pools. T, ex Ic, Cz, Fi, No. [12]

lesser water-boatman *Sigara stagnalis*
CORIXIDAE BL <6 mm. Humped body;
legs fringed with hairs, middle and hind
legs of equal length; forewings black,
mottled. Swims freely by rowing through
water, back upwards, legs below; surfaces
to take air, usually with head and thorax
uppermost. Adult can fly. Feeds on algae.
Brackish coastal pools. T, ex Ic, Cz, Fi,
No. [13]

Transparent Burnet *Zygaena purpuralis* ZYGAENIDAE WS 27–31 mm. Forewings blue with red markings. Caterpillar feeds on thyme. Cliffs. WE. [1]

plume-moth *Agdistis staticis* PTEROPHORIDAE WS 22–25 mm. Inconspicuous by day: rests with wings rolled up and pointing beyond head resembling blade of grass. Crepuscular. Green caterpillar feeds on sea-lavender; survives submergence. Cliffs, salt-marshes. WE. [2]

seaweed-fly *Ephydra riparia* EPHYDRIDAE BL 4–5 mm. Dark grey-brown with metallic blue or green sheen. Larva legless; lives on aquatic plants in brackish pools. Salt-marshes. WE, NE. [3]

kelp-fly *Coelopa frigida* COELOPIDAE BL 3–5 mm. Grey, hairy; legs hairy. In swarms near seaweed on strand-line; when disturbed, moves short distance in swarm, soon settling. Larva legless, in rotting seaweed. Upper shore. WE, rare NE. [4]

kelp-fly *Suillia ustulata* HELEOMYZIDAE BL 6–10 mm. Silvery-grey, hairy; translucent wings with row of small spines on front margin. On seaweed along strand-line. In swarms, at times abundant; often troublesome on beach, but non-biting; swift darting flight; flies only short distances when disturbed. Larva legless, feeds in rotting seaweed on strand-line; survives submergence by sea. Upper shore. WE, CE, rare NE. [5]

Red-banded Sand-wasp *Ammophila sabulosa* SPHECIDAE BL 20–23 mm. Narrow, long waist and front of abdomen. ♀ stings and immobilizes caterpillar, carries it to excavated burrow in sand; lays eggs on caterpillar; larva on hatching feeds on living but paralysed caterpillar. Sand-dunes. T, ex Ic. [6]

spider-wasp *Pompilius cinereus* POMPILIDAE BL 5–10 mm. Antennae slightly curled at tip; wings smoky esp at apex. ♀ hunts for spider on dunes; paralyses it with sting and places it in burrow; lays egg on living but immobile spider. Sand-dunes. T, ex Ic. [7]

leafcutter-bee *Megachile maritima* MEGACHILIDAE BL 13–16 mm. Resembles honeybee, ♂ with broad, yellow-tufted forelegs, ends of forelegs dilated, white, looking like glove; ♀ larger, without expanded forelegs, with pollen basket on underside. Burrows in sand, makes nest of leaf-fragments; larva feeds on stored pollen. Coastal, occasionally inland. WE, CE. [♀ 8]

rove-beetle *Bledius furcatus* STAPHYLINIDAE BL 5–7 mm. Thorax broader anteriorly. Flies freely in warm weather; locally gregarious. In damp sandy soil; feeds on algae. WE, rare Sw. [9]
Bledius arenaria (BL <3 mm) similar, but black with short red forewings. Coastal. WE, NE.

ground-beetle *Dyschirius obscurus* CARABIDAE BL 3–5 mm. Rounded thorax; legs and base of antennae darker. Burrows in sand; active in sunshine. Predatory on shore beetles, esp *Bledius*. Sandy shores. WE, local NE, rare No. [10]

ground-beetle *Pogonus chalceus* CARABIDAE BL 4–6 mm. Black with usually purplish sheen; antennae black; thorax with prominent groove in mid-line. Predatory; hunts under seaweed, esp at strand-line. Br, WE. [11]

dune cockchafer *Euchlora dubia* SCARABAEIDAE BL 8–15 mm. Short antennae with fanned end; forewings reddish-brown with thin black lines. Feeds on rotting vegetation; ♂ flies freely, swarms; ♀ stays on sand. Larva feeds on roots. Sand-dunes. T, ex Ic, but rare No. [12]

weevil *Apion limonii* CURCULIONIDAE BL 3–4 mm. Forewings broad compared with narrow head and thorax; head elongated between eyes; colour variable, forewings with black lines; black spot on thorax. Diurnal, summer. Feeds on decaying sea-lavender. Salt-marshes. Br, Fr, Be, Ne, De. [13]

Arrow-worms (Chaetognatha). Elongated, narrow, with lateral- and tail-fins; head bears curved spines, those near mouth catch prey.

arrow-worm *Spadella cephaloptera*
SAGITTIDAE L <8 mm. Body elongated, flattened; head rounded with fans of curved spines; finely papillate attachment organ on ventral side; tail-fin triangular; transparent, colourless. Amongst encrusting organisms; middle to lower shore. T, ex nBaS. [1] *Sagitta* (L <2 cm) more slender; planktonic.

Starfish, sea-urchins, sea-cucumbers (Echinodermata). Radially symmetrical; no identifiable head-region; body-wall has weak muscles, but well-developed, calcareous internal skeleton bears moveable spines and other structures, is penetrated by hydraulically controlled tube-feet; sea-urchins have round, shell-like skeleton, the test. Starfish pull bivalves apart by clamping tube-feet on to each valve; eversible suctorial pharynx digests soft bivalve body. Brittle-stars and feather-stars trap suspended particles in mucus, then waft them towards the mouth by cilia on the arms. Sea-urchins rasp encrusting organisms from rocks, using complex jaws. Sea-cucumbers trap food in mucus on modified tube-feet around mouth.

sand-burrowing starfish *Astropecten irregularis* ASTROPECTINIDAE LS <12 cm. 5 stiff arms fringed with spiny plates in 2 layers; rather flattened except for centre of disc; pink, brick-red or brownish above, pale below. Burrows in sand; lower shore to sublittoral. T, ex nBaS. [2]

starfish *Luidia ciliaris* LUIDIIDAE LS <45 cm. 7 rather broad flattened arms; tube-feet slightly knobbed at tips; orange above, creamy-white below. On sand, under weeds; lowest shore to sublittoral.

T, ex nBaS. [3] *L. sarsi* (LS <20 cm) similar but with 5 arms; shades of yellowish-brown or red above, pale below. On mud and sand; sublittoral. T, ex nBaS. [4]

Cushion Star *Asterina gibbosa* ASTERINIDAE LS <6 cm. Stubby, rather rounded arms; thick, leathery, tough; shades of sandy-fawn or greyish-green above, pale below. Under boulders; lower shore to sublittoral. Br, Ir, Fr. [5]

Common Sunstar *Crossaster papposus* SOLASTERIDAE LS <25 cm. Circular in outline, central disc large, with 8–13 rather short arms; spiny; shades of red, orange and brown, often with white markings. On sand and gravel, on shellfish beds; sublittoral. T, ex nBaS. [6]

Purple Sunstar *Solaster endeca* SOLASTERIDAE LS <30 cm. 7–13 thick, rounded, stiff arms; minutely spiny; purple shading to orange above, pale orange below. In rocky areas; sublittoral. T, ex nBaS. [7]

purple starfish *Henricia oculata* ECHINASTERIDAE LS <15 cm. Central disc small, with 5 thick arms round in cross-section; leathery, stiff; port-wine colour or purplish. Amongst rocks; lower shore to sublittoral. T, ex nBaS. [8]

Common Starfish *Asterias rubens* ASTERIIDAE LS <25 cm. Thick fleshy tapering arms; upper surface with blunt spines; shades of yellow to orange-brown above, pale below. Amongst rocks, lower shore to sublittoral. T, ex nBaS. [9]

Spiny Starfish *Marthasterias glacialis* ASTERIIDAE LS <30 cm. 5 long, stiff, very spiny arms; pale grey with touches of clear blue and bright purple above, pale yellow below. Amongst boulders; lower shore to sublittoral. T, ex nBaS. [10]

Common Brittle-star *Ophiothrix fragilis*
OPHIOTHRICHIDAE D <2 cm (disc). Disc
pentagonal, with 5 brittle arms bordered
with conspicuous spines; colour variable,
shades of brownish-red to brownish-
purple or fawn, often patterned. Under
boulders; middle shore to sublittoral. T,
ex nBaS. [1]

brittle-star *Ophiocomina nigra* OPHIO-
COMIDAE D <3 cm (disc). Disc almost
round, with 5 tapering, fairly flexible arms;
surface spines very tiny, feel velvety; may
be pinkish-brown, more usually mat
black. Under boulders; lower shore to
sublittoral. T, ex nBaS. [2]

burrowing brittle-star *Acrocnida
brachiata* AMPHIURIDAE D <1 cm (disc).
Disc pentagonal, with long, very flexible
arms; sandy-fawn. Burrows in sand; lower
shore to sublittoral. T, ex nBaS. [3]

brittle-star *Amphipholis squamata*
AMPHIURIDAE D <5 mm (disc). Disc
rounded, with 5 slender, delicate arms,
pair of plates on disc surface at base of
each arm; pale, off-white or fawn. Under
stones, amongst encrusting algae; lower
shore to sublittoral. T, ex nBaS. [4]

brittle-star *Ophiura texturata* OPHIO-
LEPIDAE D <3 cm (disc). Disc pentagonal,
thick, with stout, tapering arms, pair of
plates on disc surface at base of each arm;
reddish-brown, sometimes tinted purple.
Burrows in sand; lower shore to sublittoral.
T, ex nBaS. [5]

Rock-urchin *Paracentrotus lividus*
ECHINIDAE D <6 cm. Body somewhat
flattened; spines numerous, <3 cm; test
delicately grooved, with very fine,
transverse markings in grooves; test green,
spines dark brown, sometimes appearing
black, with dark green tints. Amongst
rocks, often bores into them; lower shore
to sublittoral. Br, Ir, Fr. [6]

Green Sea-urchin *Psammechinus
miliaris* ECHINIDAE D <5 cm. As
Paracentrotus lividus, but spines <1·5 cm;
test delicately grooved, with very fine
granules in grooves; test greenish, spines
violet, esp at tips. Under stones, amongst
encrusting organisms; lower shore to
sublittoral. T, ex nBaS. [7]

sea-urchin *Strongylocentrotus droebachiensis* ECHINIDAE D <5 cm. As
Paracentrotus lividus, but spines <2 cm
thick; test with pronounced grooves and
coarser markings; test green, spines dark
greenish-brown. On rocks, amongst weeds,
sometimes bores into rocks; probably only
sublittoral. T, ex nBaS. [8]

Edible Sea-urchin *Echinus esculentus*
ECHINIDAE D <15 cm. Body slightly
conical; spines < 1·5 cm; tube-feet long;
test reddish-brown, spines purple.
Amongst weed-covered rocks; lower
shore to sublittoral. T, ex nBaS. [9]

Pea-urchin *Echinocyamus pusillus*
FIBULARIIDAE L <1·5 cm. Body egg-
shaped in outline, flattened; spines very
short, numerous; test and spines pale
greenish-grey. Burrows in sand; lower
shore to sublittoral. T, ex nBaS. [10]

Purple Heart-urchin *Spatangus
purpureus* SPATANGIDAE L <12 cm. Body
heart-shaped, flattened; spines numerous,
relatively short, fewer and longer on
dorsal surface; test grey-purple, spines
rich purple. Burrows in sand; lower shore
to sublittoral. T, ex nBaS. [11]

Sea-potato *Echinocardium cordatum*
SPATANGIDAE L <9 cm. Body heart-
shaped, slightly flattened; spines
numerous, relatively short, on underside
longer, flattened, spoon-shaped; test
and spines sandy-fawn. Burrows in sand;
lower shore to sublittoral. T, ex nBaS.
[12]

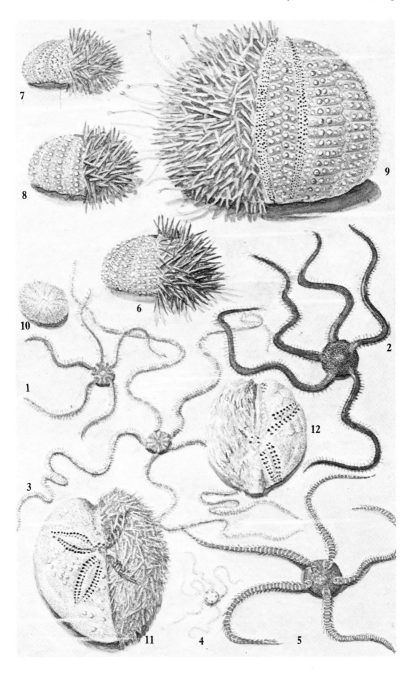

Cotton-spinner *Holothuria forskali*
HOLOTHURIIDAE BL <25 cm. Body thick,
cucumber-shaped; well-spaced, pointed
warts dorsally, 3 rows of tube-feet
ventrally; 20 feathery modified tube-
feet surround mouth; skin clammy,
slimy, slightly sticky; ejects long, sticky
threads from posterior when irritated;
brown-black above, yellowish below.
Amongst rocks, weeds; lower shore to
sublittoral. Br, Ir, Fr. [1]

Sea-gherkin *Pawsonia saxicola*
CUCUMARIIDAE BL <10 cm. Body
cylindrical; 5 distinct rows of tube-feet, 2
single, slightly zigzag rows dorsally, 3
straight, double rows ventrally; 10
branched, modified tube-feet surround
mouth; skin thin, smooth; white,
sometimes yellowish, branched tube-feet
greyish-brown. Under stones; lower shore
to sublittoral. Br, Ir, Fr. [2]

sea-cucumber *Aslia lefevrei* CUCUMARIIDAE
BL <11 cm. As *Pawsonia saxicola*, but all
tube-feet in double rows; skin thick, leathery, wrinkled; brownish-grey, darkens on
exposure to light. Under stones; lower
shore to sublittoral. Br, Ir, Fr. [3]

sea-cucumber *Ocnus lactea* CUCUMARIIDAE
BL <4 cm. As *Pawsonia saxicola*, but
with few tube-feet; skin thick, leathery,
smooth; off-white or pinkish-brown,
branched tube-feet white. Under stones;
lower shore to sublittoral. Br, Ir, Fr. [4]

sea-cucumber *Leptopentacta elongata*
CUCUMARIIDAE BL <15 cm. As *Pawsonia
saxicola*, but body tapers toward posterior;
all tube-feet in double rows; skin leathery,
tough; off-white or shades of brown. On
mud; sublittoral. T, ex nBaS. [5]

sea-cucumber *Thyone fusus* CUCUMARIIDAE
BL <20 cm. Body oval in cross-section,
plump, tapering at both ends; tube-feet
irregularly scattered over surface; 10
branched, modified tube-feet surround
mouth; off-white, dirty pink or pale
brown. On sand, mud; sublittoral. T, ex
nBaS. [6]

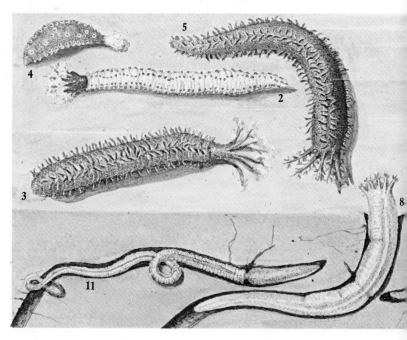

sea-cucumber *Leptosynapta inhaerens* SYNAPTIDAE BL <18 cm. Body cylindrical; no tube-feet except for 12 minutely branched ones surrounding mouth; skin semi-transparent, gut contents visible (looks like polythene tube full of sand); anchor-shaped plates in skin make it adhesive when touched; colourless or very pale pinkish-yellow. Burrows in sand, mud; lower shore. T, ex nBaS. [7]

sea-cucumber *Labidoplax digitata* SYNAPTIDAE BL <18 cm. As *Leptosynapta inhaerens*, but tube-feet surrounding mouth each have 4 stubby, finger-like branches. Br, Ir, Fr. [8]

Feather-star *Antedon bifida* ANTEDONIDAE LS <15 cm. Central disc small; 5 pairs of feathery arms; short processes on underside of disc for temporary attachment; form only clearly visible when in water, resembles tangle of knotted string when out of water; brick-red, sometimes brownish and banded white. On rocks, in shelter; lower shore to sublittoral. T, ex nBaS. [9]

Acornworms (Hemichordata). Worm-like, but body divided into 3 regions: globular or tapering proboscis (acorn), collar partially surrounding mouth, elongated trunk often penetrated by respiratory gill-openings. Cilia on proboscis and copious mucus trap microscopic particles.

acornworm *Glossobalanus sarniensis* PTYCHODERIDAE BL <20 cm. Proboscis yellow-orange, remainder pale yellow. Burrows in sand; lower shore to sublittoral. Br, Ir, Fr. [10]

acornworm *Saccoglossus ruber* GLANDICIPITIDAE BL <15 cm. As *Glossobalanus sarniensis*, but proboscis very long, tapered, rose or orange-pink, trunk cylindrical, tapering, greyish-brown. Br, Ir. [11] *S. horsti* (BL <15 cm) similar, but proboscis cream-coloured, remainder pink or orange-pink. Br, Fr.

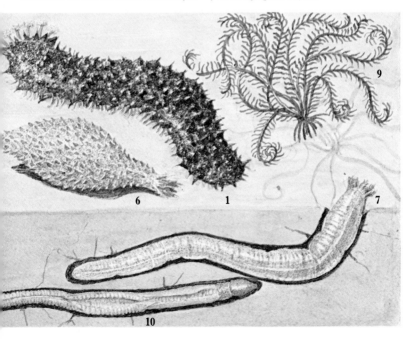

Sea-squirts (Ascidiacea). Perforated sac-like pharynx with ciliated surface, draw in large volumes of water, strain food and trap it in mucus. Body encased in rubbery sleeve (test) with inhalent and exhalent siphons. Solitary or colonial.

sea-squirt *Clavelina lepadiformis* CLAVELINIDAE H <2 cm. Vase-shaped, with inhalent and exhalent siphons at top; root-like structure connects individuals in colony; test transparent, glassy, internal organs yellow, pink, white. On solid objects; lower shore to sublittoral. T, ex nBaS. [1]

sea-squirt *Aplidium proliferum* POLY-CLINIDAE H <5 cm (colony). Gelatinous, club-shaped growths; individual animals visible at tips where orange-red siphons clustered around common orifice; orange-yellow. On solid objects, weeds; lower shore to sublittoral. T, ex nBaS. [2]

sea-squirt *Ciona intestinalis* CIONIDAE H <12 cm. Cylindrical, with distinct, tubular siphons; internal organs and muscle-bands visible; highly contractile; test pale greenish-white, siphons with clear, orange spots. On solid objects; lower shore to sublittoral. T, ex nBaS. [3]

sea-squirt *Ascidia mentula* ASCIDIIDAE H <10 cm. Upright, plump; test leathery, wrinkled; inhalent siphon at top, exhalent siphon $c\frac{1}{2}$ way up body; test opaque, greyish-white. On stones; lower shore to sublittoral. T, ex nBaS. [4]

sea-squirt *Ascidiella aspersa* ASCIDIIDAE H <12 cm. Upright, plump, but slightly flattened; inhalent siphon at top, exhalent siphon $c\frac{2}{3}$ way up body; test leathery, rough, opaque; brownish-grey. On solid objects, sometimes in mud; lower shore to sublittoral. T, ex nBaS. [5]

sea-squirt *Styela plicata* STYELIDAE H <12 cm. Upright, slender, broadening from narrow base; test tough, leathery, with longitudinal creases; light brown, siphons rosy-purple. On solid objects; lower shore to sublittoral. Br, Ir, Fr. [6]

sea-squirt *Dendrodoa grossularia* STYELIDAE H <2·5 cm. Rounded, compact, sometimes slightly flattened; test tough, smooth; many individuals occur clustered together; brick-red. Under stones, in shelter; lower shore to sublittoral. T, ex nBaS. [7]

Star Ascidian *Botryllus schlosseri* STYELIDAE. Elongated individual animals, embedded in encrusting, thick, gelatinous test, grouped around central, common orifices; colour variable, test and individual animals contrasting. On stones; middle shore to sublittoral. T, ex nBaS. [8] *Botrylloides leachi* similar, but individual animals arranged along elongated, common orifices which are often much-branched. [9]

Lancelets (Cephalochordata). Fish-like but lack jaws and gills. Conspicuous notochord (precursor of vertebrate backbone) runs length of body. Feed by filtering water sucked in through perforated pharynx.

Amphioxus, Lancelet *Branchiostoma lanceolatum* BRANCHIOSTOMIIDAE L <6 cm. Head with fringe of curved cirri; muscles in V-shaped blocks visible through body-wall; more-or-less transparent, slightly iridescent. Burrows in gravelly sand; lower shore to sublittoral. T, ex nBaS. [10]

Lamprey *Petromyzon marinus* PETRO-
MYZONIDAE BL <91 cm. Snake-like body,
sucker disc large, teeth in radiating rows,
large sharp teeth in front; dorsal fins
separate. Yellow-brown with heavy, black
mottling. Spawns in rivers, migrates to
sea aged 4–6 years. Feeds on bony fishes,
sucking blood from wound bored in flesh
of *eg* shads, cod, haddock, salmon. T, ex
BaS; in rivers T, ex Ic, Po, Fi. [1]

Dogfish *Scyliorhinus canicula* SCYLIO-
RHINIDAE BL <100 cm. Slender body;
dorsal fins far down back, the first behind
level of pelvic fins; nostril flaps almost
meet in mid-line. Sandy-brown above,
cream with small dark spots below. Sandy
and gravel bottoms, 3–110 m. Lays eggs
in elongated brown cases, mainly Jul–
Nov. Feeds on crabs, prawns, whelks,
worms. T, ex BaS, Ic, nNo. [2]

Basking Shark *Cetorhinus maximus*
CETORHINIDAE BL <11 m. Deep body,
with 5 gill slits running from back to
throat. Dark grey-brown above with
irregular darker blotches; greyish below.
Often seen swimming slowly at surface
whilst feeding on plankton. Seen mostly
May–Nov, possibly migrates S in Nov.
Live-bearing. T, ex BaS [3].

Spur-dog *Squalus acanthias* SQUALIDAE
BL <120 cm. Slender, smooth-skinned
shark with long spine in front of dorsal
fins; no anal fin. Dark grey above with
white spots on back and sides; pale grey
below. Abundant in schools, often single-
sexed, over soft bottoms, 10–200 m. Live-
bearing; in litters of 3–11. Feeds on mid-
water and bottom-living fish, squids. T,
ex BaS. [4]

Roker *Raja clavata* RAJIDAE BL <85 cm.
Right-angled 'wings', short snout and
dense prickles on back; mature ♀ esp has
broad-based spines above and below.
Variable colour, warm brown above with
cream blotches and black spots. On all
types of bottom, 10–60 m. Feeds on
crustaceans, fish. Commonest shallow-
water ray. T, ex BaS, nNo, but rare Ic. [5]

Small-eyed Ray *Raja microocellata*
RAJIDAE BL <82 cm. Right-angled 'wings',
short snout; eyes small; prickles on front
half of body only; spines on tail
numerous and bent. Medium brown on
back with thick, cream-coloured streaks
running parallel to edges of body. Locally
abundant on sandy grounds, 5–100 m.
Atlantic coasts of Br, Ir, Fr. [6]

Blonde Ray *Raja brachyura* RAJIDAE
BL <113 cm. Right-angled 'wings', short
snout; eyes large; prickles cover entire
back of adult, but strong spines only
along mid-line of tail. Light brown above
with creamy blotches, dense dark spots to
edges of body. Sandy bottoms, 10–100 m.
Feeds on crustaceans, fish. Br, Ir, Fr,
rare Be, Ne. [7]

Sting Ray *Dasyatis pastinaca* DASYATIDAE
BL <140 cm. Rounded 'wings', long whip-
like tail, no dorsal fin but 1 (rarely 2–3)
strong, serrated spine near base of tail.
Olive- or dark-brown above, white with
grey edges below. Common on sandy or
muddy bottoms, 3–70 m. Feeds on
molluscs, crustaceans (mainly crabs).
Jun–Nov. Br, Ir, Fr (common), Be, Ne,
De, Sw ex BaS. [8]

Eel *Anguilla anguilla* ANGUILLIDAE BL ♀
<1 m, ♂ <50 cm. Slender body; lower
jaw protrudes; pectoral fins rounded;
dorsal fin origin closer to anus than gill
opening. Greeny-brown to black above,
golden-yellow to silvery below. Common
in estuaries, on sea coasts; juvs reach river
mouths in spring from mid-Atlantic
spawning grounds. T, ex nIc, SC, (eGe,
Po). [9]

Conger *Conger conger* CONGRIDAE BL <274
cm. Thickset eel with upper jaw
protruding; pectoral fins pointed; dorsal
fin origin above tip of pectoral fin. Dull
brown above, golden or creamy below; in
deep water greyish. Abundant in rocky
areas, around wrecks, harbour walls, lower
shore to 100 m. Spawns in deep,
subtropical Atlantic. Feeds mainly on
crabs, octopuses. Br, Ir, Fr, occasional Be,
Ne, De, sNo. [10]

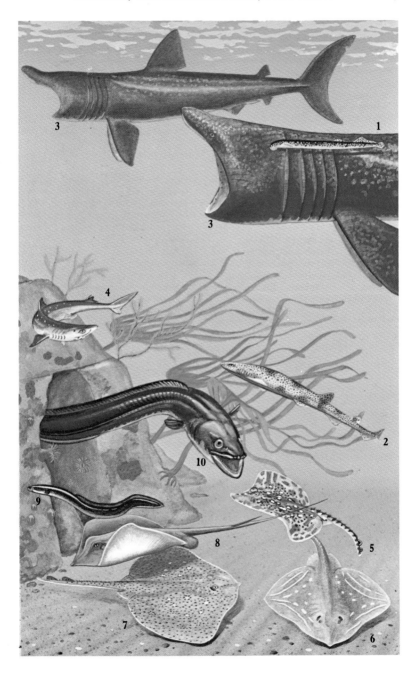

Pilchard *Sardina pilchardus* CLUPEIDAE
BL <25 cm. Herring-like, but with large, easily detached scales; rounded belly; ridges radiating from eye over gill covers. Blue-green above, shading to gold on sides. Common in schools near surface, mainly offshore. Spawns spring, summer. Feeds on plankton. T, ex BaS, Ic, nNo, but rare De, Sw, sNo. [1]

Sprat *Sprattus sprattus* CLUPEIDAE BL <16·5 cm. Herring-like with sharp, toothed keel from throat along belly. Dark green above, shading to silver on sides, golden on cheeks. Abundant in schools in estuaries and inshore waters, near surface. Spawns in spring, summer. T, ex Ic. [2]

Sea Trout *Salmo trutta* SALMONIDAE
BL <140 cm. Migratory form of freshwater brown trout, common in estuaries and coastal waters. Distinguished by depth of tail, square-cut tail fin; upper jaw bone reaches beyond eye. Silvery with black spots. Spawns in rivers Nov–Jan. Feeds on fish, shrimps. T, ex nIc. [3]

Smelt *Osmerus eperlanus* OSMERIDAE
BL <30 cm. Slender body, with fleshy fin behind dorsals; mouth large with prominent teeth. Light olive-green, with distinct silvery sides. Smells strongly of cucumber. Common in many estuaries; spawns near limit of tidal influence in rivers, Mar–Apr. Feeds on crustaceans, small fish; prey of other fish, terns. BaS, NoS, local Br, Ir, Fr. [4]

Shore Clingfish *Lepadogaster lepadogaster* GOBIESOCIDAE BL <6·5 cm. Broad, flattened anterior body, sucker dic on belly; dorsal and anal fins long-based, joined to tail fin. Pink to deep red, with yellow ringed blue eye-spots above. Rocky shores, under boulders on sheltered shores, middle shore to 10 m. Spawns Jul–Sep, eggs laid on underside of rock, guarded by parent. wBr, Ir, Fr. [5] [eggs 6]

Angler *Lophius piscatorius* LOPHIIDAE
BL <2 m. Wide, almost circular, flattened head and body, large mouth, small pelvic fins on underside; long 'fishing rod' on

mid-line of head. Colour variable, brown green and black above, white below. Bottom-living in coastal and deep water, 18–500 m. Entices small fish with 'fishing rod' to within snapping range. T, ex BaS. [7]

Whiting *Merlangius merlangus* GADIDAE BL <70 cm. Slender body with narrow, pointed head; upper jaw longer than lower; 3 dorsal fins; 2 anal, the first very long. Pale sandy-brown above, sides and belly conspicuously white. Abundant inshore, in estuaries esp Nov–Mar; mainly over sandy or muddy bottoms, 30–100 m. Young often living with jellyfishes. T, ex Po, Fi, Sw, nNo. [8]

Bib *Trisopterus luscus* GADIDAE BL <42 cm. Deep body, with 3 dorsal, 2 anal fins, all close set; anal fin origin under first dorsal; chin barbel long. Coppery-brown above, white below; 4–5 dusky bars on body. Abundant in inshore waters, young esp in estuaries Nov–Mar. Feeds on shrimps, small squids, fish. Br, Ir, Fr, Be, Ne, De, rare sSw. [9]

Shore Rockling *Gaidropsarus mediterraneus* GADIDAE BL <35 cm. Almost eel-like, with 2 dorsal fins (first a row of low, fine rays), 1 anal fin; 3 barbels (from chin and each anterior nostril). Uniform dull brown or reddish-brown above, paler below. On rocky shores down to 27 m, under boulders or algae. Spawns in deep water early summer; silvery young on shore Sep–Oct. wBr, Ir, Fr. [10]

Five-bearded Rockling *Ciliata mustela* GADIDAE BL <25 cm. Slender, eel-like; 2 dorsal fins (first a row of low, fine rays), 1 anal fin; 5 barbels (from chin, pair on upper lip, 1 from each anterior nostril). Warm brown, sometimes reddish above, grey-brown below. Common in intertidal zone on rocky and sandy shores, estuaries, down to 20 m. Spawns in winter; silvery, pelagic young form diet of many young sea-birds. T, ex BaS. [11]

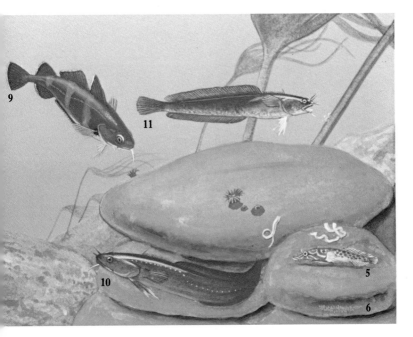

Pollack, Lythe *Pollachius pollachius*
GADIDAE BL <130 cm. 3 dorsal, 2 anal
fins; lower jaw protrudes; lateral line
curved above pectoral fin. Brownish-green
above, coppery-green on sides; lateral line
dark. Abundant around rocks, reefs and
wrecks, 10–200 m. Spawns in deep water,
Jan–Apr. Feeds on fish, crustaceans.
Young close inshore. T, ex BaS, nIc, nNo.
[1]

Saithe *Pollachius virens* GADIDAE BL <130
cm. 3 dorsal, 2 anal fins; lower jaw slightly
longer than upper; lateral line straight
from head to tail. Dark green back and
upper sides, dull silvery sides and belly;
lateral line creamy. Abundant in schools
in coastal waters, surface to 200 m; young
in tidal pools, close inshore. Spawns Jan–
Apr. Adult feeds on fish; juv on
crustaceans, fish. T, ex BaS, rare Fr. [2]

Cod *Gadus morhua* GADIDAE BL <150 cm.
3 dorsal, 2 anal fins, dorsal rounded in
outline; upper jaw overhangs lower; long
chin barbel. Variable coloration, greenish
to sandy-brown, always with light
mottling on back and sides; lateral line
white. Common in coastal waters (mostly
winter) to offshore (600 m); juv close
inshore. Schools 30–80 m above sea-bed.
Spawns Feb–Apr. Feeds on crustaceans,
worms, fish. T, ex nBaS. [3]

Ling *Molva molva* GADIDAE BL <2 m.
Slender body; 2 dorsal fins (first short), 1
anal fin; long chin barbel; jaws equal.
Dull browny-green, mottled above,
lighter below; dark blotches at ends of
fins. Common on rocky grounds, around
wrecks; on open coasts, 20–300 m. Spawns
in deep water, Mar–Jul. Feeds on fish,
crustaceans. T, ex BaS, rare sNoS. [4]

Viviparous Blenny *Zoarces viviparus*
ZOARCIDAE BL <50 cm. Slender body; 1
dorsal fin, with deep notch near tail,
continuous with tail and anal fins; pelvic
fins short. Abundant inshore, estuary
mouths; from middle shore to 40 m,
among rocks, on muddy grounds. Mates
Aug–Sep; young born Dec–Feb. Feeds
mainly on small crustaceans. T, ex sBr,
Ir, Ic, Fr. [5]

Garfish *Belone belone* BELONIDAE BL <94 cm. Long, slender body with pointed, beak-like, many-toothed jaws; 1 dorsal, 1 anal fin. Bright greeny-blue above, gleaming silver below. Surface-living, in inshore waters to N in summer. Spawns May–Jun. Feeds on surface-living fish, esp sprat, herring, sand-eels. T, ex BaS, Ic, nNo, only summer nBr. [6]

Sand-smelt *Atherina presbyter* ATHERINIDAE BL <21 cm. 2 well separated dorsal, 1 anal fins; mouth oblique; eye medium-sized; scales small. Clear green on back and sides, intense silvery stripe along sides, white below. Common inshore and in estuary mouths in schools, down to 20 m. Spawns in tidal pools, May–Jul. sBr, Ir, Fr, Be, Ne; summer nBr. [7]

Dory *Zeus faber* ZEIDAE BL <66 cm. Flattened body, huge protrusible jaws; strong spines on first dorsal and anal fins. Yellowish-brown with lighter lines; conspicuous blotch on sides. Mainly solitary, 10–50 m; often below flotsam, around rocks, wrecks. Stalks fish head-on until prey close enough to be engulfed. sBr, Ir, Fr, Be, Ne, De; summer No. [8]

Stickleback *Gasterosteus aculeatus* GASTEROSTEIDAE BL <10 cm. 3 isolated spines on back, first 2 larger, 3rd close to dorsal fin; pelvic fin a strong spine; scaleless, but variously developed plates on sides. Olive-brown above, with dusky bars, silvery below. Abundant in estuaries, coastal waters, occasional in high seas. Spawns Apr–Aug; ♂ builds nest on bottom, guards eggs and young. T. [♂ 9]

Fifteen-spined Stickleback *Spinachia spinachia* GASTEROSTEIDAE BL <20 cm. Slender body, pointed snout; 14–16 short spines on back in front of dorsal fin. Brownish or green above with dusky bars, yellowish below. Common inshore amongst algae, eelgrass. Spawns in bulky nest above bottom in seaweeds, middle shore and below, May–Aug; ♂ guards nest. Feeds on small crustaceans. T, ex nBaS, Ic. [10]

Deep-snouted Pipefish *Syngnathus typhle* SYNGNATHIDAE BL <30 cm. Long, slender body composed of hard, bony rings; snout deep, flattened. Light greeny-brown, often plain brown above, lighter below. Common amongst eelgrass on sandy bottoms, algae on rocks, 4–20 m. ♂ carries eggs in skin folds on tail, Jun-Aug. Feeds on small crustaceans, young fish. T, ex nBaS, Ic, nNo. [1]

Nilsson's Pipefish *Syngnathus rostellatus* SYNGNATHIDAE BL <17 cm. Long, slender body composed of hard, bony rings; snout short, no ridge in mid-line of head; 13–17 rings between pectoral base and anus. Warm brown above, yellowish below. Abundant in estuaries and coastal waters on sandy bottoms, 1–10 m. ♂ carries eggs in skin folds on tail, Jun-Sep. Feeds on crustaceans. T, ex BaS, nNoS, Ic. [2]

Worm Pipefish *Nerophis lumbriciformis* SYNGNATHIDAE BL <15 cm. Worm-like, with rounded body; no pectoral or tail fin; snout short. Dark brown or green; creamy bars and spots on throat. Common on rocky shores amongst fine brown algae (which it mimics); also under stones, boulders. ♂ carries eggs in shallow groove in belly, Jun-Aug. Young hatch (BL 1 cm) live 2–3 months on plankton. wBr, Ir, Fr, rare Be, Ne, De. [3]

Grey Gurnard *Eutrigla gurnardus* TRIGLIDAE BL <45 cm. Slender body, snout sharply pointed; eyes large; lateral line with sharp spines. Back and sides grey or grey-brown, with creamy spots. Inshore waters on sandy, muddy or gravel bottoms, 10–50 m. Spawns Apr-Aug. Feeds mainly on bottom-living crustaceans, small fish. T, ex BaS, nIc, nNo. [4]

Red Gurnard *Aspitrigla cuculus* TRIGLIDAE BL <40 cm. Rather deep body; snout pointed, with 3 short spines each side; lateral line with large, soft scales. Deep rose-red, pinkish-silver below. Common on sand, mud and gravel bottoms, occasional in estuaries (winter), 10–250 m. Feeds on crustaceans, fish, occasionally mid-water spp. Br, Ir, Fr, Be, Ne, rare De, Ge, Sw, sNo. [5]

Tub Gurnard *Trigla lucerna* TRIGLIDAE BL <75 cm. Rather deep body; snout pointed, with small lobes, bearing spines each side; pectoral fins reach well past anus. Back and upper sides red to reddish-brown; pectoral fins peacock-blue, green-spotted. Abundant inshore on mud and sand, 2–150 m. Feeds on fish, crustaceans. Br, Ir, Fr, Be, Ne, rare De, Sw, sNo. [6]

Sea Scorpion *Taurulus bubalis* COTTIDAE BL <17·5 cm. Broad-headed with very long preoperculum spine; small skin flap on angle of upper jaw bone; gill-cover membranes joined to throat. Variable colouring; green-brown, yellowish below. Abundant on rocky shores and below tide level to 30 m. Spawns Apr–Jun; eggs in clumps amongst algae. Feeds on fish, crustaceans. T, ex BaS, Ic. [7]

Hooknose *Agonus cataphractus* AGONIDAE BL <21 cm. Head and body encased in strong, bony armour; pair of hooks on snout; underside of head with many short barbels. Dull brown above with 4–5 darker saddles. Common on sandy or muddy bottoms, inshore and in estuary mouths, 2–40 m. Spawns Feb–May; eggs between holdfasts of seaweeds. Feeds on crustaceans, worms, brittle-stars. Br, Ir, Be, Ne, De, No, sSw. [8]

Lumpsucker *Cyclopterus lumpus* CYCLOPTERIDAE BL <60 cm. Body nearly spherical, with coarsely spined plates on skin; large sucker-disc on belly. Greenish or greenish-brown above, pale below; breeding ♂ with reddish tints. Bottom-living amongst rocks, lower shore to 200 m; also in mid-water. Spawns Feb–Jul; egg clumps, amongst seaweeds, guarded by ♂. T. [♂ 9]

Montagu's Sea Snail *Liparis montagui* LIPARIDAE BL <10 cm. Rounded, plump body with loose, gelatinous skin, finely prickled; round sucker-disc on belly; neither dorsal nor anal fins joined to tail fin. Colour variable with habitat. Shallow water, on undersides of boulders, among algae, from middle shore on rocky shores to 5 m. Eggs in small clumps near seaweeds. T, ex BaS. [10]

Bass *Dicentrarchus labrax* PERCICHTHYIDAE
BL < 1 m. 2 dorsal fins, first with 8–9 strong
spines; body fully scaled; forward-
pointing spines on lower edge of preoperculum. Greenish above, white below.
Abundant in estuaries (esp juv), and in
shallow water; schools near reefs. Spawns
in inshore waters, Mar–Jun. Feeds on
fish, squids, crustaceans. Br, Ir, Fr, Be,
Ne; summer also nBr, De, wSw, sNo. [1]

Scad *Trachurus trachurus* CARANGIDAE
BL < 50 cm. 2 dorsal fins, first with thin
spines; wide-shield-like plates along
lateral line, sharp near tail. Greenish-grey
above, sides silvery with golden tints.
Pelagic schools; juv in inshore waters,
estuaries; young commensal with
jellyfishes. Spawns May–Jul. Adult feeds
on fish, squids; juv on crustaceans. T, ex
BaS, Ic, nNo. [2]

Red Sea-bream *Pagellus bogaraveo*
SPARIDAE BL < 51 cm. Continuous dorsal
fin, spiny in front; pectoral fin long; eyes
large, teeth pointed in front. Rose-red,
sides silvery-pink; large, black blotch
behind head. Juv in schools near rocks,
wrecks, 10–35 m; adults in 100–200 m.
Spawns S of Br, Jun–Sep. Feeds on fish,
crustaceans, squids. sBr, Ir, Fr; summer
also nBr, Be, Ne, De, wSw, No. [3]

Black Sea-bream *Spondyliosoma
cantharus* SPARIDAE BL < 51 cm. Deep
body; 1 dorsal fin, spiny anteriorly; eyes
medium-sized; teeth pointed, curved,
even-sized. Greyish above, sides silvery
with 6–7 dusky, vertical bars. Adults round
reefs, wrecks offshore; juv close inshore,
5–30 m. Excavates shallow nest in sandy
sea-bed; ♂ guards eggs and loose school
of young. sBr, sIr, Fr; young in summer
nBr, Be, Ne, De, sNo. [4]

Red Mullet *Mullus surmuletus* MULLIDAE
BL < 40 cm. Body slender, head profile
steeply arched; scales large; 2 long
barbels on chin. Rose to reddish-brown
with 4–5 faint horizontal stripes. In small
schools on sandy or muddy bottoms, 3–90
m. Spawns Jun–Jul. Probes soft bottom
with barbels to find worms, molluscs,

crustaceans. sBr, Ir, Fr, Be, Ne; summer
also nBr, De, sNo. [5]

Thick-lipped Grey Mullet *Chelon
labrosus* MUGILIDAE BL < 75 cm. 2 dorsal
fins, first with 4 rays; scales large; upper
lip thick, covered with small papillae.
Grey-blue, sides silvery; 6–7 horizontal,
grey bands. Common in shallow inshore
waters, in schools near surface. Feeds on
green algae on rocks, pier pilings, on
surface layer of mud on sea-bed, esp in
harbours, near sewer outlets. T, ex BaS,
nIc, nNo; summer sIc, De, wSw, sNo. [6]

Thin-lipped Grey Mullet *Liza ramada*
MUGILIDAE BL < 60 cm. 2 dorsal fins, first
with 4 rays; pectoral fin short; scales
large; upper lip thin. Grey-blue above,
sides silvery; 6–7 horizontal, grey bands.
Inshore waters, estuaries, often far
upstream. Feeds on bottom mud and
green algae. Mainly summer migrant in
N Europe. sBr, sIr, Fr, rare nBr, nIr, Be,
Ne, De, wSw, sNo. [7]

Red Band-fish *Cepola rubescens* CEPOLIDAE
BL < 70 cm. Long, slender body; long
dorsal and anal fins; eyes large. Above and
sides orange-red; fins yellowish. In
burrows in stiff mud, 17–100 m; feeds on
crustaceans by partially emerging.
Occasionally swept out of burrows by
storms and stranded on shore. Br, Ir, Fr,
but rare eBr. [8]

Cuckoo Wrasse *Labrus mixtus* LABRIDAE
BL < 35 cm. Slender body; long, pointed
snout; scales small. ♀ and imm ♂ orange-
red with 3 dark blotches above. Close to
rocks, 35–180 m; summer migration
inshore (to 10 m). ♂ clears nest on
sea-bed and displays to ♀s; ♂ guards eggs
and young. Br, Ir, Fr, De, sSw, sNo. [♂ 9]

Ballan Wrasse *Labrus bergylta* LABRIDAE
BL < 60 cm. Deep body, blunt snout;
mouth and scales small. Colour variable;
numerous white spots below and on fins.
Around rocks, 3–20 m; juv in lower shore
pools, amongst seaweeds. Spawns in
seaweed nest in crevice. Feeds on
crustaceans, molluscs (esp mussels). Br,
Ir, Fr, Be, Ne, De, wSw, sNo. [10]

Corkwing Wrasse *Crenilabrus melops*
LABRIDAE BL <25 cm. Deep body, with
large scales extending on to cheeks; edges
of preoperculum toothed. Colour varies
with habitat; dusky crescent behind eye,
black spot near tail. Abundant around
rocks, middle shore to 30 m; common in
rock pools. Feeds on molluscs, crustaceans;
juv sometimes cleans parasites off other
fish. Br, Ir, Fr, rare Be, Ne, De, wSw,
sNo. [1]

Goldsinny Wrasse *Ctenolabrus rupestris*
LABRIDAE BL <18 cm. Slender body, with
large scales; rear edge of preoperculum
toothed. Brown or reddish-orange with
dusky spot on first dorsal fin and top of
tail. Abundant on seaweed-covered rocks,
11–50 m; on eelgrass beds, lower-shore
pools. Spawns in deeper water, May–Aug.
Feeds on crustaceans; may be parasite
cleaner. wBr, Ir, Fr, De, wSw, sNo. [2]

Rock Cook *Centrolabrus exoletus* LABRIDAE
BL <15 cm. Deep body, with large scales;
mouth small; anal fin with 4–6 stout
spines. Greenish-brown or reddish above;
dark crescent-mark near tip of tail.
Amongst algae and in eelgrass beds, 2–25
m; rarely in lower-shore pools. Feeds on
small crustaceans, both free-living and
parasitic on other fish. Fr, local wBr,
wIr, De, wSw, sNo. [3]

Lesser Weever *Echiichthys vipera*
TRACHINIDAE BL <14 cm. Short, deep
body; mouth strongly oblique; long,
venomous spines on gill cover, also first
dorsal fin. Yellow-brown above, lighter
below; first dorsal fin black. Inshore on
clean sandy bottoms, lower shore to 50 m;
enters estuaries. Burrows in sand. Feeds
on small crustaceans, fish. Inflicts danger-
ous wounds. Br, Ir, Fr, Be, Ne, De. [4]

Shanny *Lipophrys pholis* BLENNIIDAE
BL <16 cm. Slender, scaleless; long dorsal
fin notched near middle; pelvic fin of 2
rays. Colour variable; variously mottled;
dusky spot at front of dorsal fin.
Abundant on rocky shores, also in sandy
pools if seaweeds present, upper shore to
30 m. Feeds on barnacles, other small
crustaceans. Br, Ir, Fr, Be, sNo. [5]

Montagu's Blenny *Coryphoblennius galerita* BLENNIIDAE BL <8 cm. Slender, scaleless; long dorsal fin notched near middle; pelvic fin of 2 rays; fringed triangular skin-flap across head between eyes. Greenish-brown with bluish spots; ♂ with orange edge to crest above eyes. Common in pools on rocky shores, middle shore. Spawns in rock crevices, Jul. Feeds on acorn-barnacles. Br, swIr, Fr. [6]

Butterfish *Pholis gunnellus* PHOLIDAE BL <25 cm. Eel-like, but flattened body; dorsal fin spines short and sharp; pelvic fins minute, spiny. Brown or dark green; dark stripe through eyes; white-ringed black spots along back. On shores of all kinds, middle shore to 100 m; commonest amongst rocks. Spawns Jan–Feb; eggs in clumps, in crevice or mollusc shell, guarded by parent. T, ex neBaS, Fr. [7]

sand-eel *Ammodytes tobianus* AMMODYTIDAE BL <20 cm. Slender body, pointed head, protruding chin; 50–56 rays in dorsal fin. Yellow-green above, sides and belly silvery. Abundant on sandy shores, middle shore to 30 m. Burrows in clean, fine sand, or swims in schools, often head-down. Important prey for herring, mackerel, bass, puffins, terns. T, ex nBaS, nNo. [8]

Mackerel *Scomber scombrus* SCOMBRIDAE BL <66 cm. Dorsal and anal fins with series of finlets behind; tail fin with small keels at bases of lobes. Brilliant blue-green above, with black, curving lines; sides and belly white with gold reflections. Abundant in schools, near surface; inshore in summer. Feeds on smaller fish, crustaceans. T, ex nBaS. [9]

Blue-fin Tunny *Thunnus thynnus* SCOMBRIDAE BL <4 m. First dorsal fin concave in outline, with 13–15 spines, almost joins second; pectoral fin short. Dark blue above, shading to green on sides, white below. Surface-living in schools, usually offshore but migrating shorewards and N in summer. Makes transatlantic migrations. Feeds on most schooling fishes. Largest tunny in Europe. Rare due to overfishing. T, ex BaS. [10]

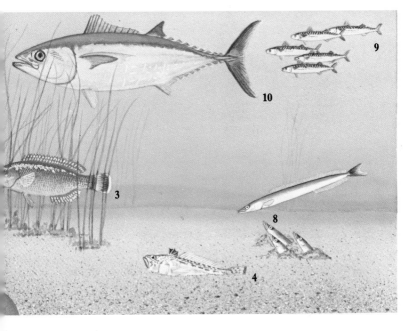

Dragonet *Callionymus lyra* CALLIONYMIDAE
BL <30 cm. Slender body, flattened
anteriorly; strong, 4-pointed spine on
lower preoperculum. Juv ♂ colouring as
♀. Common on sandy and muddy bottoms,
10–100 m; enters estuaries in winter.
Spawns Feb–Mar. Feeds on worms,
molluscs, crustaceans. T, ex BaS, nIc,
sSw, nNo, but rare sIc. [♂ 1] [♀ 2]

Two-spotted Goby *Gobiusculus flavescens*
GOBIIDAE BL <6 cm. Slender body; eyes
lateral; pelvic fins fused to form a flat
disc. Reddish-brown with 5–6 pale
saddles on back; dark spot at tail-fin base,
and behind pectoral on ♂. Active in
schools on rocky shores, lower shore to
15 m. Spawns May–Jul; ♂ guards eggs in
hollow seaweed holdfasts. Feeds on
crustaceans. T, ex BaS, Ic, nNo. [3]

Common Goby *Pomatoschistus microps*
GOBIIDAE BL <6·4 cm. Stout body, with
blunt head; pelvic fins united to form
disc; scales medium-sized, 39–52 along
each side. Sandy-brown; dusky marks on
sides, conspicuous at tail-fin and pectoral-
fin bases. Abundant on muddy or sandy
shores, far up estuaries, in brackish dykes.
Spawns inside hollow sea-shell, Apr–Aug;
eggs guarded by ♂. Feeds on small
crustaceans. T, ex Ic, nNo. [4]

Black Goby *Gobius niger* GOBIIDAE
BL <17 cm. Stout body, with blunt head;
pelvic fins united to form disc; scales large,
32–42 along each side; ♂ has long first
dorsal rays. Medium to dark brown.
Common on muddy or sandy bottoms, esp
estuaries and low salinity areas. Spawns
May–Aug; eggs in empty shell or rubble,
guarded by ♂. Feeds on crustaceans,
worms, molluscs. T, ex Ic, nNo. [5]

Rock Goby *Gobius paganellus* GOBIIDAE
BL <12 cm. Stout body, with blunt head;
pelvic fins united to form disc; scales
small, 50–57 along each side. Brown with
mottling; orange band on edge of first
dorsal fin. Confined to rocky shores,
middle shore to 15 m. Spawns Apr–Jun;
eggs in crevice, guarded by ♂. Feeds on
small crustaceans, fish. sBr, wBr, Ir, Fr. [6]

Turbot *Scophthalmus maximus*
SCOPHTHALMIDAE BL <1 m. Broad body,
thickset; eyes on left side of head; mouth
very large; no scales, but scattered, bony
tubercles in skin. Dull sandy-brown with
darker speckles. Shallow inshore waters, on
shell, sandy bottoms, lower shore to 80 m;
young on shore-line. Spawns offshore over
gravel, Apr–Sep. Feeds on fish. T, ex
nBaS, nIc, rare N of De. [7]

Dab *Limanda limanda* PLEURONECTIDAE
BL <42 cm. Slender body; eyes on right
side of head; mouth small; scales rough-
edged, on upper side. Warm sandy-brown
above, white below. Abundant on sandy
bottoms, 2–40 m; young in shallowest
depths. Adult migrates shoreward in
summer. Feeds on small crustaceans,
worms, molluscs. T, ex BaS. [8]

Flounder *Platichthys flesus* PLEURO-
NECTIDAE BL <51 cm. Diamond-shaped
body; eyes usually on right side of head;
prickles on bases of dorsal and anal fins,
also on lateral line. Dull brown with
darker blotches above, dead white below.
Abundant inshore, lower shore to 55 m;
in estuaries into freshwater. Migrates up
and down shore with tide. Feeds on
molluscs, worms, crustaceans. T, ex nBaS,
Ic. [9]

Plaice *Pleuronectes platessa* PLEURO-
NECTIDAE BL <91 cm. Diamond-shaped
body; eyes on right side of head; 4–7
bony knobs in line behind eyes. Warm
brown, with distinct bright red or orange
spots, clear white below. Abundant on
sandy and muddy bottoms, lower shore to
50 m; young close inshore. In estuary
mouths, Nov–Mar. Feeds on molluscs,
crustaceans, worms. T, ex nBaS. [10]

Sole *Solea solea* SOLEIDAE BL <60 cm.
Narrow body; snout rounded; dorsal fin
origin in front of eyes; eyes on right side
of head. Warm sandy-brown with darker
blotches, pectoral fin with black patch,
creamy-white below. On sandy and muddy
grounds, 1–100 m; young in intertidal
zone. Migrates offshore in winter. Feeds
mainly on crustaceans, worms. Br, Ir, Fr,
Be, Ne, De, sSw, sNo. [11]

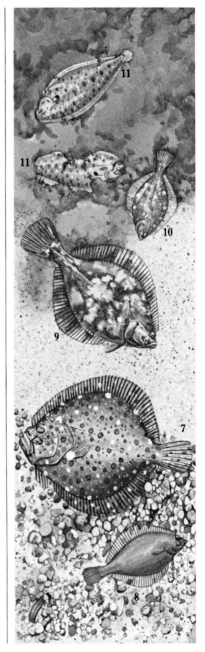

Divers and grebes nest largely by fresh-water – divers and Slavonian grebes in northern upland, tundra, forest, others more in lowlands – but winter on inshore seas, estuaries, also lakes. Colourful and easily distinguished in summer, but blackish, brown or grey, and white, in winter; noisy when breeding, otherwise mostly silent. On sea, divers and great crested grebes feed mainly on fish, some crustaceans, molluscs; other grebes more on crustaceans, esp shrimps, but also fish, molluscs; on freshwater, all take many aquatic insects.

Red-throated Diver *Gavia stellata*
GAVIIDAE L 53–58 cm. Slender uptilted bill, small head, thin neck; in winter, whitish face, speckled upperparts. Summer nBr, Ic, FS; winter T, ex Fi, nSw. [winter ad 1]

Black-throated Diver *Gavia arctica*
GAVIIDAE L 58–69 cm. White thigh-patch diagnostic in winter, when visible; told from red-throated by straight bill, blackish forehead, more uniform back and wings;

from great northern by slenderer bill, smaller head, sloping forehead, thinner neck, no pale indentation into grey hindneck, darker back than hindneck. Largely coastal in winter. Summer nBr, FS; winter T, ex Ir, Ic, Lu, Cz, Fi, nSw. [winter ad 2]

Great Northern Diver *Gavia immer*
GAVIIDAE L 68–81 cm. Heavy bill, large head, steep forehead, thick neck; in winter, white indentation into darker hindneck, back and wings paler than hindneck. Summer Ic; winter Br (has bred), Ir, Ic, Fr, Be, Ne, De, sGe, No. [winter ad 3]

White-billed Diver *Gavia adamsii*
GAVIIDAE L 76–91 cm. Like great northern diver, but bulkier, with longer, uptilted bill, often bump on forecrown increasing angle of forehead; bill yellowish, darker-based in winter but culmen (ridge) always pale (great northern can have bill pale, but culmen dark); cheeks lighter, looks white-faced like red-throated (which also has uptilted bill, but is smaller, with spotted

back and wings). Winters northern seas close to ice, esp inshore. Winter nNo, vagrant south to Br, Ne, De, Ge, Po. [winter ad **4**]

Little Grebe *Tachybaptus ruficollis* PODICIPEDIDAE L 25–29 cm. Small, dumpy, with short, stoutish bill, short neck, blunt-ended body, no white wing-patches (present on other 4 grebes); in winter, dull brown above, paler below, with white throat, grey-brown rear. T, ex Ic, Fi, all but extreme sSC, but only summer Cz, ePo, sSC. [winter ad **5**]

Great Crested Grebe *Podiceps cristatus* PODICIPEDIDAE L 46–51 cm. Large, with dagger bill, long thin neck; in winter, pink bill, blackish crown, white-headed look due to stripe above eye. T, ex nBr, Ic, all but sFS, but mainly summer Cz, Po, Fi, Sw. [winter ad **6**]

Red-necked Grebe *Podiceps grisegena* PODICIPEDIDAE L 41–46 cm. Largish, stocky, with stout bill, bulbous head, thickish neck; in winter, told from great crested by shape, dark bill with yellow base, black crown to eye-level, greyer neck. Largely coastal in winter. Summer De, Ge, Po, Fi, sSw, irregular Cz; winter eBr, nFr, Be, Ne, De, Ge, sSC, rare nPo. [winter ad **7**]

Slavonian Grebe *Podiceps auritus* PODICIPEDIDAE L 31–36 cm. Larger than little grebe; straight bill, flattish head, thin erect neck; in winter, told from black-necked grebe by bill and head shape, blackish crown extending only to eye-level, white on cheeks crossing to nape, white foreneck. Summer nBr, Ic, FS, but local; winter Br, Ir, wIc, Fr, Be, Ne, De, Ge, Po, sSw, No. [winter ad **8**]

Black-necked Grebe *Podiceps nigricollis* PODICIPEDIDAE L 28–33 cm. Told from Slavonian in winter by thin, uptilted bill, rounded head, less erect neck, blackish crown extending to ear-coverts, white smudge behind not crossing to nape, duskier foreneck. Summer De, Ge, Cz, Po, rare nBr, Fr, Be, Ne, sSw; winter sBr, Fr, Be, Ne, wGe. [winter ad **9**]

Fulmar *Fulmarus glacialis* PROCELLARIIDAE
L 45–50 cm. Superficially gull-like petrel,
but bull-necked, gliding and banking on
rigid wings, with stubby, yellow, tube-
nose bill. Swims buoyantly. When
nesting, low crooning, excited cackling.
Breeds on sea-cliffs, locally dunes,
buildings, crags < 30 km inland; inshore
Nov/Dec–Sep, otherwise offshore to
pelagic. Colonial; nest scrape on ledge, 1
egg, May–Sep. Food crustaceans,
cephalopods, fish, offal, carrion. Summer
Br, Ir, Ic, local nFr, wGe, wNo; winter
AtO, NoS, EnC. [1]

Cory's Shearwater *Calonectris diomedea*
PROCELLARIIDAE L 42–49 cm. Told from
great shearwater by heavier build, grey-
brown hood merging into unmarked white
underparts, yellow bill; sometimes pale
horseshoe at base of tail, but not so
prominent. Flight strong, fulmar-like
alternation of deep flaps and low glides on
more bowed wings. Breeds islands AtO/
Mediterranean; in WE, silent and mainly
pelagic. Food fish, cephalopods, crustaceans. Scarce passage swBr, sIr, nwFr. [2]

Great Shearwater *Puffinus gravis*
PROCELLARIIDAE L 43–51 cm. Large, with
dark bill, dark cap, pale collar, white
horseshoe at base of tail, dusky belly-
patch and brown-blotched, blackish-
bordered underwings. Flight more like
Manx than Cory's. Breeds islands sAtO;
in WE, silent and mainly pelagic.
Food chiefly fish, cephalopods, also offal.
Passage wBr, Ir, Ic, nwFr, rare NoS. [3]

Sooty Shearwater *Puffinus griseus*
PROCELLARIIDAE L 40–51 cm. Body bulky,
wings disproportionately narrow; all-dark
but for grey-white strip along centre of
underwings. Flight like Manx, but
stronger, more direct. Breeds S America/
New Zealand; in WE, silent and mainly
pelagic. Food as Cory's. Passage Br, Ir,
sIc, Fr, swNo, rarer sNoS. [4]

Manx Shearwater *Puffinus puffinus*
PROCELLARIIDAE L 30–38 cm. Smaller,
much commoner; black above, white
below with blackish wing-border. Banks
from side to side, now black, now white,
alternating glides on stiff wings with rapid

beats. Noisy when breeding: babble of raucous crowing and crooning, with howls, screams, cackles. Breeds on turfy islands, headlands, scree slopes, Feb–Sep; otherwise offshore to pelagic. Nocturnal at colonies; nest chamber, usually scantily lined, at end of burrow <180 cm long, in turfy slope, 1 egg, May–Sep. Food fish, offal, also cephalopods, small crustaceans. Breeds wBr, Ir, local sIc, nwFr; passage/feeding AtO, NoS, EnC. [5]

Storm Petrel *Hydrobates pelagicus*
HYDROBATIDAE L 14–18 cm. Sooty-black with white rump, whitish patch in wing-pit, square tail. Weak, bat-like fluttering with short glides. Harsh, sustained purring in hole, ending in hiccough; flight-call 'terr-chick'. Breeds on islands, headlands; otherwise offshore to pelagic. Nocturnal at colonies; nest sometimes lined grass, in crevice, stones, less often excavated burrow, 1 egg, Jun–Oct. Food plankton, fish, oil or fat from fish-offal, whale carrion. Summer wBr, wIr, sIc, nwFr; passage/feeding AtO, nNoS. [6]

Leach's Petrel *Oceanodroma leucorhoa*
HYDROBATIDAE L 19–22 cm. Larger, browner than storm petrel, with pale diagonal on inner wings, grey strip on rump-patch, forked tail. Flight distinctive: darts, glides, banks, hovers; seldom follows ships. Crooning or churring in burrow; staccato chattering in flight. Habitat as storm, but only islands. Nocturnal at colonies; nest in burrow, 1 egg, Jun–Oct. Food as storm. Summer nBr, local sIc, nwNo; passage/feeding AtO, NoS. [7]

Gannet *Sula bassana* SULIDAE L 87–100 cm. Goose-sized, cigar-shaped, white, with long, narrow, black-tipped wings; juv blackish speckled with white, grows white over 4 years. Deep wing-beats, short glides; plunges headlong with wings folded back. Loud, hoarse 'urrah' at nesting places. Breeds on cliffs or cliff-top slopes, esp islands, stacks; otherwise offshore to pelagic. Colonial; nest of seaweed, on ledge, slope, 1 egg, Apr–Oct. Food fish. Summer nBr, sIr, Ic, nwFr, nwNo; winter AtO, NoS, EnC. [ad 8] [imm 9]

Cormorant *Phalacrocorax carbo*
PHALACROCORACIDAE L 80–100 cm. Large, heavy, goose-like in flight, upright when perched (wings often hanging half open), with longish neck, hook-tipped bill; glossy black, fore-cheeks and chin white, back and wings bronzy pencilled with black; in summer, white thigh-patch and variable hoary whitish feathering on head; imm brown above, mainly whitish below. Swims like diver, but neck more erect, bill raised. Guttural calls when breeding. Sea-cliffs, rocky islets, estuaries, rivers, lakes. Colonial; flattish nest of seaweed, on cliff-ledge, rock (or of sticks, grass, in tree inland), 3–4 eggs, Mar–Aug. Food fish, crabs. Br, Ir, Ic, nFr, Ne, De, nGe, sCz, nPo, sSw, nNo. [summer ad **1**] [imm **2**]

Shag *Phalacrocorax aristotelis* PHALACRO-CORACIDAE L 65–80 cm. Smaller, slimmer than cormorant with slenderer bill, smaller head, shorter neck, also crest in summer; oily green-black, no white on face or thighs; imm much less white below. Clicking, grunting, hissing, when breeding. Rocky coasts, islands, esp with caves, crevices. Colonial; flattish nest of seaweed, also heather, sticks, grass, on sheltered ledge, 3 eggs, Mar–Sep. Food fish, some shrimps. Br, Ir, wIc, nwFr, No. [summer ad **3**] [imm **4**]

Barnacle Goose *Branta leucopsis*
ANATIDAE L 58–70 cm. Medium-sized, boldly pied, with longish neck, small bill; creamy face and pale grey flanks stand out from black hind-crown, neck and breast; back and wings blue-grey with white-edged black bands, white U above black tail; imm duller, browner, with dark brown and whitish bands on wings. Shrill, barking 'gnuk', flock sounding like yapping dogs. Breeds Greenland/Spitsbergen/USSR; winters salt-marshes, coastal pastures, turfy islands, sometimes mud-flats. Food lvs, seeds, of grasses, rushes, clovers. Winter nBr, nIr, Be, Ne, De, wGe; passage Ic, FS. [ad **5**]

Brent Goose *Branta bernicla* ANATIDAE
L 56–61 cm. Small, mallard-sized, dark, with short neck and legs, longish wings; head, neck and breast black but for small whitish neck-patch, back and wings dark brown-grey, stern white (black tail hardly shows); dark-bellied ssp *B. b. bernicla* has slate-grey lower breast and flanks (nearly as dark as back), pale-bellied *B. b. hrota* pale brown to whitish underparts; juv lacks neck-patch. Often silent, but throaty 'krronk' makes growling clamour in flock. Breeds circumpolar arctic; winters tidal mud-flats, estuaries, locally adjacent grassland, roosting on sea. Food eelgrass, green seaweeds, salt-marsh plants. Winter Br, Ir, Fr, Be, Ne, De, wGe; passage Ic, FS. [dark ad **6**] [pale ad **7**]

Shelduck *Tadorna tadorna* ANATIDAE
L 58–67 cm. Large, rather goose-like, looks pied at distance; green-black head, chestnut body-belt, black 'braces', flight-feathers and belly-stripe, red bill ($\male$ with knob at base), pink legs; juv grey-brown crown and back, white face, pinkish bill, grey legs. When breeding, harsh 'aark-aark', chattering 'ak-ak-ak' from $\female$, whistles from $\male$. Sandy and muddy shores, estuaries, nesting in adjacent dunes, rough ground, even woods. Nest hollow lined grass, much down, in rabbit burrow, hollow tree, haystack, under dense vegetation, 8–12 eggs, Apr–Jul. Food molluscs, crustaceans, insects, also marine worms, algae, seeds. T, ex Ic, Lu, Cz, nFS, but only summer eGe, Po, FS. [$\male$ ad **8**] [juv **9**]

Wigeon *Anas penelope* ANATIDAE L 45–51 cm. Medium-sized, short-necked dabbling-duck, with small bill, narrow wings, pointed tail; $\male$ yellow blaze on chestnut head, grey body, pinkish breast and, in flight, large white patches on inner wings, white belly contrasting with black undertail; $\female$ rufous, or greyer on back, with white belly, green-black wing-patch between whitish bars, dull blue bill. $\male$ loud whistle 'whee-oo', $\female$ purring growl. Breeds by freshwater on moors, marshes, tundra, open forests; winters muddy coasts, estuaries, salt-marshes, often resting on sea, also lakes, flooded grasslands. Food eelgrass, grasses, pondweeds, algae, seeds. Summer nBr, Ic, FS, local sBr, neGe, nPo; winter Br, Ir, swIc, Fr, Lu, Be, Ne, De, wGe, Cz, sSC. [$\male$ **10**] [$\female$ **11**]

Mallard *Anas platyrhynchos* ANATIDAE
L 55–64 cm. ♂ yellow bill, green head, white collar, purplish breast, black and white stern; ♀ mottled brown, with greenish-brown bill (often dull orange at sides). In flight, purple wing-patch between 2 white bars. Only ♀ quacks; ♂ low 'yaarb', loud whistle. Commonly winters on sea, estuaries, saltings; some also breed on coasts, but most resort to freshwater. Coastal food seeds, molluscs, crabs, shrimps, worms, fish. T, but only summer most FS. [♂ 1] [♀ 2]

Pintail *Anas acuta* ANATIDAE L 51–66 cm + <10 cm elongated tail of ♂. Large, slender, long-necked, narrow-winged dabbling-duck with long bill, pointed tail; ♂ chocolate head, white neck-stripe and underparts, black and white stern; ♀ told from ♀ mallard by shape, paler and greyer coloration, blue-grey bill, whitish belly. ♂ quiet 'whee' and teal-like whistle; ♀ quacking notes. Breeds mostly by fresh-water; largely coastal in winter, esp estuaries, adjacent floodlands. Coastal food seeds, eelgrass, molluscs, crustaceans. Summer Ic, Po, FS, local or irregular Br, Ir, Fr, Ne, De, Ge; winter T, ex Ic, Lu, eGe, Cz (passage), Po. [♂ 3] [♀ 4]

Pochard *Aythya ferina* ANATIDAE L 42–49 cm. Stocky, short-necked diving-duck with large, blue-banded bill, sloping forehead, high crown; ♂ grey with chestnut head, black breast and stern; ♀ grey-brown with hoary face, dull yellow-brown head and breast. In flight, pale grey wing-bar. Generally silent in winter. Prefers freshwater, but some winter on sheltered estuaries. Coastal food includes stoneworts, eelgrass, molluscs. Summer T, ex Lu, nFi, nSw, No, local Ic; winter T, ex Ic, ePo, Fi, all but sSC. [♂ 5] [♀ 6]

Scaup *Aythya marila* ANATIDAE L 42–51 cm. Big-headed, broad-bodied diving-duck with large bill; ♂ looks black at ends, white in middle, though back pale grey; ♀ brown, paler below, with white face and, in summer, whitish patch on ear-coverts. In flight, bold white wing-bar. Courting ♂ croons, whistles; ♀ growls. Breeds mainly by freshwater, but

on islands in BaS; winters on sea, esp estuaries, bays. Nest hollow lined grass, down, in open or under cover, 8–11 eggs, May–Aug. Coastal food molluscs, esp mussels, also crustaceans, marine worms, insects, seeds. Summer Ic, nFS, BaS coasts of Fi, Sw; winter Br, Ir, Fr, Be, Ne, De, Ge, Po, sSC. [♂ 7] [♀ 8]

Eider *Somateria mollissima* ANATIDAE
L 50–71 cm. Bulky, short-necked, long-bodied sea-duck with elongated bill, sloping forehead; ♂ only duck with white back and black belly; ♀ brown, closely barred black. ♂ low cooing or groaning; ♀ hoarse, guttural calls. Largely marine, esp sheltered rocky or sandy islands and coasts, saltings, estuaries. Often colonial; nest hollow lined grass, seaweed, abundant down (original source of eiderdowns), in open or hidden, among rocks, marram-dunes, heather, 4–6 eggs, Apr–Jul. Food mussels, periwinkles, crabs, starfish, sea-urchins. nBr, nIr, Ic, Ne, De, wGe, FS, rare Fr; winter also sBr, Fr, Be, eGe, Po. [♂ 9] [♀ 10]

King Eider *Somateria spectabilis* ANATIDAE L 47–63 cm. Large, round-headed sea-duck with short bill; ♂ told from eider by black back, as well as distinctive head shape and colours; ♀ by redder-brown tone with crescent markings on flanks, stubby bill with less uneven feather-limits, pale chin and throat. Less noisy than eider, some similarity in calls. Breeds by freshwater in arctic Canada/USSR; winters on sea, often some way offshore. Food much as eider. Winter/few summer eIc, nNo; vagrant farther south, esp Br, Ir, Fi, Sw. [♂ 11] [♀ 12]

Steller's Eider *Polysticta stelleri* ANATIDAE L 43–48 cm. Small compact sea-duck with thick-based bill; ♂ only duck with white head, black back and rufous-buff underparts; ♀ also very different from other eiders, smaller, darker, more mottled, with mallard-like purple wing-patch between white bars. ♂ silent in winter; ♀ rapid, guttural growl. Winters by rocky shores, river mouths. Food molluscs, amphipods, marine worms. Winter/few summer nNo; vagrant NoS, BaS. [♂ 13]

Harlequin *Histrionicus histrionicus*
ANATIDAE L 38–45 cm. Small, dark sea-duck with small bill, pointed tail; ♂ dark grey-blue (black at distance) with chestnut flanks, 'harlequin' pattern of black-edged white marks; ♀ brown, with 2 pale patches before eye, white circle behind. Rather silent. Breeds on islands in torrents; winters rough seas off rocky coasts. Food molluscs, crustaceans; insects in summer. Ic. [♂ 1] [♀ 2]

Long-tailed Duck *Clangula hyemalis*
ANATIDAE L 40–47 cm + <13 cm pointed tail of ♂. Small-headed, pale sea-duck with short, high-based bill, narrow wings; ♂ mainly white in winter (brown cheek-patch, breast-band, mid-back, tail, wings), mainly brown in summer (whitish face-patch, belly); ♀ also darker in summer, esp head but for whitish round eye. In flight, wings all dark, ♂ with white 'braces' in winter. ♂ loud yodelling, in flock like distant hounds; ♀ soft quack. Breeds by tundra lakes; winters on sea. Food molluscs, crustaceans, marine worms, fish, also insects. Summer Ic, sFi, nFS;

winter mainly nBr, nIr, Ic, Ne, De, Ge, Po, sSw, No. [winter ♂ 3] [winter ♀ 4]

Common Scoter *Melanitta nigra*
ANATIDAE L 44–54 cm. Squat, dark sea-duck with deep bill, pointed tail; ♂ all-black but for orange-yellow patch in front of bill-knob; ♀ brown, with clear-cut, whitish-brown cheeks, throat. ♂ plaintive, piping whistle in late winter flocks, sometimes in chorus. Breeds by freshwater, esp tundra, moors; winters on sea. Food mussels, also crustaceans, marine worms, starfish. Summer nBr, nIr, nIc, nFS; winter Br, Ir, Fr, Be, Ne, De, Ge, Po, sSw, No. [♂ 5] [♀ 6]

Velvet Scoter *Melanitta fusca* ANATIDAE L 51–58 cm. Large, heavy-headed, thick-necked sea-duck with long deep bill, pointed tail, white wing-patches, red feet; ♂ also white below eye, orange-yellow *sides* to swollen (not knobbed) bill, ♀ 2 whitish cheek-patches. Infrequent whistling (♂), growling (♀). Breeds by freshwater in forests, wooded tundra, moors, also wooded islets BaS; winters off

exposed coasts, also estuaries. Food as common scoter. Summer FS; winter Br, eIr, Fr, Be, Ne, De, Ge, Po, sSw, No. [♂ 7] [♀ 8]

Barrow's Goldeneye *Bucephala islandica* ANATIDAE L 42–53 cm. Told from ♂ golden-eye by flat crown to purple-glossed, oval head, with white *crescent* before eye, also by spur of black in front of wing, white blobs at sides of blacker upperparts; ♀ by richer brown, oval head, stubbier bill with more yellow on top, less white on wings. ♂ grunts, clicks, only in display; ♀ growling flight-call. Breeds by lakes, rivers, even torrents; winters also sheltered coastal bays. Food molluscs, crustaceans; insects in summer. Ic. [♂ 9]

Goldeneye *Bucephala clangula* ANATIDAE L 42–50 cm. Smallish, stocky, short-billed diving-duck with peak to green-glossed, triangular head; ♂ boldly pied, with white *circle* before eye, streaky white shoulders; ♀ chocolate head, whitish collar, grey-mottled upperparts, breast. In flight, white wing-patches broken by 1

(♂) or 2 (♀) black lines; wings make whistling sound. ♂ rasping and rattling calls in display; ♀ hoarse flight-call. Breeds by forest lakes; winters inland and coasts, esp estuaries, bays. Food molluscs, crustaceans, insects, fish. Summer FS, rare nBr, Ge, Cz, Po; winter T, ex Fi, nSC, but local Ic, Fr, Cz. [♂ 10] [♀ 11]

Red-breasted Merganser *Mergus serrator* ANATIDAE L 52–58 cm. Rakish sawbill-duck with narrow red bill, double crest; ♂ green-black head, wide white collar, black-spotted chestnut breast, inner wings white part-broken by 2 black lines; ♀ red-brown head merging into whitish foreneck, brown-grey upperparts, white patch at rear of inner wings broken by 1 line. In display, ♂ rattling or purring, ♀ croaking or rasping. Sheltered inlets, estuaries, esp with islands; also breeds inland. Nest hollow lined grass, down, under thick cover, in hole, rabbit burrow, 8–10 eggs, May–Jul. Food fish, also crustaceans, molluscs, worms, insects. Summer nBr, Ir, Ic, De, FS, local nGe, nPo; winter T, ex Lu, Cz, Po, Fi, nSw. [♂ 12] [♀ 13]

White-tailed Eagle *Haliaeetus albicilla*
ACCIPITRIDAE L 70–95 cm, ♂ smaller than
♀. Huge, with rectangular wings, massive
yellow bill, large pale head and short,
wedge-shaped, white tail; juv brown,
centres of tail-feathers later whitish. Shrill
chatter, gull-like croak. Sea-cliffs, islands,
forest lakes; winters also coastal marshes,
estuaries. Bulky nest of sticks, heather,
lined wood-rush, grass, on ledge, flat
islet, tree, 2 eggs, Mar–Aug. Food fish,
carrion, mammals, birds. wIc, nGe, Po,
wFi, eSw, No; winter also Ne, De, Cz.
[ad 1] [imm 2]

Peregrine *Falco peregrinus* FALCONIDAE
L 38–48 cm, ♂ smaller than ♀. Large
falcon with long, pointed, broad-based
wings; black moustache, blue-grey back,
whitish underparts barred black; imm
browner, streaked below. Chatters near
nest. Sea-cliffs, inland crags, forests, also
winters estuaries, marshes. Nest scrape on
ledge, old raptor/crow nest, 3–4 eggs,
Mar–Jul. Food birds, few mammals. T,
ex Ic, but rare in south (mainly winter),
only summer nFS. [♂ 3] [♀ 4]

Oystercatcher *Haematopus ostralegus*
HAEMATOPODIDAE L 41–45 cm. Large, pied
wader, with long orange-red bill, stout
pink legs; winter ad and browner juv have
white ½-collar on throat. Loud, shrill
'peek, ka-peek', sharp 'pik, pik'. Rocky,
shingly, sandy or grassy coasts, locally
inland; winters estuaries, saltings. Nest
scrape in open, 3 eggs, Apr–Jul. Food
molluscs, crabs, worms, insects. T, ex
Lu, Cz, rare Be, Po, only summer eGe,
Po, Fi, most SC. [summer 5] [winter ad 6]

Avocet *Recurvirostra avosetta* RECURVIROS-
TRIDAE L 41–45 cm. Graceful, black and
white, with long, slender, upcurved bill
and blue-grey legs. Fluty 'kleep'. Brackish
lagoons, salt-marshes, estuaries, adjacent
meadows; winters mud-flats, estuaries.
Nest on muddy islet, sand, turf, 3–4
eggs, May–Jun. Food insects, shrimps,
tiny molluscs, worms; sweeps bill in
water. Summer seBr, Ne, De, nGe, sCz,
sSw, rare nFr, Be; winter swBr, wFr. [7]

Ringed Plover *Charadrius hiaticula*
CHARADRIIDAE L 18·5–19·5 cm. Small,

plump, with stubby, orange-based bill and shortish, orange legs; black breast-band, black-and-white head-pattern, white wing-bar; juv duller, more scaly, no black, browner breast-band often broken, dark bill, yellowish legs. Soft whistle 'poo-i'; trilling song repeated 'qui-lee-yu'. Sand or shingle beaches, thrift turf, saltings, also inland; winters estuaries, mud-flats. Nest scrape bare or lined pebbles, debris, in open or among plants, 3–4 eggs, Apr–Aug. Food molluscs, crustaceans, insects. Summer T, ex Lu, Cz (passage); winter Br, Ir, Fr. [ad 8] [juv 9]

Kentish Plover *Charadrius alexandrinus*
CHARADRIIDAE L 15·5–16 cm. Smaller, slimmer than ringed plover, with blackish bill, legs; ♂ has rufous crown, black at sides of breast; ♀ duller, no black on head, browner breast-patches. Soft 'wit-wit-wit', alarm 'kittup'; trilling song. Sand and shingle beaches, dry mud-flats, brackish lagoons. Nest scrape bare or lined plant fragments, on sand, mud, pebbles, 3 eggs, May–Jul. Food as ringed plover. Mainly summer Fr, Be, Ne, De, Ge, sSw. [♂ 10]

Golden Plover *Pluvialis apricaria*
CHARADRIIDAE L 27–29 cm. On coasts only in winter, when dark upperparts still spangled gold, but underparts whitish, mottled gold and brown on face, breast; in flight, rump and tail dark, no wing-bar. Clear whistle 'tlui'. Breeds on tundra, moors; winters grasslands, arable, estuaries. Food as grey plover, also grasses, seeds. Summer nBr, nIr, Ic, De, Ge, FS; passage T; winter Br, Ir, Fr, Be, Ne, De. [winter 11]

Grey Plover *Pluvialis squatarola*
CHARADRIIDAE L 27–29 cm. Stouter than golden plover, hunched, with heavier bill; in summer, silver-spangled, black and white; in winter, grey-brown above (imm mottled yellowish), whitish below, told from golden plover in flight by black 'arm-pit', whitish rump, tail, wing-bar. Plaintive 'tlee-oo-ee'. Breeds tundra USSR; winters estuaries, mud-flats, sandy shores. Food worms, molluscs, crustaceans, insects. Winter/non-breeding summer Br, Ir, Fr, Be, Ne, wGe; passage De, eGe, Cz, Po, FS. [summer 12] [winter ad 13]

Knot *Calidris canutus* SCOLOPACIDAE L 25–26 cm. Larger, stockier than dunlin, short-necked, with straight bill, shortish legs; in summer, head and underparts russet; in winter, all grey and whitish, with scaly wing-coverts, pale rump and tail; juv scalier, tinged buff. Hoarse 'knut' ('knot'), whistling 'twit-wit'. Breeds high arctic Canada/Greenland/USSR; winters mud-flats. Food crustaceans, molluscs, worms, insects. Winter Br, Ir, Fr, Be, Ne; passage also De, Ge, Po, FS. [winter ad 1]

Sanderling *Calidris alba* SCOLOPACIDAE L 20–21 cm. Slightly larger than dunlin, with black bill, legs; in summer, head, breast and upperparts black-spotted rufous, belly white; in winter, very pale, with blackish shoulder-patch; juv chequered black and whitish above, tinged buff below. Darts at edge of waves like toy on wheels. Shrill or softer 'twick, twick'. Ranges as knot; winters sandy shores. Food as knot, esp sand-hoppers, shrimps. [summer ad 2] [winter ad 3]

Little Stint *Calidris minutus* SCOLOPACIDAE L *c*14·5 cm. Tiny, with short bill, black legs; in summer, rufous and white; in winter, much greyer; juv paler than summer ad, with 2 large whitish Vs on back. Short 'trit' or twitter. Breeds in grassy marshes, tundra; passage sandy shores, mud-flats, estuaries, freshwater inland. Food as sanderling. Summer nNo; passage T, ex Ic; few winter sBr, wFr. [summer ad 4] [juv 5]

Curlew Sandpiper *Calidris ferruginea* SCOLOPACIDAE L 18–20 cm. Larger, more upright than dunlin, with longer, finer down curved bill, longer neck and legs, white rump; in summer, head and underparts russet, face whitish; in winter, grey-brown above, white below; juv upperparts darker, more scaly, breast buff. Soft 'chirrip'. Breeds tundra NE Asia; passage as little stint. Food as sanderling. Passage T, ex Ic. [winter ad 6]

Purple Sandpiper *Calidris maritima* SCOLOPACIDAE L 20–22 cm. Larger than dunlin, stocky, with yellow-based bill, short yellow legs; head and breast sooty-brown, back and wings blackish, glossed purple, throat whitish, belly white, spotted on flanks; in summer, paler, back and wings scaled with rufous, throat and breast more spotted; juv similarly scaled with whitish. Piping 'weet-wit'. Breeds on arctic tundra; winters rocky coasts. Food crustaceans, molluscs, small fish, insects, algae. Summer Ic, nFS; winter T, ex Lu, Cz, Po, Fi. [summer ad 7] [winter ad 8]

Dunlin *Calidris alpina* SCOLOPACIDAE L 17–19 cm. Commonest wader in WE, small, hunched, with slightly downcurved bill; in summer, black-streaked chestnut crown and back, black belly-patch; in winter, brown-grey above, white below with greyish breast. Nasal 'tree'. Breeds on moors, bogs, salt-marshes; winters coasts, estuaries, esp mud-flats. Food as knot. Summer nBr, Ir, Ic, De, nGe, nPo, FS; passage T; winter Br, Ir, Fr, Be, Ne, De, Ge, swSC. [summer 9] [winter 10]

Black-tailed Godwit *Limosa limosa* SCOLOPACIDAE L 37–44 cm. Tall, with long, pinkish bill slightly upturned, long legs, white wing-bar, black-ended white tail; in summer, head and breast reddish (♀ duller), flanks and belly blackish-barred white; in winter, grey-brown and whitish; juv head, breast and back-markings rufous-buff. Loud 'weeka-weeka-weeka'. Breeds on water meadows, marshes; winter/passage estuaries, salt-marshes, freshwater inland. Food crustaceans, molluscs, worms, insects. Summer Ic, Ne, De, Ge, Cz, Po, local Br, nwFr, Be, sSw; passage T, ex FS; winter sBr, Ir, wFr. [winter ad 11]

Bar-tailed Godwit *Limosa lapponica* SCOLOPACIDAE L 35–38 cm. Shorter-legged than black-tailed godwit, with shorter, more upturned bill, whitish rump, barred tail; in summer, ♂ head and underparts reddish, but much duller ♀ may have white flanks and belly; juv has pinkish-buff breast streaked brown. Low 'kirrick'. Breeds on swampy tundra; winters muddy and sandy coasts, estuaries. Food as black-tailed. Summer neFS; winter/non-breeding summer Br, Ir, Fr, Be, Ne; passage also De, Ge, Po, sFS. [winter ad 12]

Whimbrel *Numenius phaeopus* SCOLO-PACIDAE L 38–41 cm. Like small, dark curlew, with shorter, kinked bill, striped crown, faster wing-beats. Rapid, whinnying titter. Breeds on moors, tundra; passage estuaries, rocky shores, coastal grassland. Food small crabs, shrimps, sand-hoppers, periwinkles, worms, insects. Summer nBr, Ic, nFS, passage T. [1]

Curlew *Numenius arquata* SCOLOPACIDAE L 53–59 cm. Large, with long, evenly downcurved bill (♀ longer); streaked brown with white rump. Ringing 'cour-lee'; bubbling trill. Breeds on moors, marshes, rough grassland, dunes; winters mud-flats, estuaries, coastal fields. Food as whimbrel, but more mussels, cockles, fish. Summer T, ex Ic, Lu, nFS; winter T, ex sGe, Cz, Po, Fi, Sw, nNo. [2]

Spotted Redshank *Tringa erythropus* SCOLOPACIDAE L 29–31 cm. Taller, slenderer than redshank, bill and legs longer, no wing-bar, but white wedge up back; mainly black in summer, grey and whitish in winter, spotted white on wings. 'Tchu-eet'. Breeds in open marshy forest; passage/winter estuaries, salt-marshes, also inland. Food insects, molluscs, shrimps, worms, tadpoles, small fish. Summer nFS; passage T, ex Ic; some winter sBr, sIr, wFr, Ne. [winter 3]

Redshank *Tringa totanus* SCOLOPACIDAE L 27–29 cm. Medium-sized, grey-brown and whitish, with orange-based bill, orange-red legs; in flight, white crescent on hindwings, white rump; more strongly streaked and spotted in summer. Shy, restless, often bobbing. Noisy, esp piping 'tu', yelping 'teuk', down-slurred 'tlu-hu-hu'. Breeds on coastal and inland marshes, saltings, dunes; winters mostly estuaries, mud-flats. Nest hollow usually in grass tussock, 4 eggs, Apr–Jul. Food as spotted redshank, also eelgrass, lvs, seeds. Summer T, ex Lu, but local Fr, Be; winter Br, Ir, Ic, Fr, Be, Ne; passage also Lu. [winter 4]

Greenshank *Tringa nebularia* SCOLO-PACIDAE L 30–32 cm. Larger, taller than redshank with slightly upturned, blackish bill, long green legs, no wing-bar, but white wedge up back; in summer, dark brown and white, streaked and spotted; in winter, greyer above, whiter face and underparts. Loud 'tew-tew-tew'. Breeds on moors, open forest; passage/winter on estuaries, marshes. Food as spotted redshank. Summer nBr, nFS; passage T, ex Ic; winter sBr, Ir, wFr. [winter 5]

Turnstone *Arenaria interpres* SCOLO-PACIDAE L 22–23 cm. Robust, with pointed black bill, short orange legs; in summer, black, white and chestnut, ♂ head whiter than ♀; in winter, dusky brown with white throat and belly. Rapid, gravelly 'kitititit'; trilling rattle when nesting. Breeds on stony coasts, islands, fells, river flats; winters rocky coasts. Nest scrape variably lined grass, lvs, lichens, in open or by rock, shrub, 3–4 eggs, May–Aug. Food insects, sand-hoppers, molluscs. Summer FS, rare De; passage T; winter/non-breeding summer Br, Ir, Be, Ne, De, Ge, swNo. [summer ♂ 6] [winter 7]

Phalaropes are dainty, tame waders that swim habitually; ♂s incubate, tend young, are smaller and, in summer, duller than ♀s. In autumn/winter, 2 spp similar, but smaller red-necked has longer, finer bill, more curved eye-patch, darker grey back with whitish streaks; grey phalarope stockier, with more oval eye-patch, uniform blue-grey back, longer tail; juvs have dark, buff-streaked backs, but grey phalarope has white areas tinged buff, while red-necked blacker above, whiter below. Both breed by freshwater, even near coast; passage mainly offshore. Food insects, tiny molluscs, crustaceans, worms.

Red-necked Phalarope *Phalaropus lobatus* SCOLOPACIDAE L 16·5–18 cm. In summer, black bill, grey head, white throat, orange on neck. Low 'whit'. Summer nBr, Ic, nFS; passage T, ex Lu, Cz, scarce. [winter ad 8]

Grey Phalarope *Phalaropus fulicarius* SCOLOPACIDAE L 19–21 cm. In summer, yellow-based bill, white sides of head, chestnut underparts. Shrill 'twit'. Summer Ic; passage/few winter sBr, sIr, Fr, Be, Ne, De, wGe, swNo. [winter ad 9]

Pomarine Skua *Stercorarius pomarinus* STERCORARIIDAE L 43–48 cm + <8 cm tail projection (broad, blunt, twisted, but may break). Larger, deeper-chested than arctic skua; similar light and (rarer) dark forms, but clearer whitish wing-flashes; light form has black cap extending to face, blackish flanks and vent, usually dusky breast-band. Passage offshore and coastal. Food as arctic. Passage eAtO, NoS, EnC, BaS, overland Fi. [light ad **1**]

Arctic Skua *Stercorarius parasiticus* STERCORARIIDAE L 37–40 cm + <9 cm tail projection (straight, pointed). Mid-sized and commonest of 3 smaller skuas; variable from dark form (all black-brown) to light (blackish cap, creamy cheeks and hindneck, white below, often dark breast-band); imm dark or barred and mottled. Breeds on moors near coast; passage inshore and offshore. Food at sea, fish (often by robbing gulls, terns), cephalopods, shrimps, other plankton, offal, refuse. Summer nBr, Ic, coastal FS; passage AtO, NoS, EnC, BaS, overland FS. [light ad **2**] [dark ad **3**]

Long-tailed Skua *Stercorarius longicaudus* STERCORARIIDAE L 34–37 cm + <20 cm tail projection (thin, flexible, but may break). Slighter than arctic skua, dark form rare; neater black cap, greyer upperparts, darker underwings, belly and undertail, no breast-band. Breeds on moors, tundra; passage offshore. Food as arctic. Summer nFS; passage AtO, NoS, BaS, overland FS. [ad **4**]

Great Skua *Stercorarius skua* STERCORARIIDAE L 56–61 cm. Large, heavy, gull-like, with stout bill, short tail, broad rounded wings; dark brown, streaked paler, with bold white wing-flashes (juv less). Often settles on water. Breeds on moors, rough grassland, mainly near sea; passage inshore and offshore. Food fish (often by forcing gulls, terns, gannets to disgorge), also birds and young, molluscs, crustaceans, offal. Summer nBr, Ic; passage AtO, NoS, EnC. [ad **5**]

Mediterranean Gull *Larus melanocephalus* LARIDAE L 38–40 cm. Taller, flatter-

crowned than black-headed gull, with droop-tipped bill, white wing-tips, in summer *black* head with broken eye-ring; imm stages more like imm common gulls, but wing-markings more contrasted. Distinctive 'kee-oo'. Coastal lagoons, marshes, estuaries, sometimes in black-headed gull colonies. Food fish, molluscs, crustaceans, worms, insects. Irregular breeding sBr, Be, Ne, Ge; winter mainly sBr, wFr. [summer 6] [winter ad 7]

Little Gull *Larus minutus* LARIDAE L 27–29 cm. Told from black-headed gull by white-tipped grey primaries, blackish undersides of more rounded wings, *black* head in summer, dark bill in winter; imm has kittiwake-like black zigzag across wings, pale underwings, black-ended tail; juv crown and back blackish. Tern-like flight. Low 'kek-kek-kek'. Breeds fresh-water marshes, lakes; winters coasts, estuaries. Food as Mediterranean gull. Summer nDe, nPo, Fi, sSw, but scarce; has also nested eBr; passage/winter T, ex Ic, most SC. [winter ad 8] [imm 9]

Sabine's Gull *Larus sabini* LARIDAE L 32–34 cm. Small, tern-like, tail forked, bill black with yellow tip; head slate-grey with black collar in summer, mottled dusky in winter; juv scaly grey-brown above, with black-ended tail. In flight, white triangle on wings divides black primaries from grey coverts. Picks food from surface in flight. Grating, tern-like call. Coastal and offshore. Passage AtO to WE, Ic. [summer 10] [juv 11]

Black-headed Gull *Larus ridibundus* LARIDAE L 35–38 cm. Smallish, bill and legs red; *brown* hood (not back of neck) in summer becomes mainly white in winter; juv mottled brown above, tail-end blackish. In flight, broad white front edge to pointed, black-tipped wings. Noisy when breeding, *eg* harsh 'kwarr', short 'kuk'. Coasts, estuaries, freshwater and fields inland. Colonial; nest scrape, or heap of plants, on marsh, dune, even in tree, 2–3 eggs, Apr–Jul. Food as Mediterranean gull, also seeds, roots, moss, refuse. T, ex nFS, but only summer Fi, most SC. [winter ad 12]

Gulls are mostly grey or black, and white, much browner when young. Unlike the 4 on page 199, these 8 do not assume dark heads in summer; all but common and ivory gulls and kittiwake have stout yellow bills with a red spot. Their usually colonial nests are variable heaps of grass, moss, seaweed, litter. Food often very varied: worms, molluscs, crustaceans, starfish, insects, fish, birds, eggs, small mammals, carrion, seaweed, seeds, turnips.

Common Gull *Larus canus* LARIDAE L 39–42 cm. Told from herring gull by slender green-yellow bill and legs, softer expression, longer and thinner wings; head strongly streaked in winter; juv/imm whiter than juv herring, with broad black tail-band. Shrill 'kee-yah'. Breeds moors, lakes, also coastal slopes, islands; winters coasts, also fields, lakes. Summer nBr, nIr, wIc, Ne, De, nGe, nPo, FS, few sBr, nFr, Be; winter T, ex Fi, nSw. [winter ad 1]

Lesser Black-backed Gull *Larus fuscus* LARIDAE L 51–60 cm. Size as herring gull, but back slate-grey (Br, Ir, Ic, Fr, Ne, wGe) to black (De, eGe, FS); told from great black-backed by yellow legs and, in winter, close head-streaking; imm like herring gull, but darker-backed. Deeper calls. Habitats also similar; more often well offshore. 2–3 eggs, May–Jul. Summer T, ex Lu, Be, Cz, Po; winter T, ex Ic, Lu, Cz (passage), FS. [summer ad 2]

Herring Gull *Larus argentatus* LARIDAE L 53–64 cm. Commonest coastal gull; grey-backed, with white-spotted, black wing-tips, heavy bill, pink legs (yellow Fi), head lightly streaked in winter; juv mottled brown with darker primaries, tail, blackish bill, becoming paler over 3 yrs. Loud 'keew', trumpeting 'kyow-kyow-kyow'; rhythmic 'gag-gag-gag' near nest. Breeds on grassy cliffs, islands, dunes, shingle, coastal towns; winters coasts, estuaries, also inland. Nest on ground, ledge, roof, 2–3 eggs, Apr–Jul. T, but breeding rare Be, Po, only passage Lu, Cz. [summer ad 3] [imm 4]

Iceland Gull *Larus glaucoides* LARIDAE L 53–66 cm. Told from glaucous gull by shorter, thinner bill, smaller rounded head, longer wings; at least ½ bill of juv/ 1st winter black. Voice, winter habitat also similar; breeds Greenland. Winter nBr, nIr, Ic, No, vagrant elsewhere. [ad 5]

Glaucous Gull *Larus hyperboreus* LARIDAE L 60–73 cm. Build of great black-backed gull; back pale grey, primaries white, legs pink; juv/2nd winter all creamy-brown, ⅔ bill pink, body becoming paler over 4 yrs. Calls shriller than herring gull. Breeds on rocky coasts, islands; winters coasts, also inland. Nest on cliff-slope, ground, 2–3 eggs, May–Jul. Summer wIc; winter Br, Ir, Ic, Ne, De, Ge, SC, irregular Fr, Be, Po, Fi. [ad 6] [imm 7]

Great Black-backed Gull *Larus marinus* LARIDAE L 64–79 cm. Large, bill massive; back and wings black, legs whitish-pink, head sparsely streaked in winter; juv/imm head and underparts whitish, back and wings chequered, 4 yrs to adult. Deep, barking, disdainful 'owk', guttural 'uk-uk-uk'. Breeds on islands, headlands, locally lakes, moors; winters coasts, estuaries. Often single pairs; nest on ridge, 2–3 eggs, Apr–Jul. Kills shearwaters, puffins. Summer Br, Ir, Ic, nwFr, De, FS; winter/ non-breeding T, ex Lu, Cz, nBaS. [ad 8]

Kittiwake *Rissa tridactyla* LARIDAE L 39–42 cm. Like dainty common gull, but plain black wing-tips, black legs, gentle dark eyes; juv grey and white (no brown), with black hind-collar, zigzag across wings and tip to slightly forked tail. 'Kitti-waak' at colonies. Breeds on sea-cliffs, locally buildings; winters offshore and pelagic. Nest on ledge, 1–3 eggs, May–Sep. Food fish, marine invertebrates. Summer Br, Ir, Ic, nwFr, No, local De, wGe; winter AtO, NoS, EnC. [ad 9] [juv 10]

Ivory Gull *Pagophila eburnea* LARIDAE L 43–46 cm. Pure white, plump, pigeon-like, with short black legs; imm also white, greyish on face, spotted black on back and wings. Harsh, tern-like calls. Breeds circumpolar arctic; winters edge of pack-ice. Food fish, crustaceans, molluscs, carrion. Occasional Ic, nNo, vagrant Br, Ir, Fr, Ne, De, FS. [ad 11]

Terns are slender, narrow-winged, graceful fliers with pointed bills, short legs, forked tails. Most are white and grey, with black caps in summer, white foreheads and streaked crowns in autumn; juvs as autumn, but mottled brown above. Most fish by hovering and plunging.

Gull-billed Tern *Gelochelidon nilotica* STERNIDAE L 35–39 cm. Resembles Sandwich, but bill stubby, all-black; tail grey and less forked, wings broader, legs longer; head whiter in autumn. Hawks over land and water, seldom plunges. Throaty 'kayhuk', 'kaahk'. Salt-marshes, saline lagoons, sandy coasts. Usually colonial; nest as Sandwich, but on lagoon shore, 2–3 eggs, May–Jul. Food insects, small mammals, young birds, lizards, frogs, fish, crabs. Local summer De, has bred seBr, Ne, Ge; scarce passage EnC, sNoS. [summer 1]

Caspian Tern *Sterna caspia* STERNIDAE L 48–56 cm. Near size of herring gull, with huge, deep, orange-red bill, rather long legs; head black to below eyes in summer, streaked and dark round eyes in autumn; juv bill paler, yellow-orange. Deep, crow-like 'kaaah', also 'kuk-kuk-kuk'. Sandy or stony coasts and islands. Usually colonial; nest scrape in open, 2–3 eggs, May–Jul. Food fish, young birds, eggs. Summer Fi, eSw, has bred De, Ge; passage also Po, rare Br, Ne, No. [summer 2] [autumn 3]

Sandwich Tern *Sterna sandvicensis* STERNIDAE L 38–43 cm. Quite large, white-looking, with long wings, shallow-forked tail and long, yellow-tipped, black bill; head shaggy, crested, forehead becoming white and crown streaked as early as Jun. Rasping 'ki-rrik'. Dunes, shingle, rocky, sandy or grassy islets. Colonial; nest scrape in open or among marram, 1–2 eggs, May–Aug. Food fish, esp sand-eels, also marine worms, some molluscs. Summer Br, Ir, nwFr, Ne, sGe, De, sSw; passage also Be, eGe, Po (has bred). [summer 4] [autumn 5]

Roseate Tern *Sterna dougallii* STERNIDAE L 35–38 cm. Breast rosy only in spring;

told from common/arctic tern by whiter appearance, mainly black bill, tail-streamers projecting well beyond closed wing-tips. Grating 'aaak, aaak', musical 'keeo'. Coastal sand, shingle, rocky or grassy islets; strictly maritime. Colonial; nest scrape in open or in hollow, 1–2 eggs, Jun–Aug. Food fish. Summer Br, Ir, nwFr, local. [summer 6] [autumn 7]

Common Tern *Sterna hirundo* STERNIDAE L 33–35·5 cm. Told from arctic tern by black tip to orange-red bill, shorter tail-streamers not projecting beyond closed wing-tips; autumn/juv by blacker shoulder-patches. Long-drawn, grating 'keeee-yaah', also 'kikikikik', 'kirri-kirri'. Coastal sand, shingle, rocky islets, freshwater inland. Colonial; nest scrape often lined thrift, marram, in open, 2–4 eggs, May–Sep. Food fish, crustaceans, marine worms, echinoderms, molluscs, insects. Summer T, ex Ic, nFS. [summer 8] [autumn 9]

Arctic Tern *Sterna paradisaea* STERNIDAE L 35–38 cm. Told from common tern by entirely blood-red bill, shorter legs (looks 'legless'), longer tail-streamers, wholly translucent primaries overhead, greyer underparts often with contrasting white streak below black cap. Calls like common tern, but shorter 'kee-yaah' with emphasis more on 2nd syllable, whistling 'kee-kee' with rising pitch. Habitat and food similar (often breed together), but more northerly, less inland. Nest as common tern, 1–3 eggs, May–Aug. Summer Br, Ir, Ic, Ne, De, Ge, FS, rare nwFr; passage also Be, Po. [summer 10] [autumn 11]

Little Tern *Sterna albifrons* STERNIDAE L 23–25 cm. Tiny, with black-tipped yellow bill, yellow legs, white forehead contrasting with black crown and eyestripe. Persistently hovers; rapid beats. Sharp 'ki-tuk', rasping 'kree-ik', chattering 'kirri-kikki, kirri-kikki'. Coastal sand, shingle, also lakes and rivers inland. Loosely colonial; nest scrape usually unlined, in open, 2–3 eggs, May–Aug. Food crustaceans, marine worms, sand-eels. Summer T, ex Ic, Lu, Fi (passage), No, but local. [summer 12] [autumn 13]

Auks are pied seabirds with short necks, standing upright on legs set far back. They hop or shuffle on their lower legs and fly with rapid, whirring beats of small, narrow wings: legs and wings are adapted for swimming underwater. Food fish, crustaceans, molluscs, marine worms. Most nest in large colonies: pelagic outside breeding season, they return early (some guillemots and razorbills in Dec–Jan), which affects 'summer' and 'winter' ranges. Common victims of oil.

Guillemot *Uria aalge* ALCIDAE L 40–43 cm. Slender pointed bill, thinnish neck; head brown in summer, some 'bridled' with white eye-ring and line behind; cheeks and throat white in winter with black line back from eye; upperparts blackish (nBr, Ic, De, Ge, FS) or dark grey-brown (sBr, Ir, Fr). Noisy at colonies: loud clamour of growling 'arrrr'. Breeds on cliff-ledges, flat-topped stacks. No nest, 1 egg on bare rock, May–Jul. Summer Br, Ir, Ic, nwFr, No, local De, Ge, Fi, Sw; winter AtO, NoS, EnC, swBaS. [summer 1] [bridled 2] [winter 3]

Brünnich's Guillemot *Uria lomvia* ALCIDAE L 40–43 cm. Told from guillemot by shorter, stouter bill with thin, pale line along base of upper mandible (imm razorbill has stubbier bill, no line) and in winter by black of crown extending down over ear-coverts. Voice as guillemot, also habitat; even more pelagic in winter. No nest, 1 egg on bare rock, Jun–Aug. Summer Ic; winter nAtO south to Ic, nNo, vagrant south to Br, Ir, Fr, Ne, De, Ge. [summer 4] [winter 5]

Razorbill *Alca torda* ALCIDAE L 39–42 cm. Told from guillemot by deeper, compressed bill crossed by white line, also by heavier head, thicker neck, and longer, pointed tail cocked up when swimming; head and upperparts blacker; in winter, black of crown extends lower, with no separate cheek-line; juv has small bill (no line), browner head. Less noisy than guillemot: deep grunts, pig-like 'kaarrrr'. Breeds on broken cliffs, steep slopes with fissures, boulders. No nest, 1 egg in rocks, on sheltered ledge, May–

Jul. Summer Br, Ir, Ic, nwFr, FS, local Ge; winter as guillemot, but not BaS. [summer 6] [winter 7] [juv 8]

Black Guillemot *Cepphus grylle* ALCIDAE L 33–35 cm. Very different auk: in summer, black but for white wing-patch; in winter, mainly whitish, with black-and-white barred back, black eye-patch, flight-feathers and tail; red feet and gape; juv darker than winter ad with blackish back, white parts mottled. Weak, whining whistle 'peeeeee', sometimes becoming trilling twitter. Rocky, boulder-strewn coasts, not necessarily cliffs, also wooded islands (BaS); inshore all year. Often solitary; no nest, 1–2 eggs in hole, burrow, May–Aug. Food includes many mussels, gastropods. nBr, Ir, Ic, De, FS, but only summer Fi, nSw; winter also Ge, Po. [summer 9] [winter ad 10]

Little Auk *Alle alle* ALCIDAE L 20–21 cm. Starling-sized, stumpy, seemingly neckless, with short tail, stubby bill; blackish upperparts streaked white on shoulders; in winter, throat, breast and ear-coverts whitish. Noisy when breeding: high, shrill, laughing chatter. Sometimes many blown ashore in winter gales. Breeds on broken rocky cliffs, locally mountains. No nest, 1 egg in crevice, among rocks, Jun–Aug. Food crustaceans, larval molluscs. Summer nIc; winter nAtO, NoS, south to eBr, sNo. [summer 11] [winter 12]

Puffin *Fratercula arctica* ALCIDAE L 29–31 cm. Stumpy, big-headed, with orange feet; in summer, bill triangular, laterally flattened, multi-coloured, and sides of head greyish; in winter, bill smaller, narrower at base, yellower, and head darker, blackish in front of eyes; juv bill much smaller, blackish. Walks more easily than other auks. Groaning 'arrr' in burrow, also deep grunts. Breeds on turf-clad tops and slopes of cliffs. Nest sometimes lined grass, feathers, in hole or burrow excavated or taken over from shearwater or rabbit, 1 egg, May–Sep. Sand-eels for young carried crosswise in bill, < 10 at once. Summer Br, Ir, Ic, No; winter AtO, NoS, south from Ic, sNo. [summer 13] [winter 14]

Skylark *Alauda arvensis* ALAUDIDAE L 17–18 cm. Crest rounded but often prominent; white sides to longish tail, whitish hind-margin of wings show in flight. Rippling 'chirrup'; musical song for minutes on end and high in air. Saltings, dunes, grasslands, cultivation, dry moors. Cup nest of grass, sometimes lined hair, on ground in grass or crop, 3–5 eggs, Apr–Aug. Food seeds, some lvs, earthworms, insects. T, ex Ic, nFS, but mainly summer Cz, Po, FS. [ad **1**]

Horned or Shore Lark *Eremophila alpestris* ALAUDIDAE L 16–17 cm. Coastal only in winter, when summer head-pattern of yellow and black partly obscured by brownish or yellowish feather-tips; pinkish-brown above, whitish below. Pipit-like 'tseep', wagtail-like 'tswe-reep'. Breeds on tundra, stony grassland above tree-line, but winters saltings, shingle, adjacent stubble. Food insects, tiny molluscs, crustaceans. Summer nFS, has bred nBr; winter seBr, neFr, Be, Ne, De, nGe, nPo, sSw, [winter ♂ **2**] [imm ♀ **3**]

Meadow Pipit *Anthus pratensis* MOTACILLIDAE L 14·5–15 cm. Olive-brown above, whitish below, heavily streaked; white-sided tail, pale brown legs. 'Tseep', 'tissip'; song gathers speed, ends in trill, during 'parachuting' descent. Breeds sand-dunes, coastal marshes, rough grassland, moors; winters coasts, marshes, farmland. Cup nest of dry grass, hair, in tussock, 3–5 eggs, Apr–Aug. Food insects, some seeds. T, but only summer Ic, Cz, Po, FS. [**4**]

Rock Pipit *Anthus spinoletta* MOTACILLIDAE L 16–16·5 cm. Larger than meadow pipit, bill longer, tail grey-sided, legs dark; in FS, less streaked and tinged pink below. Song louder, with more pronounced trill. Rocky shores, adjacent moors, tundra in FS. Cup nest of grass, hair, in rocky crevice, 4–6 eggs, Apr–Jul. Food insects, sand-hoppers, tiny molluscs, seeds. Br, Ir, Fr, nDe, summer FS. [**5**]

Wren *Troglodytes troglodytes* TROGLO-DYTIDAE L c9·5 cm. Tiny, stumpy, tail short, cocked. Hard ticking, churring; song loud, clear phrase of shrill notes with

final trill. Varied habitats include sea-cliffs, rocky shores, sand-dunes, cliff-top gorse. Domed nest of dead lvs, bracken, moss, grass, lined feathers (♂ builds several, ♀ lines 1), with side-entrance, in crevice, shrub, 5–6 eggs, Apr–Aug. Food insects, spiders, some seeds. T, ex nFS, but only summer Fi. [6]

Black Redstart *Phoenicurus ochruros* TURDIDAE L 13–14 cm. Flickering rufous tail; summer ♂ sooty-black with white wing-patch, winter ♂ much greyer, ♀ and juv grey-brown. 'Tsip', 'tik-tik'; short, warbling song interrupted by gravelly rattle. Sea-cliffs, ruins, coastal and other towns, power stations, mountains. Cup nest of grass, moss, lined hair, feathers, in crevice, on ledge, 4–6 eggs, Apr–Jul. Food insects, also berries, tiny crustaceans in winter. Summer sBr, Fr, Lu, Be, Ne, De, Ge, Cz, Po, sSw; winter sBr, sIr, Fr. [summer ♂ 7] [♀ 8]

Stonechat *Saxicola torquata* TURDIDAE L 12·5–13 cm. ♂ black head, white ½–collar and wing-patch, whitish rump, chestnut breast; ♀ and juv streaked brown above, no white on neck or rump, dull rufous below but for dark throat. 'Hweet, tsak-tsak', like 2 stones knocked together; song musical warble. Gorse, wasteland, esp near sea, sand-dunes, also moors, heaths. Cup nest of grass, moss, wool, feathers, on or near ground in dense bush, 5–6 eggs, May–Jul. Food insects, spiders, worms, some seeds. Summer T, ex Ic, nPo, FS, rare De; winter Br, Ir, Fr, Lu, Be, Ne. [♂ 9] [♀ 10]

Wheatear *Oenanthe oenanthe* TURDIDAE L 14·5–15 cm. White rump and sides to black tail; summer ♂ blue-grey above, with white-topped black mask, black wings; ♀ and autumn ♂ browner, with darker brown wings; juv more spotted. 'Weet-chak-chak', harder than stonechat; song short, rattling warble of rich and harsh notes. Rocky shores, dunes, moors, grassland. Cup nest of grass, moss, lined hair, wool, feathers, in hole, rabbit burrow, under stone, 5–6 eggs, Apr–Jul. Food insects, spiders, also centipedes, molluscs. Summer T. [summer ♂ 11] [♀ 12]

Chough *Pyrrhocorax pyrrhocorax*
CORVIDAE L 37–39 cm. Jackdaw-like, but
glossy purple-black (no grey), curved red
bill, red legs; juv duller, with more orange
bill, legs. Flight buoyant, acrobatic, with
primaries spread. Down-slurred 'kee-agh',
also 'chuff'. Sea-cliffs with caves, fissures,
also crags, ruins, mine-shafts inland.
Social; cup nest of sticks, heather, gorse,
lined wool, hair, in crevice, on ledge, 3–5
eggs, Apr–Jul. Food insects, earthworms,
also corn, crustaceans. wBr, Ir, nwFr,
local. [ad 1]

Jackdaw *Corvus monedula* CORVIDAE
L 32–34 cm. Blackish with grey nape; juv
browner. 'Chak' ('jack'), shrill 'kia'. Cliffs,
quarries, old buildings, woods, parks,
farmland. Colonial; cup nest of sticks,
rubbish, lined wool, hair, grass, in cavity
in rock-face, building, tree, rabbit burrow,
4–6 eggs, Apr–Jun. Food insects, spiders,
millipedes, earthworms, molluscs, cereals,
berries, young birds, eggs. T, ex Ic, nFS.
[ad 2]

Carrion/Hooded Crow *Corvus corone*
CORVIDAE L 46–48 cm. Bill stout; carrion
glossy black; hooded has grey back and
underparts, juv browner; intermediates
where ranges overlap. Harsh, croaking
'kraah', also motor-horn note. Sea-cliffs,
beaches, estuaries, widespread inland. Cup
nest of sticks, heather, even seaweed,
lined wool, hair, in tree, on ledge, 4–6
eggs, Mar–Jul. Food carrion, small
mammals, birds, eggs, frogs, many
invertebrates, grain, acorns, fruit. Carrion
Br, Fr, Lu, Be, Ne, sDe, wGe, wCz;
Hooded nBr, Ir, De, Ge, Cz, Po, FS, to
WE, esp coasts, in winter. [Carrion 3]
[Hooded 4]

Raven *Corvus corax* CORVIDAE L 62–65
cm. Told from other black crows by
size, massive bill, shaggy throat, wedge-
ended tail. Deep 'pruk'. Sea-cliffs, crags
inland, also forests. Cup nest of sticks,
moss, grass, lined wool, on ledge, in tree,
4–6 eggs, Feb–May. Food carrion, small
mammals, birds, eggs, frogs, some
molluscs, beetles, cereals, acorns, seeds.
T, ex seBr, Lu, Be, Ne, nDe, but local
Fr, Ge. [ad 5]

Linnet *Carduelis cannabina* FRINGILLIDAE
L 13–13·5 cm. ♂ head greyish, back
chestnut, wings and tail edged white,
forecrown and breast crimson in summer;
♀ and juv duller, more streaked, no red.
'Tsooeet', rapid twitter; song twittering
musical and twanging notes. Cliff-tops
with gorse, coastal dunes, hedgerows,
bushy grassland. Cup nest of stalks, grass,
moss, lined wool, hair, in gorse, bramble,
marram, 4–6 eggs, Apr–Sep. Food seeds,
insects in summer. T, ex Ic, nFS, but
only summer Fi, most SC. [♂ 6] [♀ 7]

Twite *Carduelis flavirostris* FRINGILLIDAE
L 13–13·5 cm. Nests on moors, rough
ground to near sea, but truly coastal only
in winter, when told from ♀ linnet by
yellow bill, less white in wings and tail,
darker upperparts, reddish-buff throat;
♂ rump pinkish. Nasal, twanging 'tsooeek'.
Winters salt-marshes, coastal stubble,
rough pastures. Food seeds, eg glasswort,
sea aster. Summer nBr, Ir, No; winter T,
ex Ic, Lu, Fi, nSC. [winter 8]

Lapland Bunting *Calcarius lapponicus*
EMBERIZIDAE L 15–15·5 cm. Coastal only in
winter when black, chestnut and white of
♂ obscured, but still chestnut on nape;
♀ and juv told from ♀ reed bunting by
stouter shape, yellowish bill, pale crown-
stripe, dark mark behind ear-coverts,
whitish wing-bars, shorter tail with less
white at sides. Runs on ground. Piping
'teu', hard notes ending in whistle
'ticky-tik-teu'. Breeds on tundra; winters
coastal stubble or rough ground. Food
seeds. Summer nFS; winter eBr, Fr, Be,
Ne, De, nGe, nPo, scarce; passage nBr
(has bred), Ir, sFS. [winter 9]

Snow Bunting *Plectrophenax nivalis*
EMBERIZIDAE L c16·5 cm. Truly coastal
only in winter, when white underparts,
white areas on wings, tail; ♂ head and
breast reddish-sandy, back mottled black;
♀ and juv duller, browner. Rippling
twitter, piping 'teu'. Breeds rocky ground,
sea-level to mountains; winters shores,
saltings, adjacent rough pastures, moors.
Food seeds, sand-hoppers, insects. Summer
nBr, Ic, nFS; winter T, ex Lu, Cz, Fi,
mainly coastal. [winter ♂ 10] [winter ♀ 11]

Natterjack Toad *Bufo calamita*
BUFONIDAE L 6–8 cm. Warty skin; grey,
olive-green or brown with irregular, grey
or reddish-brown markings; narrow
yellow stripe down middle of back.
Rather short limbs; runs rather than
jumps. Sandy places, dunes. Nocturnal;
burrows into sand by day. Migrates to
ponds to breed, Apr–May. Very loud
trilling growl during mating, usually
several ♂s calling in chorus. Eggs laid in
bands twined around weeds. Feeds on
insects, other invertebrates. Fr, Lu, Be,
Ne, De, Ge, Po, sSw, local Br, swIr. [1]

Turtles (Dermochelyidae and Cheloniidae).
Marine reptiles found throughout the
oceans of the world. Specimens have been
seen on or around north European coasts
or in the Bay of Biscay. They have an
oval or heart-shaped shell (carapace) and
flipper-like limbs; unlike tortoises, they
are unable to retract their heads. They
breed on sandy beaches in subtropical
seas, mating in the sea and laying eggs on
land. They feed on a variety of marine
animals including fish and crustaceans.
The following spp may rarely be seen in
N Europe:

Green Turtle *Chelonia mydas* CHELONIIDAE
L <150 cm. Carapace brown or olive-
green with yellow markings, underside
yellow.

Hawksbill Turtle *Eretmochelys imbricata*
CHELONIIDAE L <90 cm. Carapace brown
marbled with yellow, underside yellow.
Hooked, beak-like upper jaw. Shell is
source of true 'tortoiseshell'.

Loggerhead Turtle *Caretta caretta*
CHELONIIDAE L <100 cm. Carapace
chestnut-brown, underside yellow. [2]

Leatherback Turtle *Dermochelys coriacea*
DERMOCHELYIDAE L <270 cm. The world's
largest turtle. Carapace brown, becoming
paler with age, and with 7 raised,
longitudinal ridges.

Seals (Pinnipedia). Marine mammals
whose bodies have become adapted to
movement in water. They have a hairy
coat, hindlimbs that are used for
swimming, no dorsal fin, dog-like
head. They come ashore to rest and
to breed.

Grey Seal *Halichoerus grypus* PHOCIDAE
BL 165–230 cm, ♂ larger than ♀. Colour
variable, grey or brown; pattern of
irregular spots and blotches; muzzle long,
not separated from head in profile;
nostrils widely separated. Moaning,
wailing calls, esp in breeding season.
Rocky coasts, less often in estuaries; rests
on rocks at low tide. Breeds in autumn
in colonies on small, rocky islands, but in
spring on ice in BaS. Pup white at first,
remains on shore several weeks. Feeds on
fish. T, breeding Br, Ir, Ic, FS. [3]

Common Seal *Phoca vitulina* PHOCIDAE
BL 120–160 cm, sexes similar. Finely
spotted; head short, profile with depression
between forehead and muzzle; nostrils
close together, forming V. Usually silent.
Sheltered coasts and estuaries; rests ashore
on rocks, sandbanks. Breeds mainly on
sandbanks. Pup brown, swims from first
tide. Feeds mainly on fish, also crustaceans,
molluscs. Br, Ir, Ic, De, Ge, SC,
occasional elsewhere. [4]

Ringed Seal *Phoca hispida* PHOCIDAE
BL 120–140 cm. Like common seal but
spots larger, mostly surrounded by lighter
rings. Usually silent. Coastal waters and
large lakes; breeds on ice in spring. Pup
white at first, remains on ice for several
weeks. Feeds on fish, crustaceans. FS,
breeding Gulfs of Finland and Bothnia,
Lake Saima, Fi. [5]

Whales, dolphins and porpoises (Cetacea). Marine mammals which have a naked skin, forelimbs (flippers), no hindlimbs, a horizontally flattened tail (fluke), usually a dorsal fin, and nostrils forming a blowhole on the top of the head. They never voluntarily come ashore. Most have numerous pointed, conical teeth and catch fish or squid; a few (including most large whales) have no teeth but a filtering mechanism of horny plates (baleen) with which they strain out small animals, mainly crustaceans (krill), from the plankton.

Common Dolphin *Delphinus delphis* DELPHINIDAE BL 180–250 cm. Slender beak; dorsal fin pointed, concave behind; complex pattern forming cross centred under dorsal fin; flanks yellowish-brown. Clicks and whistles audible under water. Coastal waters. Feeds on fish. Gregarious; leaps clear of water; often accompanies ships. T, but mainly AtO, EnC. [1]

Bottle-nosed Dolphin *Tursiops truncatus* DELPHINIDAE BL 250–350 cm. Shape as common dolphin but beak thicker; colour more uniform grey, pattern less marked than in other dolphins. Coastal waters. Food and behaviour as common dolphin. T, but rare BaS. [2]

White-beaked Dolphin *Lagenorhynchus albirostris* DELPHINIDAE BL 260–310 cm. Beak short, white, only faintly demarcated from forehead; bold black and white pattern; dorsal fin large. Coastal waters and open sea. Food and behaviour as common dolphin; very gregarious. T, but commonest NoS. [3]

Killer Whale *Orcinus orca* DELPHINIDAE BL 4–9 m, ♂ larger than ♀. Dorsal fin very

large and erect in ad ♂, smaller and slightly recurved in ♀ and young; flippers broad and rounded, very large in ad ♂; pattern very distinctive. Coastal waters and open sea. Feeds on seals, dolphins, larger fish, birds; attracted to breeding colonies of seals. Usually in small groups; often swims with dorsal fin projecting from water. T. [4]

Pilot Whale *Globicephala melaena* DELPHINIDAE BL 4–6 m. Twice size of most dolphins. Dorsal fin recurved; forehead bulbous; flippers very long and narrow. Coastal waters and open sea. Feeds mainly on squid, cuttlefish, also fish. Gregarious, in schools, up to 100 or more; sometimes stranded in numbers. T, but rare BaS. [5]

Common Porpoise *Phocoena phocoena* PHOCOENIDAE BL 130–180 cm. Smallest cetacean. Dorsal fin small, blunt; no beak; white or grey patch behind head variable in extent. Coastal waters, estuaries; sometimes enters rivers. Feeds on fish, cuttlefish, crustaceans. Gregarious, in small groups; does not usually leap clear of water like dolphins; frequently stranded on beaches. T. [6]

Lesser Rorqual *Balaenoptera acutorostrata* BALAENOPTERIDAE BL 8–9 m. Smallest of baleen whales, with fringed, horny filters in mouth, no teeth. Pointed head; dorsal fin small, well behind centre of back; throat with numerous grooves; dark above, light below, white patch on flipper characteristic. Feeds by filtering crustaceans and small fish from water. Small, dispersed groups. May be detected by the blow (spray of water in air exhaled through blowhole), although blow is more conspicuous in the larger whales. T. [7]

FURTHER READING

The Sea Coast, J. A. Steers (Collins, New Naturalist Series, 1953, London)

Coasts and Beaches, J. A. Steers (Oliver and Boyd, 1969, Edinburgh)

The Sea Shore, C. M. Yonge (Collins, New Naturalist Series, 1949, London; paperback, Fontana, 1971, London)

The Open Sea : Its Natural History. Part 1 : The World of Plankton ; Part 2 : Fish and Fisheries, A. C. Hardy (Collins, New Naturalist Series, Part 1 revised edition 1971, Part 2 new impression 1970, London)

Life in the Sea, G. Thorson (Weidenfeld and Nicholson, 1972, London)

The Coastline of England and Wales, J. A. Steers (Cambridge University Press, 1964, Cambridge)

The Coastline of Scotland, J. A. Steers (Cambridge University Press, 1973, Cambridge)

Estuarine Biology, R. S. K. Barnes (Edward Arnold, 1974, London)

The Coastline, R. S. K. Barnes (John Wiley, 1977, London)

The Ecology of Rocky Shores, J. R. Lewis (Hodder and Stoughton Educational, 1977, London)

Life in Mud and Sand, S. K. Eltringham (London Universities Press, 1971, London)

The Biology of Estuarine Animals, J. Green (Sidgwick and Jackson, 1968, London)

Ecology of Salt Marshes and Sand Dunes, D. S. Ranwell (Chapman and Hall, 1972, London)

Polderlands, P. Wagret (Methuen, 1972, London)

Life in Sandy Shores, A. E. Brafield (Edward Arnold, 1978, London)

Tracks, E. A. R. Ennion and N. Tinbergen (Oxford University Press, 1967, London)

The Wild Flowers of Britain and Northern Europe, R. Fitter, A. Fitter and M. Blamey (Collins, 1974, London)

The Concise British Flora, W. Keble Martin (Ebury Press and Michael Joseph, 1976, London)

An Atlas of the Wild Flowers of Britain and Northern Europe, A. Fitter (Collins, 1978, London)

Flowers of the Coast, I. Hepburn (Collins, New Naturalist Series, 1952, London)

Coastal Vegetation, V. J. Chapman (Pergamon, 1976, Oxford)

A Handbook of British Seaweeds, L. Newton (British Museum, Natural History Publications, 1931, London)

Grasses, C. E. Hubbard (Penguin, 1968, London)

The Hamlyn Guide to the Seashore and Shallow Seas of Britain and Europe, A. C. Campbell and J. Nicholls (Hamlyn, 1976, London)

Collins Pocket Guide to the Sea Shore, J. Barrett and C. M. Yonge (Collins, 1972, London)

The Invertebrate Panorama, E. Smith *et al* (Weidenfeld and Nicholson, 1971, London)

The Oxford Book of Invertebrates, D. Nichols, J. Cooke and D. Whiteley (Oxford University Press, 1976, London)

Ray Society Monographs: *eg British Prosobranch Molluscs*, V. Fretter and A. Graham (Ray Society, British Museum, 1962, London)

The Hamlyn Guide to Shells of the World, A. P. H. Oliver and J. Nicholls (Hamlyn, 1975, London)

British Bivalve Seashells, N. Tebble (British Museum, Natural History Publications, 1976, London)

A Field Guide to the Insects of Britain and Northern Europe, M. Chinery (Collins, 1973, London)

The Fishes of the British Isles and North-West Europe, A. Wheeler *et al* (Macmillan, 1969, London)

A Field Guide to the Birds of Britain and Europe, R. Peterson, G. Mountfort and P. A. D. Hollom (Collins, 1974, London)

The Hamlyn Guide to Birds of Britain and Europe, B. Bruun and A. Singer (Hamlyn, 1970, London)

Birds of Coast and Sea, B. Campbell and R. Watson (Oxford University Press, 1977, Oxford)

The Atlas of Breeding Birds in Britain and Ireland, J. T. R. Sharrock (British Trust for Ornithology, 1976)

A Field Guide to the Mammals of Britain and Europe, F. H. van den Brink (Collins, 1967, London)

The Handbook of British Mammals, G. B. Corbet and H. N. Southern (eds.) (Blackwell, 1977, Oxford)

ACKNOWLEDGEMENTS

page

6	John Hillelson Agency/ Georg Gerster
10	Fox Photos
11	Aerofilms Ltd
15	Aerofilms Ltd
18	Dr Richard Barnes
22	Anthony and Elizabeth Bomford/Ardea London
26	Anthony and Elizabeth Bomford/Ardea London
27	Heather Angel
30 *top left*	Dr Susan Eden
top right	Dr Richard Barnes
bottom	Ardea London
34	Heather Angel
38	Heather Angel
39	Heather Angel
43	R. J. Tulloch/ Bruce Coleman Ltd
46	Dr Richard Barnes
51	Dr Richard Barnes
59	Ian Beames/Ardea London
62	R. J. Tulloch/ Bruce Coleman Ltd

INDEX

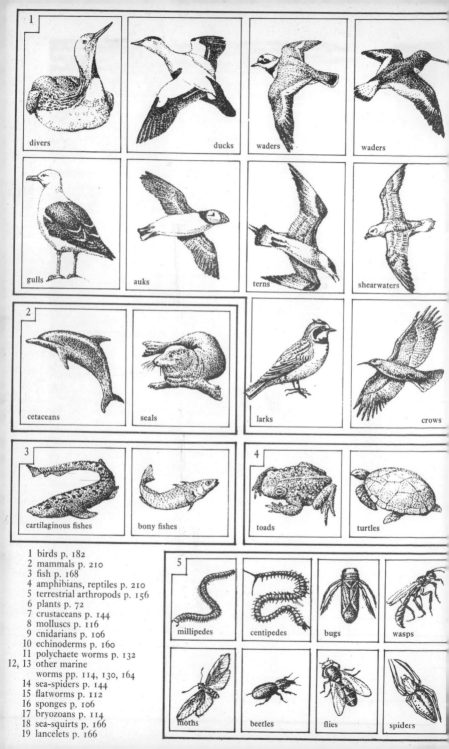

1

divers · ducks · waders · waders

gulls · auks · terns · shearwaters

2

cetaceans · seals · larks · crows

3

cartilaginous fishes · bony fishes

4

toads · turtles

1 birds p. 182
2 mammals p. 210
3 fish p. 168
4 amphibians, reptiles p. 210
5 terrestrial arthropods p. 156
6 plants p. 72
7 crustaceans p. 144
8 molluscs p. 116
9 cnidarians p. 106
10 echinoderms p. 160
11 polychaete worms p. 132
12, 13 other marine
    worms pp. 114, 130, 164
14 sea-spiders p. 144
15 flatworms p. 112
16 sponges p. 106
17 bryozoans p. 114
18 sea-squirts p. 166
19 lancelets p. 166

5

millipedes · centipedes · bugs · wasps

moths · beetles · flies · spiders